9781171935001

FURNITURE
OF THE OLDEN TIME

THE MACMILLAN COMPANY
NEW YORK · BOSTON · CHICAGO · DALLAS
ATLANTA · SAN FRANCISCO

MACMILLAN & CO., LIMITED
LONDON · BOMBAY · CALCUTTA
MELBOURNE

THE MACMILLAN COMPANY
OF CANADA, LIMITED
TORONTO

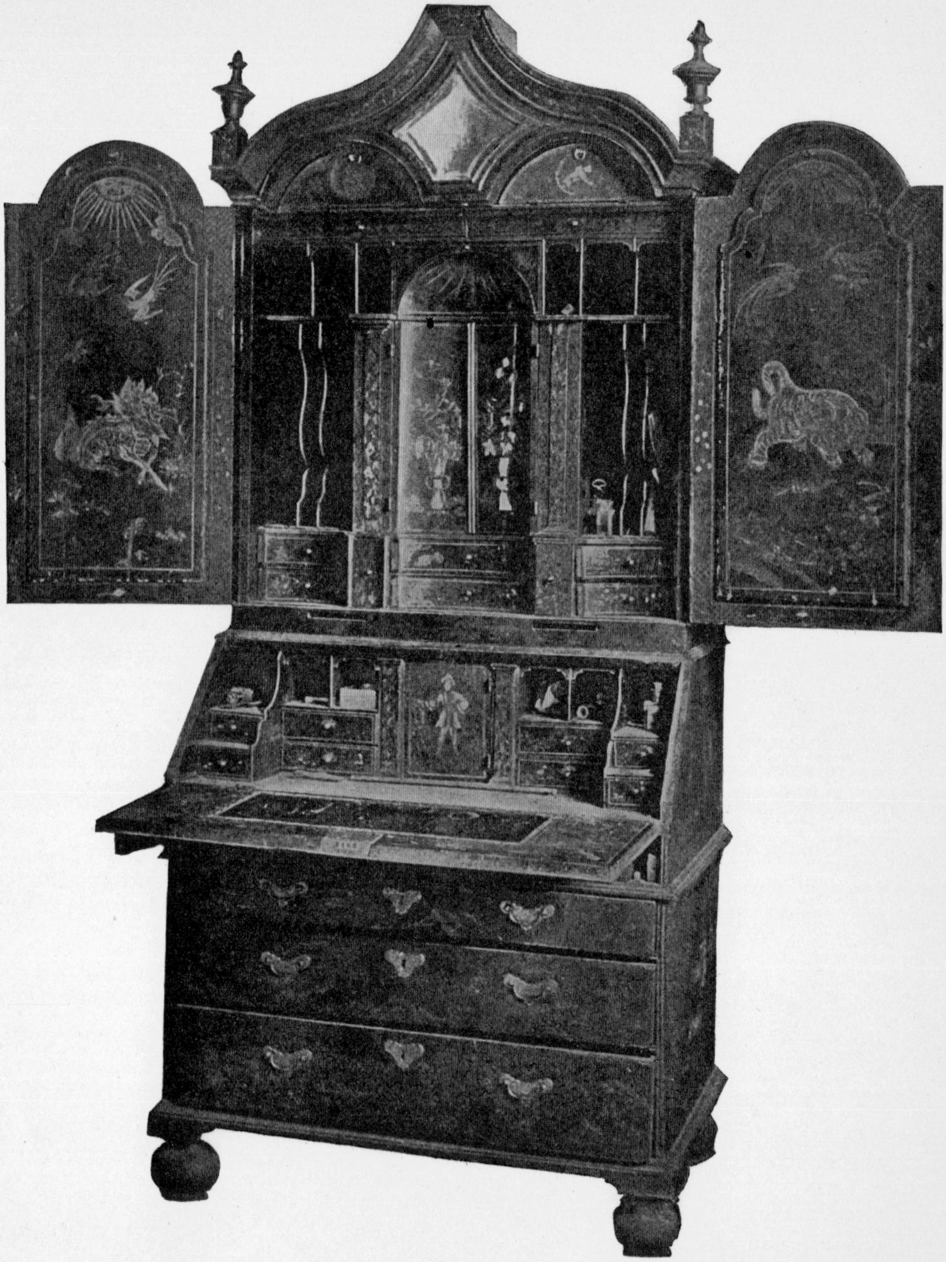

FURNITURE
OF
THE OLDEN TIME

BY

FRANCES CLARY MORSE

NEW EDITION

WITH A NEW CHAPTER AND MANY NEW ILLUSTRATIONS

"How much more agreeable it is to sit in the midst of old furniture like Minott's clock, and secretary and looking-glass, which have come down from other generations, than amid that which was just brought from the cabinet-maker's, smelling of varnish, like a coffin! To sit under the face of an old clock that has been ticking one hundred and fifty years — there is something mortal, not to say immortal, about it; a clock that begun to tick when Massachusetts was a province." — H. D. THOREAU, "Autumn."

New York
THE MACMILLAN COMPANY
1937

COPYRIGHT, 1902 AND 1917,
BY THE MACMILLAN COMPANY.

COPYRIGHT, 1930,
BY FRANCES CLARY MORSE.

All rights reserved — no part of this book may be reproduced in any form without permission in writing from the publisher, except by a reviewer who wishes to quote brief passages in connection with a review written for inclusion in magazine or newspaper.

Set up and electrotyped November, 1902. Reprinted April, 1903; July, 1905; February, 1908; September, 1910; September, 1913. New edition, with a new chapter and new illustrations, December, 1917. Reissued October, 1936. Reprinted March, 1937.

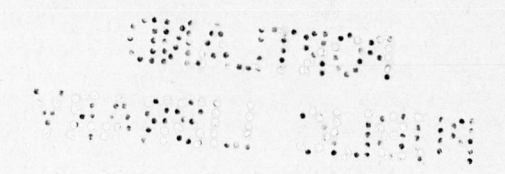

SET UP AND ELECTROTYPED BY J. S. CUSHING CO.
PRINTED IN THE UNITED STATES OF AMERICA
BY BERWICK & SMITH CO.

To my Sister

ALICE MORSE EARLE

Contents

	PAGE
INTRODUCTION	1

CHAPTER I
CHESTS, CHESTS OF DRAWERS, AND DRESSING-TABLES . 10

CHAPTER II
BUREAUS AND WASHSTANDS 41

CHAPTER III
BEDSTEADS 64

CHAPTER IV
CUPBOARDS AND SIDEBOARDS 84

CHAPTER V
DESKS 117

CHAPTER VI
CHAIRS 154

CHAPTER VII
SETTLES, SETTEES, AND SOFAS 213

CHAPTER VIII
TABLES 242

CHAPTER IX
Musical Instruments 280

CHAPTER X
Fires and Lights 315

CHAPTER XI
Clocks 348

CHAPTER XII
Looking-glasses 374

CHAPTER XIII
Doorways, Mantels, and Stairs 411

Glossary 451

Index of the Owners of Furniture 459

General Index 465

List of Illustrations

Lacquered Desk with Cabinet Top . . . *Frontispiece*

ILLUS.   PAGE

     Looking-glass, 1810–1825 10
1. Oak Chest, about 1650 11
2. Olive-wood Chest, 1630–1650 13
3. Panelled Chest with One Drawer, about 1660 . . 14
4. Oak Chest with Two Drawers, about 1675 . . 15
5. Panelled Chest with Two Drawers, about 1675 . . 16
6. Carved Chest with One Drawer, about 1700 . . 17
7. Panelled Chest upon Frame, 1670–1700 . . . 18
8. Panelled Chest upon Frame, 1670–1700 . . . 18
9. Panelled Chest of Drawers, about 1680 . . . 19
10. Panelled Chest of Drawers, about 1680 . . . 20
11. Handles 21
12. Six-legged High Chest of Drawers, 1705–1715 . . 22
13. Walnut Dressing-table, about 1700 23
14. Lacquered Dressing-table, about 1720 24
15. Cabriole-legged High Chest of Drawers with China Steps, about 1720 26
16. Lacquered High-boy, 1730 27
17. Inlaid Walnut High Chest of Drawers, 1733 . . 28
18. Inlaid Walnut High Chest of Drawers, about 1760 . 29
19. "Low-boy" and "High-boy" of Walnut, about 1740 . 30
20. Walnut Double Chest, about 1760 32
21. Double Chest, 1760–1770 33
22. Block-front Dressing-table, about 1750 . . . 34
23. Dressing-table, about 1760 35
24. Chest of Drawers, 1740 36
25. High Chest of Drawers, about 1765 37
26. Dressing-table and Looking-glass, about 1770 . . 39
27. Walnut Dressing-table, about 1770 40

List of Illustrations

ILLUS.		PAGE
	Looking-glass, 1810–1825	41
28.	Block-front Bureau, about 1770	42
29.	Block-front Bureau, about 1770	43
30.	Block-front Bureau, about 1770	45
31.	Kettle-shaped Bureau, about 1770	44
32.	Serpentine-front Bureau, about 1770	46
33.	Serpentine-front Bureau, about 1785	47
34.	Swell-front Inlaid Bureau, about 1795	48
35.	Handles	49
36.	Dressing-glass, about 1760	50
37.	Bureau and Dressing-glass, 1795	51
38.	Bureau and Dressing-glass, about 1810	52
39.	Bureau and Miniature Bureau, about 1810	53
40.	Dressing-table and Glass, about 1810	54
41.	Case of Drawers with Closet, 1810	55
42.	Bureau, about 1815	56
43.	Bureau, 1815–1820	57
44.	Empire Bureau and Glass, 1810–1820	58
45.	Basin Stand, 1770	59
46.	Corner Washstand, 1790	60
47.	Towel-rack and Washstand, 1790–1800	61
48.	Washstand, 1815–1830	62
49.	Night Table, 1785	62
50.	Washstand, 1800–1810	63
	Looking-glass, about 1770	64
51.	Wicker Cradle, 1620	65
52.	Oak Cradle, 1680	65
53.	Bedstead and Commode, 1750	66
54.	Field Bedstead, 1760–1770	67
55.	Claw-and-ball-foot Bedstead, 1774	69
56.	Bedstead, 1780	70
57.	Bedstead, 1775–1780	71
58.	Bedstead, 1789	72
59.	Bedstead, 1795–1800	74
60.	Bedstead, 1800–1810	75
61.	Bedstead, 1800–1810	76
62.	Bedstead, 1800–1810	77
63.	Bedstead, 1800–1810	78

List of Illustrations

ILLUS.		PAGE
64.	Bedstead and Steps, 1790	79
65.	Low-post Bedstead, about 1825	80
66.	Low-post Bedstead, 1820–1830	81
67.	Low Bedstead, about 1830	82
	Looking-glass, 1770–1780	84
68.	Oak Press Cupboard, 1640	85
69.	Press Cupboard, about 1650	87
70.	Carved Press Cupboard, 1680–1690	88
71.	Corner "Beaufatt," 1740–1750	90
72.	Kas, 1700	92
73.	Chippendale Side-table, about 1755	93
74.	Chippendale Side-table, 1765	94
75.	Shearer Sideboard and Knife-box, 1792	97
76.	Urn-shaped Knife-box, 1790	99
77.	Urn-shaped Knife-box, 1790	99
78.	Knife-box, 1790	100
79.	Hepplewhite Sideboard with Knife-boxes, 1790	102
80.	Hepplewhite Serpentine-front Sideboard, 1790	104
81.	Hepplewhite Sideboard, about 1795	105
82.	Sheraton Side-table, 1795	106
83.	Sheraton Side-table, 1795	107
84.	Sheraton Sideboard with Knife-box, 1795	108
85.	Sheraton Sideboard, about 1800	109
86.	Sheraton Sideboard, about 1805	110
87.	Cellarets, 1790	111
88.	Sideboard, 1810–1820	113
89.	Empire Sideboard, 1810–1820	114
90.	Mixing-table, 1790	115
91.	Mixing-table, 1810–1820	116
	Looking-glass, about 1760	117
92.	Desk-boxes, 1654	118
93.	Desk-box, 1650	118
94.	Desk, about 1680	119
95.	Desk, about 1680	120
96.	Desk, 1710–1720	121
97.	Cabriole-legged Desk, 1720–1730	124
98.	Cabriole-legged Desk, 1760	125
99.	Desk, 1760	126

List of Illustrations

ILLUS.		PAGE
100.	Desk, about 1770	127
101.	Block-front Desk, Cabinet Top, about 1770	128
102.	Block-front Desk, about 1770	129
103.	Desk with Cabinet Top, about 1770	130
104.	Block-front Desk, about 1770	133
105.	Kettle-front Secretary, about 1765	135
106.	Block-front Writing-table, 1760–1770	136
107.	Serpentine-front Desk, Cabinet Top, 1770	137
108.	Serpentine or Bow-front Desk, about 1770	138
109.	Bill of Lading, 1716	139
110.	Bookcase and Desk, about 1765	142
111.	Chippendale Bookcase, 1770	143
112.	Hepplewhite Bookcase, 1789	144
113.	Maple Desk, about 1795	146
114.	Desk with Cabinet Top, 1790	147
115.	Sheraton Desk, 1795	149
116.	Tambour Secretary, about 1800	150
117.	Sheraton Desk, 1800	151
118.	Sheraton Desk, about 1810	152
119.	Desk, about 1820	153
	Looking-glass, 1720–1740	154
120.	Turned Chair, Sixteenth Century	155
121.	Turned High-chair, Sixteenth Century	156
122.	Turned Chair, about 1600	157
123.	Turned Chair, about 1600	157
124.	Wainscot Chair, about 1600	158
125.	Wainscot Chair, about 1600	159
126.	Leather Chair, about 1660	160
127.	Chair originally covered with Turkey Work, about 1680	160
128.	Flemish Chair, about 1690	161
129.	Flemish Chair, about 1690	161
130.	Cane Chair, 1680–1690	162
131.	Cane High-chair and Arm-chair, 1680–1690	163
132.	Cane Chair, 1680–1690	164
133.	Cane Chair, 1680–1690	166
134.	Cane Chair, 1680–1690	166
135.	Turned Stool, 1660	167
136.	Flemish Stool, 1680–1690	167

List of Illustrations xiii

ILLUS.		PAGE
137.	Cane Chair, 1690–1700	168
138.	Queen Anne Chair, 1710–1720	168
139.	Banister-back Chair, 1710–1720	169
140.	Banister-back Chair, 1710–1720	169
141.	Banister-back Chair, 1710–1740	170
142.	Roundabout Chair, about 1740	170
143.	Slat-back Chairs, 1700–1750	171
144.	Five-slat Chair, about 1750	172
145.	Pennsylvania Slat-back Chair, 1740–1750	173
146.	Windsor Chairs, 1750–1775	174
147.	Comb-back Windsor Rocking-chair, 1750–1775	175
148.	High-back Windsor Arm-chair and Child's Chair, 1750–1775	176
149.	Windsor Writing-chair, 1750–1775	177
150.	Windsor Rocking-chairs, 1820–1830	178
151.	Dutch Chair, 1710–1720	179
152.	Dutch Chair, about 1740	180
153.	Dutch Chair, about 1740	180
154.	Dutch Chair, 1740–1750	181
155.	Dutch Chair, 1740–1750	181
156.	Dutch Chairs, 1750–1760	182
157.	Dutch Roundabout Chair, 1740	183
158.	Easy-chair with Dutch Legs, 1750	184
159.	Claw-and-ball-foot Easy-chair, 1750	185
160.	Chippendale Chair	186
161.	Chippendale Chair	186
162.	Chippendale Chair	187
163.	Chippendale Chair	187
164.	Chippendale Chair	189
165.	Chippendale Chairs	188
166.	Chippendale Chair	190
167.	Roundabout Chair	190
168.	Extension-top Roundabout Chair, Dutch	191
169.	Roundabout Chair	192
170.	Chippendale Chair	192
171.	Chippendale Chair	193
172.	Chippendale Chair	193
173.	Chippendale Chair	194

List of Illustrations

ILLUS.		PAGE
174.	Chippendale Chair	194
175.	Chippendale Chair in "Chinese Taste"	195
176.	Chippendale Chair	196
177.	Chippendale Chair	196
178.	Hepplewhite Chairs	198
179.	Hepplewhite Chair	197
180.	Hepplewhite Chair, 1785	199
181.	Hepplewhite Chair, 1789	199
182.	Hepplewhite Chair, 1789	200
183.	French Chair, 1790	201
184.	Hepplewhite Chair, 1790	201
185.	Arm-chair, 1790	202
186.	Transition Chair, 1785	202
187.	Hepplewhite Chair	203
188.	Hepplewhite Chair	203
189.	Hepplewhite Chair	204
190.	Hepplewhite Chair	204
191.	Sheraton Chair	205
192.	Sheraton Chairs	206
193.	Sheraton Chair	207
194.	Sheraton Chair	207
195.	Sheraton Chair	208
196.	Sheraton Chair	208
197.	Sheraton Chair	209
198.	Painted Sheraton Chair, 1810–1815	209
199.	Late Mahogany Chairs, 1830–1845	210
200.	Maple Chairs, 1820–1830	212
	Looking-glass, 1770–1780	213
201.	Pine Settle, Eighteenth Century	214
202.	Oak Settle, 1708	215
203.	Settee covered with Turkey work, 1670–1680	216
204.	Flemish Couch, 1680–1690	217
205.	Dutch Couch, 1720–1730	218
206.	Chippendale Couch, 1760–1770	218
207.	Chippendale Settee, 1760	219
208.	Sofa, 1740	220
209.	Chippendale Settee	221
210.	Double Chair, 1760	222

List of Illustrations

ILLUS.		PAGE
211.	Chippendale Double Chair and Chair in "Chinese Taste," 1760–1765	224
212.	Chippendale Double Chair, 1750–1750	225
213.	Chippendale Settee, 1770	226
214.	French Settee, 1790	227
215.	Hepplewhite Settee, 1790	228
216.	Sheraton Settee, 1790–1795	229
217.	Sheraton Sofa, 1790–1800	230
218.	Sheraton Sofa, about 1800	230
219.	Sheraton Settee, about 1805	231
220.	Sheraton Settee, 1805–1810	232
221.	Empire Settee, 1800–1810	232
222.	Empire Settee, 1816	233
223.	Sheraton Settee, 1800–1805	234
224.	Sofa in Adam Style, 1800–1810	235
225.	Sofa, 1815–1820	236
226.	Sofa, about 1820	237
227.	Cornucopia Sofa, about 1820	238
228.	Sofa and Miniature Sofa, about 1820	239
229.	Sofa about 1820	239
230.	Sofa and Chair, about 1840	240
231.	Rosewood Sofa, 1844–1848	241
	Looking-glass, 1750–1780	242
232.	Chair Table, Eighteenth Century	243
233.	Oak Table, 1650–1675	244
234.	Slate-top Table, 1670–1680	245
235.	"Butterfly Table," about 1700	245
236.	"Hundred-legged" Table, 1675–1700	246
237.	"Hundred-legged" Table, 1680–1700	247
238.	Gate-legged Table, 1680–1700	248
239.	Spindle-legged Table, 1740–1750	249
240.	"Hundred-legged" Table, 1680–1700	250
241.	Dutch Table, 1720–1740	251
242.	Dutch Card-table, 1730–1740	251
243.	Claw-and-ball-foot Table, about 1750	252
244.	Dutch Stand, about 1740	253
245.	"Pie-crust" Table, 1750	253
246.	"Dish-top" Table, 1750	254

ILLUS.		PAGE
247.	Tea-tables, 1750–1760	254
248.	Table and Easy-chair, 1760–1770	255
249.	Tripod Table, 1760–1770	256
250.	Chinese Fret-work Table, 1760–1770	256
251.	Stands, 1760–1770	258
252.	Tea-table, about 1770	258
253.	Chippendale Card-table, about 1765	259
254.	Chippendale Card-table, 1760	260
255.	Chippendale Card-table, about 1765	261
256.	Pembroke Table, 1760–1770	262
257.	Pembroke Table, 1780–1790	262
258.	Lacquer Tea-tables, 1700–1800	263
259.	Hepplewhite Card-table with Tea-tray, 1785–1790	264
260.	Hepplewhite Card-tables, 1785–1795	265
261.	Sheraton Card-table, 1800	266
262.	Sheraton Card-table, 1800–1810	266
263.	Sheraton "What-not," 1800–1810	267
264.	Sheraton Dining-table and Chair, about 1810	267
265.	Sheraton Work-table, about 1800	268
266.	Sheraton Work-table, 1810–1815	268
267.	Maple and Mahogany Work-tables, 1810–1820	269
268.	Work-table, 1810	270
269.	Work-table, 1810	270
270.	Hepplewhite Dining-table, 1790	271
271.	Pillar-and-claw extension Dining-table, 1800	272
272.	Pillar-and-claw Centre-table, 1800	273
273.	Extension Dining-table, 1810	274
274.	Accordion Extension Dining-table, 1820	274
275.	Card-table, 1805–1810	275
276.	Phyfe Card-table, 1810–1820	275
277.	Phyfe Card-table, 1810–1820	276
278.	Phyfe Sofa-table, 1810–1820	277
279.	Pier-table, 1820–1830	278
280.	Work-table, 1810–1820	279
	Looking-glass, 1760–1770	280
281.	Stephen Keene Spinet, about 1690	282
282.	Thomas Hitchcock Spinet, about 1690	284
283.	Broadwood Harpsichord, 1789	285

List of Illustrations

ILLUS.		PAGE
284.	Clavichord, 1745	288
285.	Clementi Piano, 1805	290
286.	Astor Piano, 1790–1800	292
287.	Clementi Piano, about 1820	293
288.	Combination Piano, Desk, and Toilet-table, about 1800	294
289.	Piano, about 1830	295
290.	Peter Erben Piano, 1826–1827	296
291.	Piano-stool, 1820–1830	298
292.	Piano, 1826	299
293.	Piano-stools, 1825–1830	300
294.	Table Piano, about 1835	301
295.	Piano, 1830	302
296.	Music-stand, about 1835	303
297.	Music-stand, about 1835	303
298.	Dulcimer, 1820–1830	304
299.	Harmonica or Musical Glasses, about 1820	305
300.	Music-stand, 1800–1810	306
301.	Music-case, 1810–1820	307
302.	Harp-shaped Piano, about 1800	308
303.	Cottage Piano, or Upright, 1800–1810	309
304.	Chickering Upright Piano, 1830	310
305.	Piano, about 1840	311
306.	Hawkey Square Piano, about 1845	312
307.	Harp, 1780–1790	313
	Looking-glass, 1785–1795	315
308.	Kitchen Fireplace, 1760	316
309.	Andirons, Eighteenth Century	317
310.	Andirons, Eighteenth Century	317
311.	"Hessian" Andirons, 1776	318
312.	Fireplace, 1770–1775	319
313.	Steeple-topped Andirons and Fender, 1775–1790	320
314.	Andirons, Creepers and Fender, 1700–1800	321
315.	Brass Andirons, 1700–1800	322
316.	Brass-headed Iron Dogs, 1700–1800	322
317.	Mantel at Mount Vernon, 1760–1770	324
318.	Mantel with Hob-grate, 1776	325
319.	Franklin Stove, 1745–1760	327
320.	Iron Fire-frame, 1775–1800	328

List of Illustrations

ILLUS.		PAGE
321.	Betty Lamps, Seventeenth Century	329
322.	Candle-stands, First Half of Eighteenth Century	330
323.	Mantel with Candle Shade, 1775–1800	332
324.	Candlesticks, 1775–1800	333
325.	Crystal Chandelier, about 1760	334
326.	Silver Lamp from Mount Vernon, 1770–1800	335
327.	Glass Chandelier for Candles, 1760	336
328.	Embroidered Screen, 1780	338
329.	Sconce of "Quill-work," 1720	340
330.	Tripod Screen, 1770	341
331.	Tripod Screen, 1765	341
332.	Candle-stand and Screen, 1750–1775	342
333.	Chippendale Candle-stand, 1760–1770	343
334.	Bronze Mantel Lamps, 1815–1840	344
335.	Brass Gilt Candelabra, 1820–1840	345
336.	Hall Lantern, 1775–1800	346
337.	Hall Lantern, 1775–1800	346
338.	Hall Lantern, 1760	347
	Looking-glass, First Quarter of Eighteenth Century	348
339.	Lantern or Bird-cage Clock, First Half of Seventeenth Century	349
340.	Lantern Clock, about 1680	350
341.	Friesland Clock, Seventeenth Century	350
342.	Bracket Clocks, 1780–1800	352
343.	Walnut Case and Lacquered Case Clocks, about 1738	354
344.	Gawen Brown Clock, 1765	356
345.	Gawen Brown Clock, 1780	356
346.	Maple Clock, 1770	357
347.	Rittenhouse Clock, 1770	357
348.	Tall Clock, about 1770	359
349.	Miniature Clock and Tall Clock, about 1800	360
350.	Tall Clock, 1800–1810	361
351.	Wall Clocks, 1800–1825	362
352.	Willard Clock, 1784	363
353.	Willard Clocks, 1800–1815	364
354.	Hassam Clock, 1800	366
355.	"Banjo" Clock, 1802–1820	367
356.	Presentation Clock, 1805	368

List of Illustrations xix

ILLUS.		PAGE
357.	Banjo Clock or Timepiece, 1802–1810	368
358.	Willard Timepiece, 1802–1810	369
359.	Lyre Clock, 1810–1820	369
360.	Lyre-shaped Clock, 1810–1820	370
361.	Eli Terry Shelf Clocks, 1824	371
362.	French Clock, about 1800	372
	Looking-glass, First Quarter of the Eighteenth Century	374
363.	Looking-glass, 1690	375
364.	Looking-glass, 1690	376
365.	Looking-glass, about 1730	378
366.	Pier Glass in "Chinese Taste," 1760	380
367.	Looking-glass, about 1760	382
368.	Looking-glass, 1770–1780	383
369.	Looking-glass, 1725–1750	384
370.	Looking-glass, 1770–1780	386
371.	Mantel Glass, 1725–1750	387
372.	Looking-glass, 1770	388
373.	Looking-glass, 1770	388
374.	Looking-glass, 1776	389
375.	Looking-glass, 1780	390
376.	Looking-glasses, 1750–1790	392
377.	Looking-glass, 1790	393
378.	Looking-glass, 1780	393
379.	Enamelled Mirror Knobs, 1770–1790	394
380.	Girandole, 1770–1780	395
381.	Looking-glass, Adam Style, 1780	396
382.	Looking-glass, 1790	397
383.	Hepplewhite Looking-glass, 1790	398
384.	Mantel Glass, 1783	399
385.	Looking-glass, 1790–1800	400
386.	"Bilboa Glass," 1770–1780	402
387.	Mantel Glass, 1790	403
388.	Mantel Glass, 1800–1810	404
389.	Cheval Glass, 1830–1840	405
390.	Looking-glass, 1810–1825	406
391.	Looking-glass, 1810–1815	407
392.	Looking-glass, 1810–1825	408
393.	Pier Glass, 1810–1825	409

ILLUS.		PAGE
394.	Looking-glass, 1810–1825	410
	Looking-glass	411
395.	Doorway and Mantel, Cook-Oliver House	413
396.	Doorway, Dalton House	414
397.	Mantel, Dalton House	416
398.	Mantel, Dalton House	417
399.	Hall and Stairs, Dalton House	418
400.	Mantel, Penny-Hallett House	419
401.	Doorway, Parker-Inches-Emery House	420
402.	Mantel, Lee Mansion	421
403.	Landing and Stairs, Lee Mansion	422
404.	Stairs, Harrison Gray Otis House	424
405.	Mantel, Harrison Gray Otis House	425
406.	Stairs, Robinson House	426
407.	Stairs, Allen House	427
408.	Balusters and Newel, Oak Hill	428
409.	Stairs, Sargent-Murray-Gilman House	429
410.	Mantel, Sargent-Murray-Gilman House	430
411.	Mantel, Kimball House	431
412.	Mantel, Lindall-Barnard-Andrews House	432
413.	Doorway, Larkin-Richter House	433
414.	Doorway, "Octagon"	434
415.	Mantel, "Octagon"	435
416.	Mantel, Schuyler House	436
417.	Mantel and Doorways, Manor Hall	438
418.	Mantel and Doorways, Manor Hall	439
419.	Mantel, Manor Hall	440
420.	Doorway, Independence Hall	441
421.	Stairs, Graeme Park	442
422.	Mantel and Doorways, Graeme Park	443
423.	Doorway, Chase House	445
424.	Entrance and Stairs, Cliveden	446
425.	Mantel, Cliveden	447
426.	Fretwork Balustrade, Garrett House	448
427.	Stairs, Valentine Museum	449
428.	Mantel, Myers House	450

FURNITURE
OF THE OLDEN TIME

Furniture of the Olden Time

INTRODUCTION

THE furniture of the American colonies was at first of English manufacture, but before long cabinet-makers and joiners plied their trade in New England, and much of the furniture now found there was made by the colonists. In New Amsterdam, naturally, a different style prevailed, and the furniture was Dutch. As time went on and the first hardships were surmounted, money became more plentiful, until by the last half of the seventeenth century much fine furniture was imported from England and Holland, and from that time fashions in America were but a few months behind those in England.

In the earliest colonial times the houses were but sparsely furnished, although Dr. Holmes writes of leaving —

"The Dutchman's shore,
With those that in the *Mayflower* came, a hundred souls or more,
Along with all the furniture to fill their new abodes,
To judge by what is still on hand, at least a hundred loads."

If one were to accept as authentic all the legends told of various pieces, — chairs, tables, desks, spinets, and even pianos, — Dr. Holmes's estimate would be too moderate.

The first seats in general use were forms or benches, not more than one or two chairs belonging to each household. The first tables were long boards placed upon trestles. Chests were found in almost every house, and bedsteads, of course, were a necessity. After the first chairs, heavy and plain or turned, with strong braces or stretchers between the legs, came the leather-covered chairs of Dutch origin, sometimes called Cromwell chairs, followed by the Flemish cane chairs and couches. This takes us to the end of the seventeenth century. During that period tables with turned legs fastened to the top had replaced the earliest "table borde" upon trestles, and the well-known "hundred legged" or "forty legged" table had come into use.

Cupboards during the seventeenth century were made of oak ornamented in designs similar to those upon oak chests. Sideboards with drawers were not used in this country until much later, although there is one of an early period in the South Kensington Museum, made of oak, with turned legs, and with drawers beneath the top.

Desks were in use from the middle of the seventeenth century, made first of oak and later of cherry and walnut. Looking-glasses were owned by the wealthy, and clocks appear in inventories of the latter part of the century. Virginals were mentioned during the seventeenth century, and spinets were not uncommon in the century following.

With the beginning of the eighteenth century came the strong influence of Dutch fashions, and chairs and tables were made with the Dutch cabriole or bandy leg, sometimes with the shell upon the knee, and later with the claw-and-ball foot. Dutch high chests with turned legs had been in use before this, and the high chest with bandy legs like the chairs and tables soon became a common piece of furniture. With other Dutch fashions came that of lacquering furniture with Chinese designs, and tables, scrutoirs or desks, looking-glass frames, stands, and high chests were ornamented in this manner.

The wood chiefly used in furniture was oak, until about 1675, when American black walnut came into use, and chests of drawers, tables, and chairs were made of it; it was the wood oftenest employed in veneer at that time.

Sheraton wrote in 1803: "There are three species of walnut tree, the English walnut, and the white and black Virginia. Hickory is reckoned to class with the white Virginia walnut. The black Virginia was much in use for cabinet work about forty or fifty years since in England, but is now quite laid by since the introduction of mahogany."

Mahogany was discovered by Sir Walter Raleigh in 1595. The first mention of its use in this country is in 1708. Mr. G. T. Robinson, in the London *Art Journal* of 1881, says that its first use in England was in 1720, when some planks of it were brought to Dr. Gibbon by a West India captain. The wood was pronounced too hard, and it was not until Mrs. Gibbon wanted a candle-box that any use was made of the planks, and then only because the obstinate doctor insisted upon it. When the candle-box was finished, a bureau (*i.e.* desk) was made of the wood, which was greatly admired, and as Mr. Robinson says, "Dr. Gibbon's obstinacy and Mrs. Gibbon's candle-box revolutionized English household furniture; for the system of construction and character of design were both altered by its introduction." It is probable that furniture had been made in England of mahogany previous to 1720, but that may be the date when it became fashionable.

The best mahogany came from Santiago, Mexican mahogany being soft, and Honduras mahogany coarse-grained.

The earliest English illustrated book which included designs for furniture was published by William Jones in 1739. Chippendale's first book of designs was issued in 1754. He was followed by Ince and Mayhew, whose book was undated; Thomas Johnson — 1758; Sir William Chambers — 1760; Society of Upholsterers — about 1760; Matthias Lock — 1765; Robert Manwaring — 1766; Matthias Darly — 1773; Robert and J. Adam — 1773; Thomas Shearer (in "The Cabinet-makers' London Book of Prices") — 1788; A. Hepplewhite & Co. — 1789; Thomas Sheraton — 1791-1793 and 1803.

Sir William Chambers in his early youth made a voyage to China, and it is to his influence that we can attribute much of the rage for Chinese furniture and decoration which was in force about 1760 to 1770.

Thomas Chippendale lived and had his shop in St. Martin's Lane, London. Beyond that we know but little of his life. His book, "The Gentleman's and Cabinet-Maker's Director," was published in 1754, at a cost of £3.13.6 per copy. The second edition followed in 1759, and the third in 1762. It contains one hundred and sixty copper plates, the first twenty pages of which are taken up with designs for chairs, and it is largely as a chair-maker that Chippendale's name has become famous. His furniture combines French, Gothic, Dutch, and Chinese styles, but so great was his genius that the effect is thoroughly harmonious, while he exercised the greatest care in the construction of his furniture — especially chairs. He was beyond everything a carver, and his designs show a wealth of delicate carving. He used no inlay or painting, as others had done before him, and as others did after him, and only occasionally did he employ gilding, lacquer, or brass ornamentation.

Robert and James Adam were architects, trained in the classics. Their furniture was distinctly classical, and was designed for rooms in the Greek or Roman style. Noted painters assisted them in decorating the rooms and the furniture, and Pergolesi, Angelica Kaufmann, and Cipriani did not scorn to paint designs upon satinwood furniture.

Matthias Lock and Thomas Johnson were notable as designers of frames for pier glasses, ovals, girandoles, etc.

Thomas Shearer's name was signed to the best designs of those published in 1788 in "The Cabinet-Makers' Book of Prices." His drawings comprise tables of various sorts, dressing-chests, writing-desks, and sideboards, but there is not one chair among them. He was the first to design the form of sideboard with which we are familiar.

As Chippendale's name is used to designate the furniture of 1750–1780, so the furniture of the succeeding period may be called Hepplewhite; for although he was one of several cabinet-makers who worked together, his is the best-known name, and his was probably the most original genius. His chairs bear no resemblance to those of Chippendale, and are lighter and more graceful; but because of the attention he paid to those qualifications, strength of construction and durability were neglected. His chair-backs have no support beside the posts which extend up from the back legs, and upon these the shield or heart-shaped back rests in such a manner that it could endure but little strain.

Hepplewhite's sideboards were admirable in form and decoration, and it is from them and his chairs that his name is familiar in this country. His swell or serpentine front bureaus were copied in great numbers here.

His specialty was the inlaying or painting with which his furniture was enriched. Satinwood had been introduced from India shortly before this, and tables, chairs, sideboards, and bureaus were inlaid with this wood upon mahogany, while small pieces were veneered entirely with it. The same artists who assisted the Adam brothers painted medallions, wreaths of flowers or arabesque work upon Hepplewhite's satinwood furniture. Not much of this painted furniture came to this country, but the fashion was followed by our ancestresses, who were taught, among other accomplishments, to paint flowers and figures upon light wood furniture, tables and screens being the pieces usually chosen for decoration.

Thomas Sheraton published in 1791 and 1793, "The Cabinet-Maker and Upholsterer's Drawing Book"; in 1803, his "Cabinet Dictionary"; in 1804, "Designs for Household Furniture," and "The Cabinet-Maker, Upholsterer, and General Artist's Encyclopedia," which was left unfinished in 1807.

"The Cabinet-Maker and Upholsterer's Drawing Book" is largely taken up with drawings and remarks upon perspective, which are hopelessly unintelligible. His instructions for making the pieces designed are most minute, and it is probably due to this circumstantial care that Sheraton's furniture, light as it looks, has lasted in good condition for a hundred years or more.

Sheraton's chairs differ from Hepplewhite's, which they resemble in many respects, in the construction of the backs, which are usually square, with the back legs extending to the top rail, and the lower rail joining the posts a few inches above the seat. The backs were ornamented with carving, inlaying, painting, gilding, and brass. The lyre was a favorite design, and it appears in his chair-backs and in the supports for tables, often with the strings made of brass wire.

Sheraton's sideboards are similar to those of Shearer and Hepplewhite, but are constructed with more attention to the utilitarian side, with sundry conveniences, and with the fluted legs which Sheraton generally uses. His designs show sideboards also with ornamental brass rails at the back, holding candelabra.

His desks and writing-tables are carefully and minutely described, so that the manifold combinations and contrivances can be accurately made.

Sheraton's later furniture was heavy and generally ugly, following the Empire fashions, and his fame rests upon the designs in his first book. He was the last of the great English cabinet-makers, although he had many followers in England and in America.

After the early years of the nineteenth century, the fashionable furniture was in the heavy, clumsy styles which were introduced with the Empire, until the period of ugly black walnut furniture which is familiar to us all.

While there have always been a few who collected antique furniture, the general taste for collecting began with the interest kindled by the Centennial Exposition in 1876. Not many years ago the collector of old furniture and china was jeered at, and one who would, even twenty years since, buy an old "high-boy" rather than a new black walnut chiffonier, was looked upon as "queer." All that is now changed. The chiffonier is banished for the high-boy, when the belated collector can secure one, and the influence of antique furniture may be seen in the immense quantity of new furniture modelled after the antique designs, but not made, alas, with the care and thought for durability which were bestowed upon furniture by the old cabinet-makers.

Introduction

Heaton says: "It appears to require about a century for the wheel of fashion to make one complete revolution. What our great-grandfather bought and valued (1750–1790); what our grandfathers despised and neglected (1790–1820); what our fathers utterly forgot (1820–1850), we value, restore, and copy!"

Since the publication of this book in 1902, many old houses in this country have been restored by different societies interested in the preservation of antiquities. These historic houses have been carefully and suitably furnished, thus carrying out what should be our patriotic duty, the gathering and preserving of everything connected with our history and life. Thus much furniture has been rescued, not only from unmerited oblivion, but from probable destruction.

CHAPTER I

CHESTS, CHESTS OF DRAWERS, AND DRESSING-TABLES

THE chest was a most important piece of furniture in households of the sixteenth and seventeenth centuries. It served as table, seat, or trunk, besides its accepted purpose to hold valuables of various kinds.

Chests are mentioned in the earliest colonial inventories. Ship chests, board chests, joined chests, wainscot chests with drawers, and carved chests are some of the entries; but the larger portion are inventoried simply as chests.

All woodwork — chests, stools, or tables — which was framed together, chiefly with mortise and tenon, was called joined, and joined chests and wainscot chests were probably terms applied to panelled chests to distinguish them from those of plain boards, which were common in every household, and which were brought to this country on the ships with the colonists, holding their scanty possessions.

The oldest carved chests were made without drawers beneath, and were carved in low relief in designs which appear upon other pieces of oak furniture of the same period.

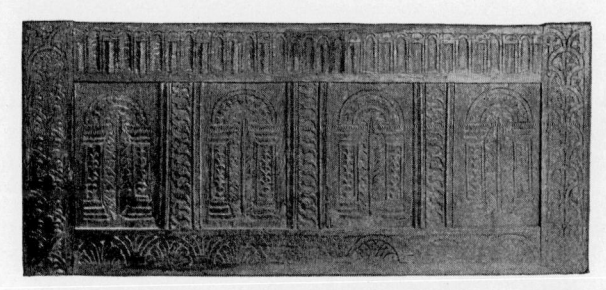

Illus. 1.— Oak Chest, about 1650.

Illustration 1 shows a chest now in Memorial Hall, at Deerfield, which was taken from the house where the Indians made their famous attack in 1704. The top of the chest is missing, and the feet, which were continuations of the stiles, are worn away or sawed off. The design and execution of the carving are unusually fine, combining several different patterns, all of an early date. Chests were carved in the arch design with three or four panels, but seldom as elaborately as this, which was probably made before 1650.

Illustration 2 shows a remarkable chest now owned by Mrs. Caroline Foote Marsh of Claremont-on-the-James, Virginia. Until recently it has remained in the family of D'Olney Stuart, whose ancestor, of the same name, was said to be of the royal Stuart blood, and who brought it with him when he fled to Virginia after the beheading of Charles I.

The feet have been recently added, and should be large balls; otherwise the chest is original in every respect. It is made entirely of olive-wood, the body being constructed of eight-inch planks. The decoration is produced with carving and burnt work. Upon the inside of the lid are three panels, the centre one containing a portrait in burnt work of James I. with his little dog by his side. The two side panels portray the Judgment of Solomon, the figures being clad in English costumes; in the left panel the two kneeling women claim the child; in the right the child is held up for the executioner to carry out Solomon's command to cut it in two. The outside of the lid has the Stuart coat of arms burnt upon it. Upon the front of the chest are four knights, and between them are three panels, surrounded by a moulding, which is now missing around the middle panel. These three panels are carved and burnt with views of castles; and around the lock, above the middle panel, are carved the British lions supporting the royal coat of arms. The chest measures six feet in length and is twenty-four inches high.

Chests with drawers are mentioned as early as 1650, and the greater number of chests found in New England have one or two drawers.

Illus. 2.—Olive-wood Chest, 1630-1650.

Illustration 3 shows a chest with one drawer owned by the Connecticut Historical Society, made about 1660. There is no carving upon this chest, which is panelled and ornamented with turned spindles and drops. The stiles are continued below the chest to form the feet.

Illus. 3. — Panelled Chest with One Drawer, about 1660.

A chest with two drawers is shown in Illustration 4, made probably in Connecticut, as about fifty of this style have been found there, chiefly in Hartford County. The top, back, and bottom are of pine, the other portions of the chest being of American oak. The design of the carving is similar upon all these chests, and the turned drop ornament upon the stiles, and the little egg-shaped pieces upon the drawers, appear upon all. They have been found with one or two drawers or none, but usually with two. This chest is in Memorial Hall, at Deerfield.

A chest with two drawers owned by Charles R. Waters, Esq., of Salem, is shown in Illustration 5. The mouldings upon the front of the frame are carved in a simple design. The wood in the centre of the panels is stained a dark color, the spindles and mouldings being of oak like the rest of the chest.

Illus. 4.—Oak Chest with Two Drawers, about 1675.

A number of chests carved in a manner not seen elsewhere have been found in and about Hadley, Massachusetts, and this has given them the name of Hadley chests. The carving in all is similar, upon the front only, the ends being panelled, and all have three panels above the drawers, with initials carved in the middle panel. The other two panels have a conventionalized tulip design, which is carved upon the rest of the front, in low relief. The carving is usually stained while the background is left the natural color of the wood.

Illustration 6 shows a Hadley chest with one drawer owned by Dwight M. Prouty, Esq., of Boston.

Illus. 5. — Panelled Chest with Two Drawers, about 1675.

Carved chests with three drawers are rarely found in any design, although the plain board chests were made with that number.

Illustration 7 and Illustration 8 show chests mounted upon frames. Illustration 8 stands thirty-two inches high and is thirty inches wide, and is made of oak, with one drawer. It is in the collection of Charles R. Waters, Esq., of Salem. Illustration 7 is slightly taller, with one drawer. This chest is in the collection of the late Major Ben: Perley Poore, at Indian Hill. Such chests upon frames are rarely found, and by some they are supposed to have been made for use as desks; but it seems more probable that they were simple chests for linen, taking the

Illus. 6. — Carved Chest with One Drawer, about 1700.

place of the high chest of drawers which was gradually coming into fashion during the latter half of the seventeenth century, and possibly being its forerunner. Chests continued in manufacture and in use until after 1700, but they were probably not made later than 1720 in any numbers, as several years previous to that date they were inventoried as "old," a word which was as condemnatory in those years as now, as far as the fashions were concerned.

Chests of drawers appear in inventories about

1645. They were usually made of oak and were similar in design to the chests of that period.

The oak chest of drawers in Illustration 9 is owned by E. R. Lemon, Esq., of the Wayside Inn, Sudbury. It has four drawers, and the decoration is simply panelling. The feet are the large balls which were used upon chests finished with a deep moulding at the lower edge. The drop handles are of an

Illus. 7 and Illus. 8.— Panelled Chests upon Frames, 1670–1700.

unusual design, the drop being of bell-flower shape. This chest of drawers was found in Malden.

Illustration 10 shows a very fine oak chest of four drawers, owned by Dwight M. Prouty, Esq., of Boston. The spindles upon this chest are unusually good, especially the large spindles upon the stiles. There is a band of simple carving between the drawers. The ends are panelled and the handles are wooden knobs.

Chests, Chests of Drawers, Dressing-tables 19

From the time that high chests of drawers were introduced, during the last part of the seventeenth century, the use of oak in furniture gradually ceased, and its place was taken by walnut or cherry, and later by mahogany. With the disuse of oak came

Illus 9.—Panelled Chest of Drawers, about 1680.

a change in the style of chests, which were no longer made in the massive panelled designs of earlier years.

The moulding around the drawers is somewhat of a guide to the age of a piece of furniture. The earliest moulding was large and single, upon the frame around the drawers. The next moulding con-

20   Furniture of the Olden Time

sisted of two strips, forming a double moulding. These strips were in some cases separated by a plain band about half an inch in width. Later still, upon

Illus. 10.— Panelled Chest of Drawers, about 1680.

block front pieces a small single moulding bordered the frame around the drawers, while upon Hepplewhite and Sheraton furniture the moulding was upon the drawer itself. Early in the eighteenth century, about 1720, high chests were made with no moulding about the drawers, the edges of which lapped over the frame.

Another guide to the age of a piece of furniture made with drawers is found in the brass handles, which are shown in Illustration 11 in the different styles in use from 1675. The handle and escutcheon lettered A, called a "drop handle," was used upon six-legged high chests, and sometimes upon chests. The drop may be solid or hollowed out in the back. The shape of the plate and escutcheon varies, being round, diamond, or shield shaped, cut in curves or points upon the edges, and generally stamped. It is fastened to the drawer front by a looped wire, the ends of which pass through a hole in the wood and are bent in the inside of the drawer.

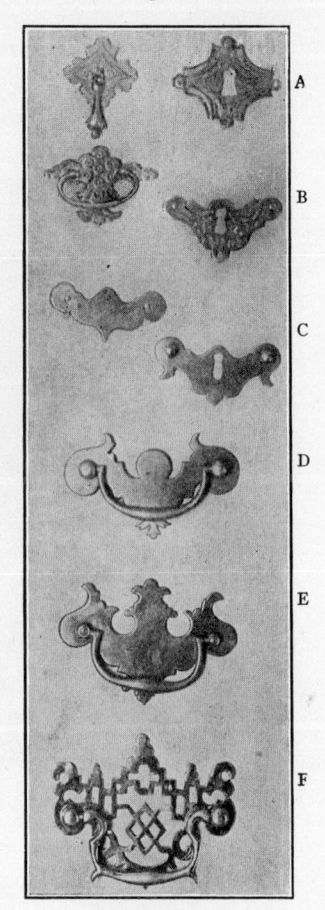

Illustration 11.

A handle and escutcheon of the next style are lettered B. They are found upon six-legged and early bandy-legged high chests. The plate of the handle is of a type somewhat earlier than the escutcheon. Both are stamped, and the bail of the handle is fastened with looped wires. Letter C shows the earliest styles of handles with the bail fastened into bolts which screw into the drawer. Letters D, E, and F give the succeeding styles of brass handles, the design growing more elaborate and increasing in size. These are found upon desks, chests of drawers, commodes, and other pieces of furniture of the Chippendale period.

Illus. 12.—Six-legged High Chest of Drawers, 1705–1715.

The earliest form of high chest of drawers had six turned legs, four in front and two in the back, with stretchers between the legs, and was of Dutch origin, as well as the high chest with bandy or cabriole legs, which was some years later in date. Six-legged chests were made during the last quarter of the seventeenth century, and were usually of walnut, either solid or veneered upon pine or whitewood; other woods were rarely employed. The earliest six-legged chests were made with the single moulding upon the frame about the drawers, and with two drawers at the top, which was always flat, as the broken arch did not appear in furniture until about 1730. The lower part had but one long drawer, and the curves of the lower edge were in a single arch.

The six-legged high chest of drawers in Illustration 12 belongs to F. A. Robart, Esq., of Boston. It is veneered with the walnut burl and is not of the earliest type of the six-legged chest, but was made about 1705–1715. The handles are the drop handles shown in letter A, and the moulding upon the frame around the drawers is double. There is a shallow drawer in the heavy cornice at the top, and the lower part contains three drawers.

Illus. 13. — Walnut Dressing-table, about 1700.

Dressing-tables were made to go with these chests of drawers, but with four instead of six legs. Their tops were usually veneered, and they were, like the high chests, finished with a small beading around the curves of the lower edge.

The dressing-table in Illustration 13 also belongs to Mr. Robart, and shows the style in which that piece of furniture was made.

The names "high-boy" and "low-boy" or "high-daddy" and "low-daddy" are not mentioned in old records and were probably suggested by the

Illus. 14.— Dressing-table, 1720.

appearance of the chests mounted upon their high legs.

High chests, both six-legged and bandy-legged, with their dressing-tables were sometimes decorated with the lacquering which was so fashionable during the first part of the eighteenth century.

Illustration 14 shows a dressing-table or low-boy

from the Bolles collection in the Metropolitan Museum of Art. It is covered with japanning, in Chinese designs. This dressing-table is the companion to a lacquered high-boy, with a flat top, in the Bolles collection. The handle is like letter C, in Illustration 11. That and the moulding around the drawers place its date about 1720.

Coming originally from the Orient, japanned furniture became fashionable, and consequently the process of lacquering or japanning was practised by cabinet-makers in France and England about 1700, and soon after in this country.

The earliest high chests with cabriole or bandy legs are flat-topped, and have two short drawers, like the six-legged chests, at the top. They are made of walnut, or of pine veneered with walnut. The curves at the lower edge are similar to those upon six-legged chests and are occasionally finished with a small bead-moulding.

The bandy-legged high-boy in Illustration 15 is owned by Dwight Blaney, Esq. It is veneered with walnut and has a line of whitewood inlaid around each drawer. The moulding upon the frame surrounding the drawers is the separated double moulding, and the handles are of the early stamped type shown in Illustration 11, letter B. The arrangement of drawers in both lower and upper parts is the same as in six-legged chests. A reminder of the fifth and sixth legs is left in the turned drops between the curves of the lower edge.

Steps to display china or earthenware were in use during the second quarter of the eighteenth century.

They were generally movable pieces, made like the steps in Illustration 15, in two or three tiers, the lower tier smaller than the top of the high chest, forming with the chest-top a set of graduated shelves upon the front and sides.

The broken arch, which had been used in chimney pieces during the seventeenth century, made its appearance upon furniture in the early years of the eighteenth century, and the handsomest chests were made with the broken arch top.

A lacquered or japanned high-boy in the Bolles collection, owned by the Metropolitan Museum of Art, is shown in Illustration 16. It is of later date than the lacquered dressing-table in Illustration 14, having the broken arch. The lacquering is inferior in

Illus. 15.—Cabriole-legged High Chest of Drawers with China Steps, about 1720.

Chests, Chests of Drawers, Dressing-tables 27

design to that upon the dressing-table, and at the top is a scroll design following the outline of the top drawers and the moulding of the broken arch. A large and a small fan are lacquered upon the lower middle drawer, and on the upper one is a funny little pagoda top, with a small fan, both in lacquer. The handles are of an early type, and the moulding around the drawers is a double separated one. Such japanned pieces are rare and of great value.

A fine high chest is shown in Illustration 17, from the Warner house in Portsmouth. It is of walnut and is inlaid around each drawer. The upper middle drawer is inlaid in a design of pillars with the rising sun

Illus. 16.—Lacquered High-boy, 1730.

between them, and below the sun are inlaid the initials J. S. and the date 1733. The lower drawer has a star inlaid between the pillars, and a star is inlaid upon each end of the case. The knobs at the top are inlaid with the star, and the middle knob ends in a carved flame.

J. S. was John Sherburne, whose son married the daughter of Colonel Warner. The legs of this chest were ruthlessly sawed off many years ago, in order that it might stand in a low-ceilinged room, and it is only in comparatively recent years that it has belonged to the branch of the family now owning the Warner house.

Illus. 17. — Inlaid Walnut High Chest of Drawers, 1733.

A double moulding runs upon the frame around the drawers, and the original handles were probably small, of the type in Illustration 11, letter C.

Chests, Chests of Drawers, Dressing-tables 29

A walnut high chest of a somewhat later type is shown in Illustration 18, belonging to Mrs. Rufus Woodward of Worcester. It is of walnut veneered upon pine, and the shells upon the upper and lower middle drawers are gilded, for they are, of course, carved from the pine beneath the veneer. The frame has the separated double moulding around the drawers. A row of light inlaying extends around each drawer, and in the three long drawers of the upper part the inlaying simulates the division into two drawers, which is carried out in the top drawers of both the upper and lower parts. The large handles and the fluted columns at the sides would indicate that this chest was made about 1760–1770.

Illus. 18. — Inlaid Walnut High Chest of Drawers, about 1760.

Illustration 19 shows a "high-boy" and "low-boy" of walnut, owned by the writer. The drawers, it will be seen, lap over the frame. The "high-boy" is original in every respect except the ring handles, which are new, upon the drawers carved with the rising sun or fan design. It was found in the attic of an old house, with the top separate from the lower part and every drawer out upon the floor, filled with seeds, rags, and — kittens, who, terrified by the invasion of the antique hunter, scurried from their resting-places, to the number of nine or ten, reminding one of Lowell's lines in the "Biglow Papers": —

Illus. 19. — "Low-boy" and "High-boy" of Walnut, about 1740.

> "But the old chest won't sarve her gran'son's wife,
> (For 'thout new furnitoor what good in life?)
> An' so old claw foot, from the precinks dread
> O' the spare chamber, slinks into the shed,
> Where, dim with dust, it fust and last subsides
> To holdin' seeds an' fifty other things besides."

But carefully wrapped up and tucked away in one of the small drawers were the torches for the upper and the acorn-shaped drops for the lower part. These drops were used as long as the curves followed those of the lower part of six-legged chests, but were omitted when more graceful curves and lines were used, as the design of high chests gradually differed from the early types.

The "low-boy," or dressing-table, was made to accompany every style of high chest. The low-boy in Illustration 19 shows the dressing-table which was probably used in the room with the bandy-legged high-boy, flat-topped or with the broken arch cornice. It is lower than the under part of the high-boy, which is, however, frequently supplied with a board top and sold as a low-boy, but which can be easily detected from its height and general appearance. The measurements of this high-boy and low-boy are

HIGH-BOY, lower part	LOW-BOY
3 feet high	2 feet 4 inches high
3 feet 1½ inches long	2 feet 6 inches long
21 inches deep	18 inches deep

The high-boy measures seven feet from the floor to the top of the cornice.

High chests and dressing-tables were made of maple, often very beautifully marked, in the same style as the chests of walnut and cherry. The high chest was sometimes made with the drawers extending nearly to the floor, and mounted upon bracket, ogee, or claw-and-ball feet. This was called a double chest, or chest-upon-chest.

The double chest in Illustration 20 is in the Warner house at Portsmouth. It is of English walnut, and the lower part is constructed with a recessed cupboard like the writing-table in Illustration 106. The handles upon this chest are very massive, and upon the ends of both the upper and lower parts are still larger handles with which to lift the heavy chest.

Illus. 20.—Walnut Double Chest, about 1760.

A double chest which was probably made in New-

Illus. 21.— Mahogany Double Chest, 1765.

port, Rhode Island, about 1760–1770, is shown in Illustration 21. The lower part is blocked and is carved in the same beautiful shells as Illustration 31 and Illustration 106. This double chest was made for John Brown of Providence, the leader of the party who captured the *Gaspee* in 1772, and one of the four famous Brown brothers, whose name is perpetuated in Brown University. This chest is now owned by a descendant of John Brown, John Brown Francis Herreshoff, Esq., of New York.

Illus. 22.— Block-front Dressing-table, about 1750.

A low-boy of unusual design, in the Warner house, is shown in Illustration 22. The front is blocked, with a double moulding upon the frame around the drawers. The bill of lading in Illustra-

Chests, Chests of Drawers, Dressing-tables 35

tion 109 specified a dressing-table, brought from England to this house in 1716, but so early a date cannot be assigned to this piece, although it is undoubtedly English, like the double chair in Illustration 212, which has similar feet, for such lions' feet are almost never found upon furniture made in this country. The shape of the cabriole leg is poor, the curves being too abrupt, but the general effect of the low-boy is very rich. The handles are the original ones, and they with the fluted columns and blocked front determine the date of the dressing-table to be about 1750.

Illus. 23.—Dressing-table, about 1760.

The low-boy in Illustration 23 is probably of slightly later date. It has the separated double moulding upon the frame around the drawers, and the curves of the lower part are like the early high chests, but the carving upon the cabriole legs, and the fluted columns at the corners, like those in Chippendale's designs, indicate that it was made after 1750. Upon the top are two pewter lamps, one with glass lenses to intensify the light; a smoker's tongs, and a pipe-case of mahogany, with a little drawer in it to hold the tobacco. This dressing-table is owned by Walter Hosmer, Esq.

The little chest of drawers in Illustration 24 belongs to Daniel Gilman, Esq., of Exeter, New Hampshire, and was inherited by him. It is evidently adapted from the high-boy, in order to make

Illus. 24.—Chest of Drawers, 1740.

a smaller and lower piece, and it is about the size of a small bureau. The upper part is separate from the lower part, and is set into a moulding, just as the upper part of a high-boy sets into the lower. The handles and the moulding around the drawers are of the same period as the ones upon the chest in Illustration 20.

The furniture made in and around Philadelphia was much more elaborately carved and richly or-

Illus. 25. — High Chest of Drawers, about 1765.

namented than that of cabinet-makers further north, and the finest tables, high-boys, and low-boys that are found were probably made there. They have large handles, like letter F, in Illustration 11, and finely carved applied scrolls.

The richest and most elaborate style attained in such pieces of furniture is shown in the high chest in Illustration 25, which is one of the finest high chests known. The proportions are perfect, and the carving is all well executed. This chest was at one time in the Pendleton collection, and is now owned by Harry Harkness Flagler, Esq., of Millbrook, New York.

Such a chest as this was in Nathaniel Hawthorne's mind when he wrote: "After all, the moderns have invented nothing better in chamber furniture than those chests which stand on four slender legs, and send an absolute tower of mahogany to the ceiling, the whole terminating in a fantastically carved summit."

The dressing-table and looking-glass in Illustration 26 are also owned by Mr. Flagler. The looking-glass is described upon page 385. The dressing-table is a beautiful and dainty piece of furniture of the same high standard as the chest last described. The carving upon the cabriole legs is unusually elaborate and well done. It will be noticed that the lower edge of these pieces is no longer finished in the simple manner of the earlier high-boys and low-boys, but is cut in curves, which vary with each piece of furniture.

In Illustration 365 upon page 378 is a low-boy of walnut, owned by the writer, of unusually graceful

Chests, Chests of Drawers, Dressing-tables 39

proportions, the carved legs being extremely slender. The shell upon this lowboy is carved in the frame below the middle drawer instead of upon it, as is usual.

The dressing-table in Illustration 27 also belongs to the writer. It is of walnut, like the majority of similar pieces, and is finely carved but is not so graceful as Illustration 365. The handles are the original ones and are very large and handsome.

High chests and the accompanying dressing-tables continued in use until the later years of the eighteenth cen-

Illus. 26.—Dressing-table and Looking-glass, about 1770.

40   Furniture of the Olden Time

tury. Hepplewhite's book, published in 1789, contains designs for chests of drawers, extending nearly to the floor, with bracket feet, one having

Illus. 27.— Walnut Dressing-table, about 1770.

fluted columns at the corners, and an urn with garlands above the flat top. It is probable, however, that high chests of drawers were not made in any number after 1790.

CHAPTER II

BUREAUS AND WASHSTANDS

THE word "bureau" is now used to designate low chests of drawers. Chippendale called such pieces "commode tables" or "commode bureau tables." As desks with slanting lids for a long period during the eighteenth century were called "bureaus" or "bureau desks," the probability is that chests of drawers which resembled desks in the construction of the lower part went by the name of "bureau tables" because of the flat table-top. Hepplewhite called such pieces "commodes" or "chests of drawers." As the general name by which they are now known is "bureau," it has seemed simpler to call them so in this chapter.

Bureaus were made of mahogany, birch, or cherry, and occasionally of maple, while a few have been found of rosewood. Walnut was not used in serpentine or swell front bureaus, although walnut chests of drawers are not uncommon, which look like the top part of a high chest, with bracket feet, and handles of an early design; and so far as the writer's observation goes, few bureaus with three or four drawers were made of walnut.

Illus. 28.— Block-front Bureau, about 1770.

The wood usually employed in the finest bureaus is mahogany, and the earliest ones are small, with the serpentine, block, or straight front, and with the top considerably larger than the body, projecting nearly an inch and a half over the front and sides, the edge shaped like the drawer fronts. The early handles are large and like letter E in Illustration 11.

Bureaus and Washstands 43

The block front is, like the serpentine or yoke front, carved from one thick board. It is found more frequently in this country than in England. The block-front bureau in Illustration 28 is owned by Dwight M. Prouty, Esq., of Boston, and is a very good example, with the original handles.

Illus. 29.— Block-front Bureau, about 1770.

The small bureau in Illustration 29 is in the Warner house in Portsmouth. It is of mahogany, with an unusual form of block front, the blocking being rounded. The shape of the board top corresponds to the curves upon the front of the drawers. The handles are large, and upon each end is a massive handle to lift the bureau by.

Illustration 30 shows a block-front bureau owned by the writer. Chippendale gives a design of a bureau similar to this, with three drawers upon rather high legs, under the name of "commode table."

Illus. 31.— Kettle-shaped Bureau, about 1770.

The height of the legs brings the level of the bureau top about the same as one with four drawers. One handle and one escutcheon were remaining upon this bureau, and the others were cast from them. The block front with its unusually fine shells would indicate that this piece, which came from Colchester, Connecticut, was made by the same Newport cabinet-maker as the writing-table in Illustration 106, and

Illus. 30. — Block-front Bureau, about 1770.

the double chest in Illustration 21, which were made about 1765. The looking-glass in the illustration is described upon page 410.

Illustration 31 shows a mahogany bureau of the style known as "kettle" shape, owned by Charles R. Waters, Esq., of Salem. Desks and secretaries were occasionally made with the lower part in this style, and many modern pieces of Dutch marqueterie with kettle fronts are sold as antiques. But little marqueterie furniture was brought to this country in old times, and even among the descendants of Dutch families in New York State it is almost impossible to find any genuine old pieces of Dutch marqueterie.

Illus. 32.— Serpentine-front Bureau, about 1770.

A bureau with serpentine front is shown in Illustration 32. It is made in two sections, the upper part with four drawers being set into the moulding around the base in the same manner as the top part of a high-boy sets into the lower part. The bureau is owned by Charles Sibley, Esq., of Worcester.

The bureaus described so far all have the small single moulding upon the frame around the drawer. From the time when the designs of Shearer and

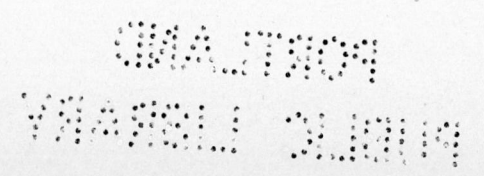

Bureaus and Washstands

Hepplewhite became fashionable, bureaus were made with a fine bead moulding upon the edge of the drawer itself or without any moulding.

The serpentine-front bureau in Illustration 33 belongs to Mrs. Johnson-Hudson of Stratford, Connecticut. The corners are cut off so as to form the effect of a narrow pillar, which is, like the

Illus. 33.—Serpentine-front Bureau, about 1785.

drawers and the bracket feet, inlaid with fine lines of holly. The bracket feet and the handles would indicate that this bureau was made before 1789.

A bureau of the finest Hepplewhite type is shown in Illustration 34, owned by Mrs. Charles H. Carroll of Worcester. The base has the French foot which was so much used by Hepplewhite, which is entirely different from Chippendale's French foot. The

Illus. 34.— Swell-front Inlaid Bureau, about 1795.

curves of the lower edge, which are outlined with a line of holly, are unusually graceful; the knobs are brass.

Illustration 35 shows the styles of handles chiefly found upon pieces of furniture with drawers, after **1770**. A is a handle which was used during the last years of the Chippendale period, and the first years of the Hepplewhite. B and C are the oval pressed brass handles found upon Hepplewhite furniture. They were made round as well as oval, and

Bureaus and Washstands

were in various designs; the eagle with thirteen stars, a serpent, a beehive, a spray of flowers, or heads of historic personages — Washington and Jefferson being the favorites. D is the rosette and ring handle, of which E shows an elaborate form. These handles were used upon Sheraton pieces and also upon the heavy veneered mahogany furniture made during the first quarter of the nineteenth century. F is the brass knob handle used from 1800 to 1820. G is the glass knob which, in clear and opalescent glass, came into use about 1815 and which is found upon furniture made for twenty years after that date, after which time wooden knobs were used, often displacing the old brass handles.

Looking-glasses made to swing in a frame are mentioned in inventories of 1750, and about that date may be given to the dressing-glass with drawers, shown in Illustration 36. It was owned by Lucy Flucker, who took it with her when, in opposition to her parents' wishes, she

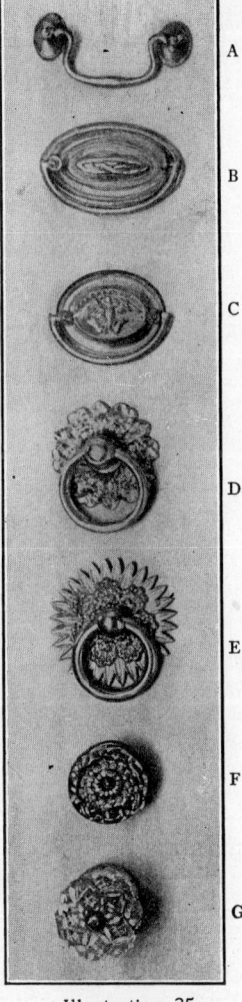

Illustration 35.

E

married in 1774 the patriot General Knox. It is now in the possession of the Hon. James Phinney Baxter, Esq., of Portland, Maine. Such dressing-glasses were intended to stand upon a dressing-table or bureau.

A bureau and dressing-glass owned by the writer are shown in Illustration 37. The bureau is of cherry, with the drawer fronts veneered in mahogany edged with satinwood. A row of fine inlaying runs around the edge of the top and beneath the drawers. This lower line of inlaying appears upon inexpensive bureaus of this period, and seems to have been considered indispensable to the finish of a bureau. The dressing-glass is of mahogany and satinwood with fine inlaying around the frame of the glass and the edge of the stand. The base of the bureau is of a plain type, while that of the dressing-glass has the same graceful curves that appear in Illustration 34.

Illus. 36.— Dressing-glass, about 1760.

Bureaus and Washstands

The bureaus in Illustration 34 and Illustration 37 are in the Hepplewhite style. The bureau and dressing-glass in Illustration 38 are distinctly Sheraton, of the best style. They are owned by Dwight Blaney, Esq., of Boston, and were probably made about 1810. The carving upon the bureau legs and upon the corners and side supports to the dressing-glass is finely executed. The handles to the drawers are brass knobs.

A bureau of the same date is shown in Illustration 39. It was owned originally by William F. Lane, Esq., of Boston. Mr. Lane had several children, for whom he had miniature pieces of furniture made, the little sofa in Illustration 228 being one. The small bureau upon the

Illus. 37. — Bureau and Dressing-glass, 1795.

top of the large one was part of a bedroom set, which included a tiny four-post bedstead. This

Illus. 38. — Bureau and Dressing-glass, about 1810.

miniature furniture was of mahogany like the large pieces. The handles upon the large bureau are not original. They should be rosette and ring, or knobs similar to those upon the small bureau. The bureaus are now owned by a daughter of Mr. Lane, Mrs. Thomas H. Gage of Worcester.

Bureaus of this style were frequently made of cherry with the drawer fronts of curly or bird's-eye maple, the fluted pillars at the corner and the frame around the drawers being of cherry or mahogany.

Illus. 39.— Bureau and Miniature Bureau, about 1810.

There was added to the bureau about this time — perhaps evolved from the dressing-glass with drawers — an upper tier of shallow drawers, usually three. The dressing-table shown in Illustration 40 is owned by Charles H. Morse, Esq., of Charlestown, New Hampshire. It stands upon high legs turned and reeded, and a dressing-glass is attached above the three little drawers. The handles should be rings or knobs.

The case of drawers with closet above, in Illustration 41, is owned by Mrs. Thomas H. Gage, of Worcester. It is of mahogany, the doors of the

Illus. 40. — Dressing-table and Glass, 1810.

closet being of especially handsome wood. The carving at the top of the fluted legs is fine, and the piece of furniture is massive and commodious.

The bureau in Illustration 42 is also owned by

Bureaus and Washstands   55

Mrs. Gage, and is a very good specimen of the furniture in the heavy style fashionable during the first quarter of the nineteenth century. It was probably made to match a four-post bedstead with twisted posts surmounted by pineapples. The drawer fronts are veneered, like those of all the bureaus illustrated in this chapter except the first four, and there is no moulding upon the edge of the drawers.

Illustration 43 shows the heaviest form of bureau, made about the same time as the last one shown, with heavily carved pillars and bears' feet. The drawer fronts are veneered and have no moulding upon the edge. This bureau is owned

Illus. 41.—Case of Drawers with Closet, 1810.

by Mrs. S. B. Woodward of Worcester, and it is a fine example of the furniture after the style of Empire pieces.

The bureau in Illustration 44 is owned by Charles H. Morse, Esq., of Charlestown, and shows the latest type of Empire bureau, with ball feet, and large round veneered pillars. The three Empire

Illus. 42.— Bureau, about 1815.

bureaus shown have the last touch that could be added, a back piece above the tier of small drawers. The bureaus have the top drawer of the body projecting beyond the three lower drawers, and supported by the pillars at the sides. This and the shallow tier of small drawers, and the back piece are typical features of the Empire bureau, which may have the rosette and ring handle or the knob of brass or glass.

Illus. 43.—Bureau, 1815-1820.

The toilet conveniences of our ancestors seem to our eyes most inadequate, and it is impossible that a very free use of water was customary, with the tiny bowls and pitchers which were used and the small and inconvenient washstands. A "bason frame" appears in an inventory of 1654. Chippendale designed "bason stands" which were simply a tripod stand, into the top of which the basin fitted. They were also called wig stands because they

Illus. 44. — Empire Bureau and Glass, 1810–1820.

were kept in the dressing-room where the fine gentleman halted to remove his hat, and powder his wig. The basin rested in the opening in the top, and in the little drawers were kept the powder and other accessories of the toilet. The depression in the

Bureaus and Washstands

shelf was for the ewer, probably bottle shaped, to rest in, after the gentleman had poured the water into the basin, to dip his fingers in after powdering his wig.

The charming little basin or wig stand in Illustration 45 is in the Metropolitan Museum of Art. The wood is mahogany and the feet are a flattened type of claw and ball, giving the little stand, with its basin and ewer, some stability, unless an unwary pointed toe should be caught by the spreading legs. The acanthus leaf is carved on the knees, and the chamfered corners above have an applied fret.

The drawings of Shearer, Hepplewhite and Sheraton show both square and corner washstands of mahogany with slender legs.

Illus. 45.— Basin Stand, 1770.

The washstand in Illustration 46 is of mahogany, and differs from the usual corner stand in having the enclosed cupboard. It was made from a Hepplewhite design and is owned by Francis H. Bigelow, Esq., of Cambridge.

The corner washstand in Illustration 47 is owned by the writer. It is of mahogany, and the drawers are finely inlaid, probably after a Sheraton design. The little towel-rack is of somewhat later date and is made of maple, stained. The washbowl and pitcher are dark-blue Staffordshire ware, with the well-known design of the "Tomb of Franklin" upon them.

While the corner washstand possessed the virtues of taking up but little room, and being out of the way, the latter consideration must have been keenly felt by those who, with head thrust into the corner, were obliged to use it.

A square washstand of more convenient shape, but still constructed for the small bowl and pitcher, is shown in Illustration 48. It is of mahogany and is in the style that was used from 1815 to 1830. This washstand is owned by Mrs. E. A. Morse of Worcester.

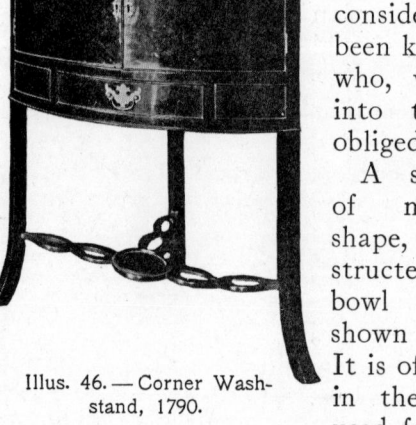

Illus. 46.— Corner Washstand, 1790.

Both corner and square washstands have an opening in the top, into which was set the washbowl, and two — sometimes three — small openings for the little cups which were used to hold the soap.

Hepplewhite's book, published in 1789, shows

designs of "night tables" like the one in Illustration 49, but they are not often found in this country. This table is of mahogany, with tambour doors, and

Illus. 47. — Towel-rack and Washstand, 1790–1800.

a carved rim around the top, pierced at each side to form a handle. The wood of the interior of the drawer is oak, showing that the table was probably made in England. It is owned by the writer.

There are several drawings in the books of Hepplewhite and Sheraton of washstands and toilet-tables with complicated arrangements for looking-glasses and toilet appurtenances, but such pieces of furniture could not have been common even in England, and certainly were not in this country.

In Illustration 288 upon page 294 is shown a

Illus. 48.—Washstand, 1815–1830.

Illus. 49.—Night Table, 1785.

piano which can be used as a toilet-table, with a looking-glass and trays for various articles, but it must have been, even when new, regarded less from the utilitarian side, and rather as a novel and ornamental piece of furniture.

A washstand of different design is shown in Illustration 50. The front is of bird's-eye maple and mahogany, and the top is of curly maple with mahogany inlay around the edge. The sides are mahogany. The two drawers are shams, and the top lifts on a hinge disclosing a compartment for a pitcher and bowl. The tapering legs end in a spade foot, and a large brass handle is upon each side. The other handles are brass knobs.

Illus. 50. — Washstand, 1800–1810.

This stand was made after instructions given by Sheraton thus, " The advantage of this kind of basin stand is, that they may stand in a genteel room, without giving offense to the eye, their appearance being somewhat like a cabinet." The washstand is owned by the writer.

CHAPTER III

BEDSTEADS

ONE of the most valuable pieces of furniture in the household of the seventeenth and eighteenth centuries was the bedstead with its belongings. Bedsteads and beds occupy a large space in inventories, and their valuation was often far more than that of any other article in the inventory, sometimes more than all the others. In spite of the great value placed upon them, none have survived to show us exactly what was meant by the "oak Marlbrough bedstead" or the "half-headed bedstead" in early inventories. About the bedstead up to 1750 we know only what these inventories tell us, but the inference is that bedsteads similar to those in England at that time were also in use in the colonies. The greater portion of the value of the bedstead lay in its furnishings, — the hangings, feather bed, bolster, quilts, blankets, and coverlid,

Bedsteads

— the bedstead proper, when inventoried separately, being placed at so low a sum that one concludes it must have been extremely plain. Several cradles made in the seventeenth century are still in existence. Illustration 51 shows one which is in Pilgrim Hall, Plymouth, and which is said to have sheltered Peregrine White, the first child born in this country to the Pilgrims. It is of wicker and of Oriental manufacture, having been brought from Holland upon the *Mayflower*, with the Pilgrims.

Illus. 51.—Wicker Cradle, 1620.

The cradle in Illustration 52 is of more substantial build. It is of oak, and was made for John Coffin, who was born in Newbury, January 8, 1680. Sergeant Stephen

Illus. 52.—Oak Cradle, 1680.

F

Jaques, "who built the meeting house with great needles and little needles pointing downward," fashioned this cradle, whose worn rockers bear witness to the many generations of babies who have slept within its sturdy frame. It is now in the rooms of the Newburyport Historical Society.

Another wooden cradle is in Pilgrim Hall, made of oak and very similar, with the turned spindles at

Ilus. 53.— Bedstead and Commode, 1750.

the sides of its wooden hood, to a cradle dated 1691, in the South Kensington Museum.

"Cupboard bedsteads" and "presse bedsteads" are mentioned in the inventories. They were probably the same as the Dutch "slaw-bank," and when not in use they were fastened up against the wall in a closet made to fit the bed, and the closet doors were closed or curtains were drawn over the bedstead. There is a slaw-bank in the old Sumner house in Shrewsbury, Massachusetts, built in 1797.

Bedsteads

Illustration 53 shows a curious bedstead made about 1750, when it was used by Dr. Samuel Johnson, president of King's College, New York. It is now owned by his descendant, Mrs. Johnson-Hudson of Stratford, Connecticut. The slanting back of the bedstead is like the back of an early

Illus. 54. — Field Bedstead, 1760–1770.

Chippendale chair, and the effect is similar to that of the couches shown in Illustration 205 and Illustration 206; but this piece was evidently intended for a bed, as it is considerably wider than the couches, which were "day beds." The wood of this bedstead is mahogany. The commode which stands beside the bed is of a slightly later date. It is also of mahogany, with massive brass handles.

Illustration 54 shows a bedstead of about 1760–1770. It is what was called a field bed, the form of its top suggesting a tent. The frames for the canopy top were made in different shapes, but the one in the illustration was most common. The drapery is made of the netted fringe so much used in those days for edging bedspreads, curtains, and covers. This deep fringe was made especially for canopy tops for bedsteads. Its manufacture has been revived by several Arts and Crafts Societies. The slat-back chair is one of the rush-bottomed variety common during the eighteenth century. This room, with its wooden rafters, is in the Whipple house at Ipswich, built in 1650.

The claw-and-ball foot bedstead in Illustration 55 was a part of the wedding outfit of Martha Tufts, who was married in 1774, in Concord. It was then hung with the printed cotton draperies, hand spun and woven, which still hang from the tester, albeit much darned and quite dropping apart with age. The draperies are of a brownish color, possibly from age, but at all events they are now dingy and unattractive, whatever they may have been in 1774. The posts above the cabriole legs are small and plain, and there is no headboard. The wood is mahogany. This bedstead is now owned by the Concord Antiquarian Society. Although Chippendale's designs do not show a bedstead with claw-and-ball feet, he probably did make such bedsteads, and this may be called Chippendale, as it belongs to that period.

Illus. 55. — Claw-and-Ball Foot Bedstead, 1774.

A bedstead with plain, simple posts, with the cover and hangings of old netting, is shown in Illustration 56. There is a good comb-back Windsor armchair and a mahogany cradle of the period in the

Illus. 56.— Bedstead, 1780.

room, which is a bedroom in the Lee Mansion, Marblehead, Mass.

A splendid bedstead found in Charleston, S. C., and now owned by J. J. Gilbert, Esq., of Baltimore, is shown in Illustration 57. All four posts are carved and reeded, and are after the manner of Chippendale. The tester and headboard show the Adam influence, placing the date of the bedstead about 1770.

Illus. 57. — Bedstead, 1775–1785.

Illustration 58 shows a bedstead made from one of Hepplewhite's designs, about 1789. The lower posts are slender and fluted, and end in a square foot. The cornice is japanned after the fashion which Hepplewhite made so popular, and the style in which this bedstead is draped is extremely attractive. It is at Indian Hill, the residence of the late Major Ben: Perley Poore.

The four-post bedsteads had sometimes canvas stretched across the frame and laced with ropes, similar to the seat of the couch in Illustration 206, and in other cases they were corded entirely with ropes. Mrs. Vanderbilt in her "Social History of Flatbush" thus describes the process of cording

Illus. 58.— Bedstead, 1789.

a bed: "It required a man's strength to turn the machine that tightened the ropes, in cording these beds when they were put together. Some one was stationed at each post to keep it upright, while a man was exhausting his strength and perhaps his stock of patience and good temper, in getting the ropes sufficiently tight to suit the wife or mother. When the bedstead was duly corded and strung to the tension required, then a straw bed, in a case of brown home-made linen, was first placed over these cords, and upon this were piled feather beds to the number of three or four, and more if this was the spare-room bed." The height of the top one of these feather beds from the floor was so great that steps were required to mount into it, and sets of mahogany steps are sometimes found now, which were made for this purpose. A set is shown in Illustration 64.

Illustration 59 shows one of the finest bedsteads known in this country. It is in the house of Charles R. Waters, Esq., of Salem. The two lower posts are exquisitely carved with garlands of flowers, and every detail is beautiful; the upper posts are plain. The size of the posts is somewhat larger than during the previous years, and the style of the lower part with the fluted leg would place the date of the bedstead about 1795–1800, when the influence of Sheraton was strong. The cornice is painted with flowers in colors, and the painted band is framed in gilt; the ornaments at the corners, the basket with two doves, and the ropes and tassels are all of gilt.

About 1800, when the Empire styles commenced to influence the makers of furniture, the posts of

Illus. 59. — Bedstead, 1795-1800.

bedsteads became larger, and they were more heavily carved, with acanthus leaves twining around the post, or a heavy twist or fluting, with pineapples at the top.

Illustration 60 shows a bedstead at Indian Hill, with the heavy posts and tester, the lower posts be-

Illus. 60.— Bedstead, 1800–1810.

ing fluted. The bedstead is draped on the side and foot with curtains which could be let down at night in cold weather, thus shutting out the bitter draughts. The coverlid for this bed is made of linen, spun and woven by hand, and embroidered in shades of blue with a quaint design. The easy-chair at the foot of the bed is covered with old chintz, printed in figures that would afford a child unlimited entertainment.

A bedstead with massive twisted posts is shown in Illustration 61. The lower posts only are carved, as was usual, the draperies at the head of the bed concealing the plain upper posts. Twisted posts were quite common during the early years of the nineteenth century, and more bed-posts are found that are carved in a twist than in any other design. The coverlid is similar to the one in Illustration 63. This bedstead stands in one of the panelled rooms of the Warner house in Portsmouth.

Illus. 61. — Bedstead, 1800–1810.

Illustration 62 shows a fine example of the four-post bedstead made from 1805 to 1810. It is unusual in having all four posts carved, and for its splendid feet, which are carved in massive lions' claws. Each post is carved with festoons of drapery, and is surmounted with a pineapple. The headboard is elaborately carved with a basket of fruit. This mahogany bedstead is owned by Mrs. E. A. Morse of Worcester.

Illustration 63 shows another bedstead with all four mahogany posts carved in the acanthus leaf and pineapple design. Each post is finished at the top with a pineapple, and the bases are set into brass sockets. Upon the plain sections of the posts may be seen pressed brass ornaments, of which there are six, two for each lower post and one for each upper

Illus. 62. — Bedstead, 1800–1810.

one. These ornaments cover the holes through which the bed-screws are put in to hold the frame

Illus. 63. — Bedstead, 1800–1810.

together. There is a headboard of simple design upon this bedstead. The coverlid is an old, handspun and woven, cotton one, with a design of stars in

Bedsteads

little cotton tufts. Such coverlids were made about 1815 to 1830. This bedstead is owned by the writer.

Illus. 64.—Bedstead and Steps, 1790.

Illustration 64 shows a bed owned by the Colonial Dames, in their house, "Stenton," in Philadelphia. It has the large, plain and heavy posts found

80   Furniture of the Olden Time

in the South. The hangings are the original ones. Beside the bed is a set of steps used to assist in mounting to the top of the feather beds used in those days. The cradle is of about the same date.

Illustration 65 shows a low-post mahogany bedstead which is owned by Dr. S. B. Woodward of

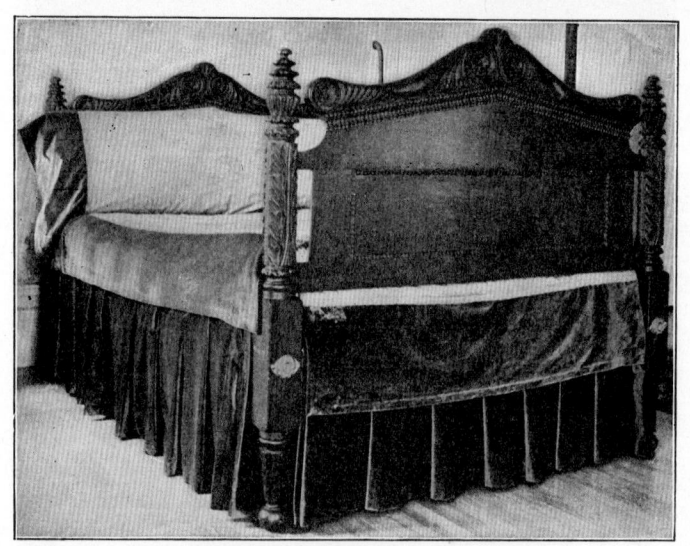

Illus. 65.—Low-post Bedstead, about 1825.

Worcester, having been inherited by him. It was made about 1825. The four posts are carved with the acanthus leaf, and both head and foot board are elaborately carved. It can be seen that the bed in this illustration is not so high from the floor as those of earlier date. The low French bedstead became fashionable soon after this time, and the high four-poster was relegated to the attic, from which it has of late years been rescued, and set up, draped with all of its old-time hangings.

The latest style of low-post bedsteads is shown in Illustration 66. It was probably made about

Illus. 66.—Low-post Bedstead, 1820–1830.

1820–1830, when the light woods, maple and birch, were, with cherry, largely used for such bedsteads. The wood of this bed is curly birch, and all four posts are carved alike with the pineapple and acanthus design, similar to the tall posts of the previous period. Low-post bedsteads are often found with posts plainly turned, of curly maple, beautifully marked.

Illustration 67 shows a low French bedstead, found in Canada and owned by George Corbett, Esq., of Worcester. The bedstead is made of finely grained old walnut, the rounding top of the head and foot boards and the face of the large

Illus. 67.— Low Bedstead, about 1830.

drawer under the footboard being veneered. This drawer may have been intended to use to keep blankets in. It has a little foot so that it remains firm when pulled out. At each side of the low bed is a carved shell, which slides out, showing a covered rest, perhaps for kneeling upon to pray. Both the head and foot boards are covered with canvas, which was probably, when the bedstead was new, about 1830, covered with a rich brocade. All the lines of the bedstead are most graceful, and the carving is unusually well done. Plainer bedsteads in this style were made, veneered with mahogany, and they are sometimes called sleigh beds, on account of their shape. These bedsteads were fashionable from 1830 to 1850, when they were superseded by the black walnut bedsteads familiar to everybody.

CHAPTER IV

CUPBOARDS AND SIDEBOARDS

CUPBOARDS appear in English inventories as early as 1344. Persons of rank in England had their cupboards surmounted by a set of shelves to display the silver and gold plate. Each shelf was narrower than the one beneath, like a set of steps, and the number of shelves indicated the rank of the owner, five being the greatest number, to be used by the king only.

The first cupboard consisted of an open framework, a "borde" upon which to set cups, as the name implies. Later it was partially enclosed below, and this enclosed cupboard was used to hold valuables, or sometimes the food which was afterward distributed by the lady of the house. This was known as an almery or press cupboard, the former

Illus. 68.—Oak Press Cupboard, 1640.

name corresponding to the French word *armoire*. The names "court cupboard" or "livery cupboard" were used to designate a piece of furniture without an enclosed cupboard, low or short, as the French word *court* implies, and intended for a serving-table, as the word "livery," from the French *livrer*, to deliver, indicates. In Europe such pieces were called *dressoirs*.

Cupboards abound in colonial inventories, under various names — "small cupboard," "great cupboard," "press cupboard," "wainscot cupboard," "court cupboard," "livery cupboard," "hanging cupboard," "sideboard cupboard." The cupboard formed an important part of the furniture owned by men of wealth and position in the colonies.

These cupboards were generally of oak, but those made in this country have the backs and bottoms of the cupboards and drawers of pine. The interior is similar in all, the lower cupboard usually having shelves, which seldom appear in the upper cupboard. Sometimes the lower part of the piece is divided into drawers for holding linen.

Such a cupboard is shown in Illustration 68. This fine example is known as the "Putnam cupboard." It is now owned by the Essex Institute, of Salem, to which it was presented by Miss Harriet Putnam Fowler of Danvers, Massachusetts. It descended to her from John Putnam, who brought it from England about 1640. Upon the back may be seen marks of a fire which two hundred years ago destroyed the house in which the cupboard stood. The wood is English oak, and the mouldings used in the panelling are of cedar. The cupboard is in two parts, the upper section with the enclosed cupboard resting upon the lower section with its three drawers.

Another panelled cupboard is shown in Illustration 69, in which both the upper and lower parts are made with a recessed cupboard, enclosed, with a drawer below. The wood is oak, with the turned pieces painted black. This cupboard is in the house of Charles R. Waters, Esq., of Salem. Upon the top are displayed some good pieces of old glass.

Illus. 69.— Press Cupboard, about 1650.

Many press cupboards were carved in designs similar to those upon the early chests. Illustration 70 shows a carved press cupboard owned by

Walter Hosmer, Esq., of Wethersfield. The wood is American oak and the cupboard was probably made in Connecticut, where there must have been

Illus. 70. — Carved Press Cupboard, 1680–1690.

unusually good cabinet-makers during the last half of the seventeenth century, for many of the best oak chests and cupboards existing in this country were made in Connecticut. This cupboard is very large, measuring five feet in height and four feet in width.

All cupboards were provided with cupboard cloths or cushions, the latter probably made somewhat thicker than the simple cloth, by the use of several layers of goods or of stuffing. These cloths or cushions were placed on the top of the cupboard, to set the glass or silver upon, and the early inventories have frequent mention of them. By 1690 the press cupboard had gone out of fashion, and but few were made after 1700, although they continued to be used by those who already owned them.

About 1710 the corner cupboard made its appearance, often under the name "beaufet" or "beaufatt." It was generally built into the corner, and was finished to correspond with the panelling around the room. The lower part was closed by panelled doors, and the upper part had sometimes one glass door, sometimes two, opening in the middle; but more often it was left without a door. The top of the beaufatt was usually made in the form of an apse, and in the finest specimens the apse was carved in a large shell. The shelves were not made to take up the entire space in the cupboard, but extended around the back, and were cut in curves and projections, evidently to fit pieces of glass or china, for the display of which the beaufatt was built rather than to serve as a simple closet. A fine beaufatt is shown in Illustration 71, which is in the Deerfield Museum. From the construction of the pillars at the side it is evident that it was not intended to use a door to the upper part.

That there was some distinction between the corner cupboard and the beaufatt would appear from the difference in their valuation in inventories, but what was the difference in their construction we do not know. Cupboards were made, during the latter part of the eighteenth century, of mahogany and other woods, and such corner cupboards, made as a piece of furniture and not built into the house, were common in the Southern States, about 1800. The corner cupboard, or beaufatt, was both convenient and ornamental, taking up but little room and filling what was often an empty space. Our ancestors frequently

Illus. 71.— Corner "Beaufatt," 1740–1750. utilized the large

chimney also, by making the sides into small closets or cupboards, and occasionally a door with glass panes was set into the chimney above the mantel, with shelves behind it to hold glass or china.

While the New England inventories speak of cupboards, the word *kas*, or *kasse*, appears in Dutch inventories in New York. The kas was the Dutch cupboard, and was different in style from the cupboard in use in New England. It was of great size, and had large doors, behind which were wide shelves to hold linen. The kas was usually made in two parts, the upper one having two doors and a heavy cornice above. The lower part held a long drawer, and rested upon large ball feet. A panelled kas of somewhat different form is shown in Illustration 72, without the ball feet, and made in three parts; the lower section with the drawer, the middle cupboard section, enclosed with large doors, and a second cupboard above that, the whole surmounted with a cornice. This kas is made of kingwood, a hard wood with a grain not unlike that of oak, but with darker markings. The bill of lading is still preserved, dated 1701, when the kas, packed full of fine linen, was imported from Holland by the father of Dr. Samuel Johnson, president of King's College from 1754 to 1763. It is now owned by Dr. Johnson's descendant, Mrs. Johnson-Hudson of Stratford, Connecticut.

Inventories during the latter years of the seventeenth century speak of a "sideboard cupboard," "sideboard table," and "side-table," but the sideboard, in our acceptance of the word, dates to the

Illus. 72.— Kas, 1700.

latter half of the eighteenth century. Chippendale designed no sideboards with drawers and compartments, but he did design side-tables, or sideboard tables, with marble or mahogany tops and carved frames. A Chippendale side-table is shown in Illustration 73. The wood is mahogany, and the frame is carved elaborately and beautifully in designs similar to those of Chippendale and his contemporaries,

Illus. 73.—Chippendale Side-table, about 1755.

which abound in flowers, birds, and shells. The cabriole legs end in massive lion's paws. This table is what is called Irish Chippendale.

In Ireland, working at the same period as Chippendale, drawing their ideas from the same sources, and probably from Chippendale as well, were cabinet-makers, much of whose work has come down, notably side-tables. The shell plays a prominent part; on this table beside the large shell are two small ones upon each leg. The carving of the Irish school

Illus. 74.—Chippendale Side-table, 1765.

is not so fine as its English model, but is very rich. This table is five feet long and the original top was of marble. It is owned by Harry Harkness Flagler, Esq., of Millbrook, New York.

A Chippendale side-table is shown in Illustration 74, which was evidently made in England, from Chippendale's designs, if not by Chippendale himself. It is very long and has had to sustain a great weight in the heavy marble top, but it is in splendid condition, perhaps because it is so heavy that it is seldom moved. It has passed through many vicissitudes, — war, fire and earthquake, — in Charleston, South Carolina, since it was brought there by the ancestor of its present owner, George W. Holmes, Esq., of Charleston.

These long side-tables were designed not only by Chippendale, but by the other cabinet-makers and designers of the day, Ince and Mayhew, and Manwaring; but the tables of these less noted men usually are made after the prevailing Chinese style, with applied fretwork and legs which are pierced, thus depriving them of the strength necessary in so large a piece. Chippendale made these also, but in this table the cabinet-maker chose a design which looks and is strong. The carving is in scrolls done in the solid wood, and is French in design. The bracket at the top of the leg is made in a scroll, which extends entirely around the table.

The earliest mention of a sideboard, the description of which implies a form of construction similar to that of the later sideboard, is in 1746, when an advertisement in a London newspaper speaks of "a Large marble Sideboard Table with Lavatory and Bottle Cistern." Chippendale's designs, published in 1753 and 1760, contain nothing answering to this description, and both he and other cabinet-makers of that period give drawings of side-tables only, without even a drawer beneath. Such a sideboard as this advertisement of 1746 mentions, may have given the idea from which, forty years later, was developed the sideboard of mahogany, often inlaid, with slender legs and curved front, which is shown in the majority of antique shops as "Chippendale," while the heavy veneered sideboard, with claw feet and compartments extending nearly to the floor, made after 1800, goes under the name of "Colonial." One name is as incorrect as the other. Thomas Shearer, an English cabinet-maker, designed the first of the slender-legged sideboards, and they appear in his drawings published in 1788. Hepplewhite's book, published in 1789, gave similar drawings, as did Sheraton's in 1791, and these three cabinet-makers designed the sideboards which were so fashionable from 1789 to 1805. The majority which are found in this country were probably made here, but one is shown in Illustration 75, which has a most romantic history of travel and adventure. It is in the half-circle shape which was Shearer's favorite design, and was probably of English make, although it was brought from France to America.

In 1792 the ship *Sally*, consigned to Colonel Swan, sailed from France, laden with rich furniture, tapestries, robes, everything gathered together in Paris which might have belonged to a royal lady.

Cupboards and Sideboards 97

The *Sally* came to Wiscasset, Maine, and the story told "down East" is that there was a plot to rescue Marie Antoinette, and the *Sally* was laden for that

Illus. 75. — Shearer Sideboard and Knife-box, 1792.

purpose; and that a house had been built in a Maine seaport for the queen, whose execution put an end to the plot, and sent the *Sally* off to America with her rich cargo. I cannot help thinking that if the story be true, Marie Antoinette was spared many weary days of discontent and homesickness; for the temperament of the unfortunate queen, luxury loving, gay, and heedless, does not fit into the life of a little Maine seaport town one hundred years ago. When the *Sally* arrived, her cargo of beautiful things was sold. Legends of Marie Antoinette furniture crop up all around the towns in the neighborhood of Wiscasset, but, singularly enough, I have been unable to trace a single piece in Maine except this sideboard. Miss Elizabeth Bartol of Boston, whose mother was a granddaughter of Colonel Swan, owns several pieces. Colonel Swan's son married the daughter of General Knox and took the sideboard with him to General Knox's home in Thomaston, Maine, where it remained for many years.

The sideboard is made of oak (showing its English origin) veneered with mahogany. The lines upon the front and the figures upon the legs are inlaid in satinwood, and the knife-box is inlaid in the same wood. The top of the sideboard is elaborately inlaid with satinwood and dark mahogany, in wide bands, separated by lines of ebony and satinwood, and crossed by fine satinwood lines radiating from the centre. The handles and escutcheons are of silver, and the top of the knife-box is covered by a silver tray with a reticulated railing. The coffee-urn is of Sheffield plate, and the sideboard with its appurtenances appears to-day as it did one hundred years ago in the house of General Knox. It is now owned by the Hon. James Phinney Baxter of Portland, Maine.

Knife-boxes were made of different shapes, to hold knives, forks, and spoons, and a pair of knife-boxes was the usual accompaniment to a handsome sideboard. The most skilled cabinet-makers were employed in their manufacture, as each curved section had to be fitted most carefully.

Illustration 76 shows an urn-shaped knife-box of mahogany inlaid in lines of holly. The interior of the box is fitted with circular trays of different heights, and through the little openings in these trays the knives and spoons were suspended.

Illus. 76. — Urn-shaped Knife-box, 1790.

Illustration 77 shows an urn-shaped knife-box opened. The top rests upon a wooden rod which extends through the middle of the box, and instead of turning back with a hinge, the top slides up on this rod, and when it is raised to a certain height it releases a spring which holds the rod firmly in its place. This urn knife-box is in the Pendleton collection in Providence, Rhode Island.

Urn-shaped boxes were designed by Adam, and are shown in his drawings, to stand upon pedestals at each end of the side table, to be used, one for ice-

Illus. 77. — Urn-shaped Knife-box, 1790.

water, and one for hot water, for the butler to wash the silver, not so plentiful then as now. Very soon the urn-shaped boxes were utilized to hold the knives, forks and spoons. Adam, Shearer, Hepplewhite and Sheraton show designs for knife-boxes, many of them elaborately carved or inlaid, but they must have been very costly, and within the means only of such noblemen, who, in Sheraton's words, "are unrestrained with the thoughts of expensiveness."

The usual shape of knife-box found is shown in Illustration 78, owned by Mrs. Clarence R. Hyde, of Brooklyn, N. Y. It is inlaid both outside and inside and the handles and fittings are of silver. The books of designs show boxes of this shape, with the lid put back, as in this illustration, and used to support a large silver plate.

Illus. 78.—Knife-box, 1790.

Mahogany was chiefly used in sideboards, with inlaying of satin-wood, holly, king, tulip, snake, zebra, yew, maple, and other woods. Occasionally one finds a sideboard veneered with walnut. The curves at the front vary considerably, the ends being convex, and the centre straight; or the ends concave, forming with the centre a double curve. A sideboard with rounded ends and only four legs was made in large numbers around Philadelphia.

Cupboards and Sideboards

Illustration 79 shows a Hepplewhite sideboard owned by the writer. It is of mahogany veneered upon pine, and it was probably the work of a Connecticut cabinet-maker of about 1790. Six chairs, made to go with the sideboard, are similarly inlaid, and the knife-boxes, which have always stood upon this sideboard, have fine lines of inlaying. There is one central long drawer, beneath which, slightly recessed, are doors opening into a cupboard, and two bottle drawers, each fitted with compartments to hold four bottles. There is a cupboard at each curved end, with a drawer above. The coloring of the wood used in this sideboard is very beautiful. Each drawer and door is veneered with a bright red mahogany, with golden markings in the grain, and this is framed in dark mahogany, outlined in two lines of satinwood with an ebony line between. The oval pieces above the legs and the bell-flower design upon the legs are of satinwood. The combination of the different shades of mahogany with the light satinwood is most effective. The handles are new. When this sideboard came into the possession of the writer, the old handles had been removed and large and offensive ones of pressed brass had been fastened upon every available spot, with that love for the showy which seizes upon country people when they attempt the process known as "doing over." The lids of the knife-boxes open back with hinges, and the interior is fitted with a slanting tray, perforated with openings of different shapes to hold knives, with the handles up, and spoons with the bowls up. A fine line of inlaying goes round each

Illus. 79.—Hepplewhite Sideboard and Knife-boxes, about 1790.

of the openings. The handles and escutcheons of the knife-boxes are of silver. Upon the top of the sideboard are several pieces of Sheffield plate. At each end is a double coaster upon wheels, with a long handle. Another double coaster, somewhat higher and with reticulated sides, stands beside the coffee-urn, and two single coasters are in front. All of these coasters have wooden bottoms, and were used to hold wine decanters, the double coasters upon wheels having been designed, so the story goes, by Washington, for convenience in circulating the wine around the table.

Illustration 80 shows a Hepplewhite sideboard with a serpentine front, the doors to the side cupboards being concave, as well as the space usually occupied by bottle drawers, while the small cupboard doors in the middle are convex. A long rounding drawer extends across the centre and projects beyond the cupboard below it, while a slide pulls out, forming a shelf, between the long drawer and the small cupboard. There are no bottle drawers in this sideboard. The doors are inlaid with a fan at each corner, and fine lines of holly are inlaid around the legs, doors, and drawer. The silver pieces upon the sideboard top are family heirlooms. The large tea-caddies at each end are of pewter finely engraved. This sideboard is owned by Francis H. Bigelow, Esq., of Cambridge.

A charming little sideboard owned by Mr. Bigelow is shown in Illustration 81. The ordinary measurements of sideboards like the last two shown are six feet in length, forty inches in height, and twenty-eight inches in depth. These measures, with slight variations, give the average size of Hepplewhite sideboards. Occasionally one finds a small piece like Illustration 81, evidently made to fit some space. This sideboard measures fifty-four inches in

Illus. 80. — Hepplewhite Serpentine-front Sideboard, 1790.

length, thirty-four in height, and twenty-three in depth. It has no cupboard, the space below the slightly rounding drawer in the centre being left open. There are fine lines and fans of inlaying in satinwood, and in the centre of the middle drawer is an oval inlay with an urn in colored woods. The handles are not original, and should be of pressed brass, oval or round. The silver service upon the sideboard is of French plate, made about 1845, and is of unusually graceful and elegant design.

Hepplewhite's sideboards seldom had fluted legs, which seem to have been a specialty of Sheraton, though the latter used the square leg as well. A feature in some of Sheraton's designs for sideboards

Illus. 81.—Hepplewhite Sideboard, about 1795.

was the brass railing at the back, often made in an elaborate design.

Illustration 82 shows a Sheraton sideboard, or sidetable, with brass rods extending across the back, and branches for candles at each end. This railing was designed to support the plates which were stood at the back of the sideboard, and also to keep the lids of knife and spoon boxes from falling back against the wall. The branches for candles were recommended for the light which the candles would throw upon the silver. This side-table is very large, measuring six feet eight inches in length, thirty inches in depth, and thirty-eight from the floor to the top of the table. The wood is mahogany, inlaid with satin-

Illus. 82.—Sheraton Side-table, 1795.

wood. It is unusual to find such a piece in this country, and this is the only example of an old Sheraton side-table or sideboard with the brass railing which I have ever seen here. It is owned by John C. MacInnes, Esq., of Worcester, and it was inherited by him from a Scotch ancestor.

Sheraton speaks of a "sideboard nine or ten feet

Cupboards and Sideboards 107

long, as in some noblemens' houses," but he admits that "There are other sideboards for small dining-rooms, made without either drawers or pedestals."

A charming little side-table, or sideboard, is shown in Illustration 83, belonging to Dwight M. Prouty, Esq., of Boston. It is of mahogany, and is

Illus. 83.—Sheraton Side-table, 1795.

inlaid with three oval pieces of satinwood, giving the little piece a very light effect. The legs also add to that appearance, the reeded upper section tapering down to a turning and ending in a plain round foot, which looks almost too small for such a piece. The outline of the body is curved down to the legs, making an arch upon the front and sides.

A sideboard of distinctly Sheraton design is shown

in Illustration 84. It has the reeded legs which are the almost unmistakable mark of Sheraton. The ends of this sideboard are straight, and only the front is rounding in shape, unlike the sideboard in Illus-

Illus. 84.—Sheraton Sideboard with Knife-box, 1795.

tration 75, which forms a complete semicircle. The wood is of mahogany, inlaid with fine lines of holly. The little shield-shaped escutcheons at the keyholes are of ivory. There are three drawers above the cupboards and two bottle drawers. Upon the top, at each end, is a wine-cooler of Sheffield plate, and in the centre is a mahogany inlaid knife-box similar to the one in Illustration 78. This sideboard is owned by Dwight Blaney, Esq., of Boston.

A Sheraton sideboard of later date is shown in Illustration 85. It is of mahogany, and was prob-

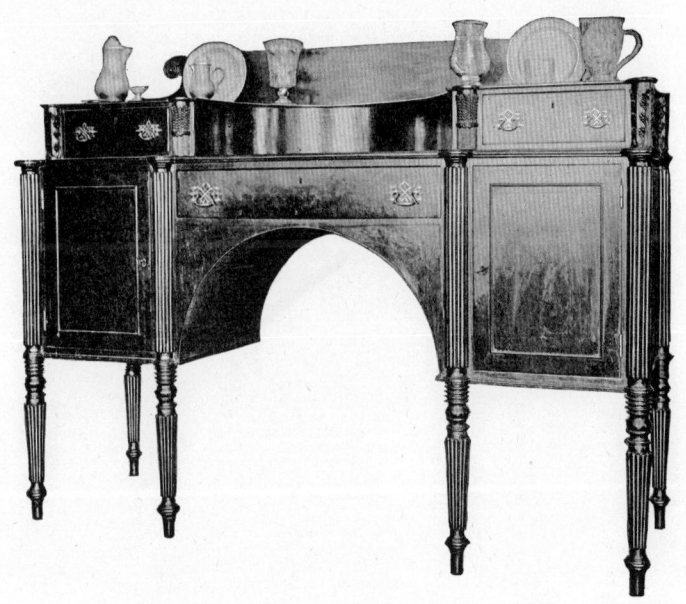

Illus. 85.— Sheraton Sideboard, about 1800.

ably made about 1800. The arched open space in the middle was left for the cellaret, which was the usual accompaniment of the sideboard in those days of hard drinking. The top of this sideboard is surmounted by drawers, with a back above the drawers.

The legs and the columns above them are reeded, and the little columns at the corners of the upper drawers are carved, the inner ones with a sheaf of wheat, and the two outside corners with the acanthus leaf. This sideboard was formerly owned by Rejoice Newton,

Illus. 86.—Sheraton Sideboard, about 1805.

Esq., of Worcester, from whom it has descended to Waldo Lincoln, Esq., of Worcester.

Illustration 86 shows the latest type of a Sheraton sideboard, owned by the Colonial Dames of Pennsylvania, and now in "Stenton," the house built in 1727 by James Logan, William Penn's secretary.

Cupboards and Sideboards

The sideboard stands where it was placed, about 1805, by George Logan, the great-great grandson of James. The wood is mahogany, and the large square knife-boxes were evidently made to fit the sideboard. The legs, with spade feet, are short, bringing the body of the sideboard close to the floor. The handles are brass knobs.

Illus. 87.— Cellarets, 1790.

Cellarets were made as a part of the dining-room furniture. They were lined with zinc, to hold the ice in which the wine bottles were packed to cool, and at the lower edge of the body of the cellaret was a faucet, or some arrangement by which the water from the melted ice could be drawn off. They were designed by Chippendale and all of his contemporaries and by the later cabinet-makers, — Adam, Hepplewhite, and Sheraton.

Illustration 87 shows two cellarets of different styles. The cellaret of octagonal shape, brass bound, with straight legs, is of the style most commonly found. It is in the Poore collection, at Indian Hill. Cellarets of this shape figure in books of designs from 1760 to 1800. The other is oval in form, and has the leg usually attributed to the Adam brothers. This cellaret belongs to Francis H. Bigelow, Esq., of Cambridge. Both cellarets are of mahogany.

We now come to sideboards of the type called "Colonial"; why, it would be difficult to trace, since sideboards of this heavy design were not made until over twenty-five years after the time that the United States took the place of the American colonies.

The heavy Empire fashions gained such popularity in the early years of the nineteenth century that furniture made after those fashions entirely superseded the graceful slender-legged styles of Shearer, Hepplewhite, and Sheraton, and sideboards were made as heavy and clumsy as the others had been light and graceful. The cupboards were extended nearly to the floor, from which the sideboard was lifted by balls or by large carved bears' feet. Round pillars, veneered, or carved similar to bedposts of the period, with a twist, or the pineapple and acanthus leaf, were used upon the front, and small drawers were added to the top. At about this time glass handles came into fashion, and many of these heavy sideboards have knobs of glass, either clear or opalescent. The brass handles that were used were either the rosette and ring or the knob shape.

Illustration 88 shows a sideboard of this period, 1810–1820, made of mahogany; the panels to the doors, the veneered pillars, and the piece at the back of the top being of a lighter and more finely

Illus. 88.— Sideboard, 1810–1820.

marked mahogany than the rest, which is quite dark. There is a little panel inlaid in colors upon the lower rail in the centre. The handles are the rosette and ring, the smaller handles matching the large ones. This sideboard belonged to the late Colonel DeWitt of Oxford, Massachusetts, and it is now owned by W. S. G. Kennedy, Esq., of Worcester.

I

Another type of mahogany Empire sideboard, and one often seen, is shown in Illustration 89. It is owned by L. J. Shapiro, Esq., of Norfolk, Virginia. The body of the sideboard is raised from the floor by very handsome bears' feet, and the posts extending up to the drawers are carved, and topped by

Illus. 89. — Empire Sideboard, 1810–1820.

typical Empire carvings of wing effect, which separate the drawers. The centre section of doors is curved outward slightly, and there is a band of carving across the lower edge, below the doors.

In the eighteenth and early nineteenth century the temperance question did not enter the heads of the fine gentlemen of the day, and the serving of wine was an important consideration. The cellaret or wine cooler accompanied the sideboard, which in the drawings of Hepplewhite, Shearer, and Sheraton had bottle drawers. What Shearer called "a gentle-

Illus. 90.—Sheraton Mixing-table, 1790.

man's social table" was designed by several, with conveniences for bottles, glasses, and biscuit, and for facilitating the progress of the wine around the table. In this country the mixing of punch or other beverages was furthered by a piece of furniture called a mixing table.

Mrs. Charles Custis Harrison, of St. David's, Pennsylvania, owns the mixing table in Illustration 90, and a sideboard to match it. Both pieces were inherited from Robert Morris, in whose famous mansion in Philadelphia they stood. The wood of the table is mahogany and the drawers and doors are of satinwood, finely inlaid. There is a well in the top for a bowl, in which was brewed the punch of the Philadelphia forefathers. The cover of the table is hinged, and the four shelves which show in the illustration fold flat when the cover is down.

Illus. 91.—Mixing-table, 1810–1820.

The table in Illustration 91 belongs to the Misses Garrett of Williamsburg, Virginia, and is known as a "mint julep" table, having been made for the concocting of that Southern beverage by a Baltimore cabinet-maker. There are shelves behind the door for the accessories to the julep, and for the mixing of it the top of the table is marble.

CHAPTER V

DESKS

FROM 1644 to about 1670 desks appear in colonial inventories. During those years the word "desk" meant a box, which was often made with a sloping lid for convenience in writing, or to rest a book upon in reading. This box was also used to hold writing-materials and papers or books, and was sometimes called a Bible-box, from the fact that the Bible was kept in it. Illustration 92 shows two of these desks from the collection of Charles R. Waters, Esq., of Salem. The larger desk is twenty inches in length and thirteen and one-half in height, and formerly had a narrow shelf in the inside across the back. The front is carved with the initials A. W. and the date 1654. The smaller desk measures thirteen and one-half inches in length and eight in height.

The desk with flat top in Illustration 93 is also in the Waters collection. It measures twenty-six inches in length by seventeen in width. It is

Illus. 92. — Desk-boxes, 1654.

made of oak, like the smaller desk in the preceding illustration.

The next style of desk made its appearance in the inventories of about 1660, under a name with French derivation: "scrutoir," "scriptor," "scrittore," "scrutor," "scriptoire," down to the phonetically spelled "screwtor." About 1720 the word "bureau," also from the French, came into use in combination with the word "desk," or "table." It has continued to be employed up to the present time, for the slant-top desk is even now, in country towns, called a bureau-desk. As the word "desk" seems to have been more or less in use through these early

Illus. 93. — Desk-box, 1650.

years, while for the last hundred years it has been almost entirely employed, alone or in combination

Illus. 94. — Desk, about 1680.

with other words, I have designated as desks all pieces of furniture made for use in writing.

A cabinet and writing desk used by perhaps all of the Dutch Patroons, of Albany, is shown in Illustration 94. It has stood in the same house, Cherry

Hill, Albany, since 1768, when the house was built by Philip Van Rensselaer, the ancestor of the present owner, Mrs. Edward W. Rankin. It was probably

Illus. 95. — Desk, about 1680.

brought from Holland by Killian Van Rensselaer, and in it were kept the accounts of the manor. The desk is open in Illustration 95, showing the compartments for papers and books. The wood of this splendid piece is oak, beautifully panelled and carved, and the fine panel seen when the desk is closed forms, when lowered, the shelf for writing. Similar pieces appear in paintings by old Dutch masters.

Illus. 96. — Desk, 1710–1720.

Illustration 96 shows a desk owned by Miss Gage, of Worcester, of rather rude construction, and apparently not made by a skilled cabinet-maker. It has two long drawers with two short drawers above them. The space above these two short drawers is reached from an opening or well with a slide, directly in front of the small drawers of the interior, which may be seen in the illustration. The pillars at each side of the middle compartment pull out as drawers. The handles are new, and should be drop handles, or early stamped ones. The characteristics which determine the date of this desk are the single moulding around the drawers, the two short drawers, and the well opening with a slide. The bracket feet would indicate a few years' later date than that of similar pieces with ball feet.

During the first half of the eighteenth century slant-top desks appeared with a bookcase or cabinet top. The lower or desk part was made usually with a moulding around the top, into which the upper part was set. The doors were of panelled wood or had looking-glasses set in them, but occasionally they were of glass.

The frontispiece shows an extraordinary piece of furniture owned by Samuel Verplanck, Esq., of Fishkill, New York. It has belonged in the family of Mr. Verplanck since 1753, when it was bought by an ancestor, Governor James de Lancey, at an auction sale of the effects of Sir Danvers Osborne, who was governor of the Province of New York for the space of five days, as he landed at Whitehall Slip, New York, from the good ship *Arundel* on Friday, and the following Wednesday he committed suicide. Sir Danvers had brought his household goods with him upon the *Arundel*, and among them was this secretary.

Lacquered furniture was fashionable during the first quarter of the eighteenth century, and while the first lacquered pieces came through Holland, by 1712

"Japan work" was so popular, even in the American colonies, that an advertisement of Mr. Nehemiah Partridge appeared in a Boston paper of that year, that he would do "all sorts of Japan work."

The wood of this secretary is oak, and the entire piece is covered with lacquer in brilliant red, blue, and gold. The upper part, or cabinet, has doors which are lacquered on the inside, with looking-glasses on the outside. A looking-glass is also set into the middle of the top. These glasses are all the original ones and are of heavy plate with the old bevel upon the edges. Above the compartments, and fitting into the two arches of the top are semi-circular-shaped flap doors, which open downward. Between these and the pigeonholes are two shallow drawers extending across the cabinet. The middle compartment has two doors with vases of flowers lacquered upon them, and there is a drawer above, while the spaces each side of the doors are occupied by drawers. The slides for candlesticks are gone, but the slits show where they were originally. The lower or desk part is divided by a moulding which runs around it above the three lower drawers, and the space between this and the writing-table is taken by two short drawers, but it has no well with a slide like the desk in Illustration 96. The arrangement of the small drawers and compartments is the same as in the desk in Illustration 96, and the lacquered pillars form the fronts of drawers which pull out, each side of the middle compartment, which has upon its door a jaunty little gentleman in European costume of the period. The moulding upon the frame around the drawers and the two short upper drawers would place the date of this piece early in the eighteenth century. The first thought upon seeing the feet of the desk, is that they were originally brackets which were sawed off and the large ball feet added, but it must have been made originally as it now stands, for both the brackets and the balls under them are lacquered with the old "Japan work" like the rest of the secretary.

A style of desk of a somewhat later date is occasionally found, generally made of maple. Its form and proportions are similar to those of a low-boy with the Dutch bandy-leg and foot, and a desk top, the slanting lid of which lets down for use in writing. The top sets into a moulding around the edge of the lower part, in the same manner as the top part of a high-boy is set upon its base. Illustration 97 shows a desk of this style in the building of the

Illus. 97.—Cabriole-legged Desk, 1720–1730.

Pennsylvania Historical Society, labelled as having belonged to William Penn, but which is of a later date than that would imply, as it was made from 1720 to 1730, while Penn left this country in 1701, never to return to it.

The mahogany desk shown in Illustration 98 belongs to Walter Hosmer, Esq., and is a most graceful and charming little piece, intended probably for a lady's use. It measures twenty-four and a half inches in length and forty-one and a half inches in height. There are three square drawers in the lower part, and the upper part has two small square drawers for pens, with a third between them. The two pen drawers pull out and support the lid when lowered. The interior of the desk has eighteen small drawers, shaped and placed so that their fronts form a curve, and each little drawer at the top is carved with the rising sun, or fan, like the middle drawer in the lower part. The entire design of the interior is like that in a large block-front desk now owned by George S. Palmer,

Illus. 98.—Cabriole-legged Desk, 1760.

Esq., of Norwich, which was made by Benjamin Dunham in 1769, and it is possible that the two pieces were made by the same Connecticut cabinet-maker.

Another desk belonging to Mr. Hosmer is shown in Illustration 99. The bandy-legs end in a claw-and-ball of a flattened shape, and instead of the drawer, plain or with a carved sunburst, usually seen between the side drawers of the lower part, the wood of the frame is sawed in a simple design. The upper part has three drawers, and the lid when down rests upon two slides which pull out for the purpose. The interior is quite simple, having four drawers with eight small compartments above. This desk measures twenty-six inches in width and thirty-nine inches and a half in height.

Illus. 99.— Desk, 1760.

The desk in Illustration 100 is now owned by the American Antiquarian Society of Worcester, and belonged formerly to Governor John Hancock. It measures four feet six inches from the floor, and is of the sturdy, honest build that one would expect

Desks 127

in a desk used by the man whose signature to the Declaration of Independence stands out so fearless and determined. The slanting lid has a moulding across the lower edge, probably to support a large

Illus. 100.— Desk, about 1770.

book, or ledger, and as it is at the right height for a man to write standing, or sitting upon a very high stool, it may have been used as an office desk. Below the slanting lid are two doors behind which are

Illus. 101.—Block-front Desk.
Cabinet Top, about 1770.

shelves. Two drawers extend across the lower part, and at each end of the desk two small, long drawers pull out. The desk was made about 1770.

Illustration 101 shows a mahogany block-front desk with cabinet top, owned by Charles R. Waters, Esq., of Salem, which was bought by Mr. Waters's grandfather, about 1770. It is a fine example of the best style of secretary made during the eighteenth century. The doors are of panelled wood. The lid of the desk is blocked like the front, and like the lid of the desk in Illustration 109, requiring for the blocked lid and drawer fronts wood from two to three inches thick, as each front is carved from one thick plank.

Illus. 102. — Block-front Desk, about 1770.

Illustration 102 shows a block-front mahogany desk, owned by Francis H. Bigelow, Esq., of Cambridge. It formerly belonged to Dr. John Snelling Popkin, who was Professor of Greek at Harvard University from 1826 to 1833, and probably descended to him, as it was made about 1770. The legs, with claw-and-ball feet, are blocked like the drawers, as was usual in block-front pieces, another feature of which is the moulding upon the frame around the drawers.

In all the desks shown, the pillars at each side of the middle door in the interior pull out as drawers. These were supposed to be secret drawers. Often

K

Illus. 103.— Desk with Cabinet Top, about 1770.

the little arched pieces above the pigeonholes are drawer fronts. The middle compartment is sometimes a drawer, or if it has a door, behind this door is a drawer which, when taken entirely out, proves to have a secret drawer opening from its back. Occasionally an opening to a secret compartment is found in the back of the desk. All these were designed at a time when banks and deposit companies did not abound, and the compartments were doubtless utilized to hold papers and securities of value. There are traditions of wills being discovered in these secret compartments, and novelists have found them of great convenience in the construction of plots.

The secretary in Illustration 103 is an extraordinarily fine piece. It is of mahogany, and tradition says that it was brought from Holland, but it is distinctly a Chippendale piece, from the fine carving upon the feet and above the doors, and from the reeded pilasters with exquisitely carved capitals. There are five of these pilasters, — three in front and one upon each side, at the back. The doors hold looking-glasses, the shape of which, straight at the bottom and in curves at the top, is that of the early looking-glasses. The two semicircular, concave spaces in the interior above the cabinet are lacquered in black and gold.

The middle compartment in the desk, between the pigeonholes, has a door, behind which is a large drawer. When this drawer is pulled entirely out, at its back may be seen small drawers, and upon taking out one of these and pressing a spring, secret compartments are disclosed.

Dr. Holmes, in "The Professor at the Breakfast Table," has written of this secretary thus: —

"At the house of a friend where I once passed a night, was one of those stately, upright cabinet desks and cases of drawers which were not rare in prosperous families during the past century [*i.e.* the eighteenth]. It had held the clothes and the books and papers of generation after generation. The hands that opened its drawers had grown withered, shrivelled, and at last had been folded in death. The children that played with the lower handles had got tall enough to open the desk, — to reach the upper shelves behind the folding doors, — grown bent after a while, — and followed those who had gone before, and left the old cabinet to be ransacked by a new generation.

"A boy of twelve was looking at it a few years ago, and, being a quick-witted fellow, saw that all the space was not accounted for by the smaller drawers in the part beneath the lid of the desk. Prying about with busy eyes and fingers, he at length came upon a spring, on pressing which, a secret drawer flew from its hiding-place. It had never been opened but by the maker. The mahogany shavings and dust were lying in it, as when the artisan closed it, and when I saw it, it was as fresh as if that day finished.

"Is there not one little drawer in your soul, my sweet reader, which no hand but yours has ever opened, and which none that have known you seemed to have suspected? What does it hold? A sin? I hope not."

The "quick-witted boy, with busy eyes and fingers," was the present owner of the secretary, the Rev. William R. Huntington, D.D., of Grace Church, New York, and since Dr. Holmes wrote of the secretary, new generations have grown up to

Illus. 104. — Block-front Desk, about 1770.

reach the handles of the drawers and to ransack the old cabinet.

The middle ornament upon the top was gone many years ago, but Dr. Huntington remembers, as a boy with his brother, playing with the two end figures which, it is not astonishing to relate, have not been seen since those years. The figures were carved from wood, of men at work at their trade of cabinet-making, and the boys who were given the carved figures for toys played that the little workmen were the ones who made the secretary. The great handles upon the sides are large and heavy enough for the purpose for which they were intended, to lift the massive piece of furniture.

The block-front mahogany desk in Illustration 81 shows the blocked slanting lid. The brasses are original and are unusually large and fine. This desk belongs to Dwight Blaney, Esq., of Boston.

A splendid mahogany secretary owned by Albert S. Rines, Esq., of Portland, Maine, is shown in Illustration 105. The lower part is bombé or kettle-shaped, but the drawers, which swell with the shape in front, do not extend to the corners, like the kettle-shaped bureau in Illustration 30, but leave a vacant space in the interior, not taken up at the ends. Three beautiful, flat, reeded columns with Corinthian capitals are upon the doors, which still hold the old bevelled looking-glasses. The handles are original, but are not as large as one usually finds upon such a secretary. There are larger handles upon the sides, as was the custom. The cabinet in the upper part is very similar to the one in Illustration 103, but there is no lacquering upon the curved tops behind the doors. With the thoroughness of workmanship and dislike of sham which characterized the cabinet-makers of the eighteenth century, there are fine pieces of mahogany inside at the back of the looking-glasses. The cabinet in the desk proper, which

Illus. 105. — Kettle-front Secretary, about 1765.

is covered by the slanting lid when closed, is unusually good, with the curved drawers, set also in a curve. This secretary is generous in secret compartments, of which there are six. The centre panel of the cabinet is the front of a drawer, locked by a concealed spring, and at the back of this drawer are two secret drawers; beneath it, by sliding a thin

Illus. 106.— Block-front Writing-table, 1760–1770.

piece of mahogany, another drawer is disclosed; a fourth is at the top, behind a small drawer, and at each end of the curved drawers is a secret drawer. The secretary is over eight feet in height.

Illustration 106 shows a beautiful little piece of furniture, modelled after what Chippendale calls a writing-table or a bureau table, by the latter term meaning a bureau desk with a flat top. The same unusually fine shells are carved upon this as upon the double chest of drawers in Illustration 21, and upon the low chest of drawers in Illustration 31. In the inside of one of the drawers of this writing-table is written in a quaint old hand a name which is illegible, and "Newport, R.I., 176–," the final figure of the date not being sufficiently plain to determine it. Desks, secretaries, and chests of drawers have been found with block fronts and these fine shells. All were originally owned in Rhode Island or near there, and nearly all can be traced back to Newport, probably to the same cabinet-maker. This writing-table was bought in 1901 from the heirs of Miss Rebecca Shaw of Wickford, Rhode Island.

Illus. 107.—Serpentine-front Desk, Cabinet Top, 1770.

Miss Shaw died in 1900 at over ninety years of age. The writing-table is now owned by Harry Harkness Flagler, Esq., of Millbrook, New York. It measures thirty-four inches in height and thirty-six and three-quarters inches in length. A door with a shell carved upon it opens into a recessed cupboard. A writing-table like this

Illus. 108.— Serpentine or Bow-front Desk, about 1770.

is in the Pendleton collection, also found in Rhode Island.

Illustration 107 shows a desk with cabinet top and serpentine or ox-bow front. It is made of English walnut of a fine golden hue which has never been stained or darkened. The doors are of panelled wood, with fluted columns at each side. It was

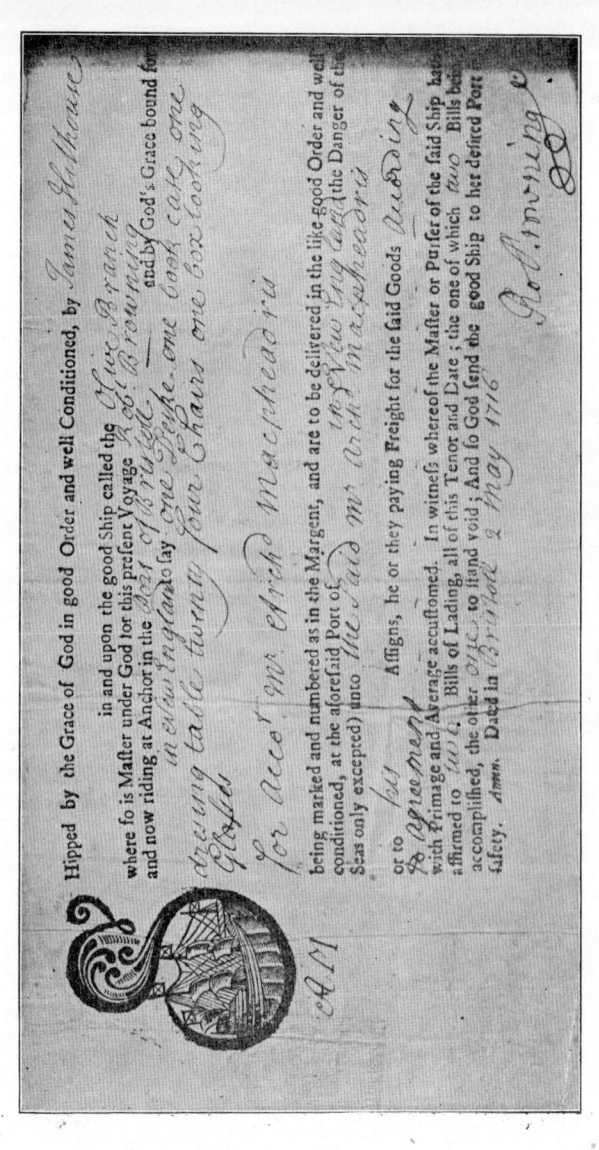

Illus. 109. — Bill of Lading, 1716.

owned in the Bannister family of Newburyport until 1870, when it was given to the Newburyport Library. It now stands in the old Prince mansion, occupied by the Library.

Illustration 108 shows a mahogany desk with serpentine front and claw-and-ball feet, owned by Mrs. Alice Morse Earle, of Brooklyn. The serpentine drawers of this piece and the one preceding are carved from a solid block, not quite so thick as is necessary for the block-front drawers. This desk was made at about the same time as the secretary in the last illustration.

The bill of lading in Illustration 109 is preserved in the house known as the "Warner House," in Portsmouth, New Hampshire, built by Archibald Macphaedris, a member of the King's Council. It was commenced in 1712, and occupied in 1716, but not finished until 1718. Mr. Macphaedris died in 1729, and his widow, upon her second marriage, gave the house to her daughter, married then to Colonel Jonathan Warner, and the house has remained ever since in the possession of their descendants.

The rooms are panelled, and are filled with the furniture bought by successive generations. Upon the walls hang Copley portraits of Colonel Warner and his wife and her haughty mother, Mrs. Macphaedris (who was a daughter of Lieutenant-Governor Wentworth), and of Colonel Warner's young daughter Mary, in her straight little stays, which are still preserved, along with the garments, stiff with gold embroideries, which Colonel Warner and his wife wore upon state occasions. A number of the illustrations for this book were taken in the Warner house, which is one of the best-preserved old houses in the country, and which, with its furnishings and decorations, presents an unusually good picture of the home of the wealthy colonist.

The quaint wording of this bill of lading, and the list of furniture mentioned, make it interesting in this connection, but none of the pieces of that date remain in the house, which was evidently refurnished with great elegance, after 1760, when the old furniture was probably discarded as "old-fashioned."

Illustration 110 shows a bookcase built into the Warner house. It is made of mahogany, and stands in every particular exactly as it was originally made. The bill of lading of 1716, shown in Illustration 85, mentions a bookcase, but this bookcase is of later date, and was probably bought by Colonel Warner for his daughter, as the books in the case are all bound alike in a golden brown leather, with gilt tooling, and each book has "Miss. Warner" stamped in gilt letters upon the cover. The books are the standard works of that time, — Shakespeare, Milton, Spenser, "The Spectator," Fox's "Book of Martyrs," and all the books which a wealthy man of those days would buy to furnish a library. The dates of the editions vary from 1750 to 1765, so the latter date may be given to this bookcase. It was once entirely filled with "Miss. Warner's" books, but early in the nineteenth century, during a great fire in Portsmouth, the books were removed for safety, and all were not brought back.

142   Furniture of the Olden Time

Illus. 110.— Bookcase and Desk, about 1765.

At the top of the bookcase is a row of Chinese fretwork, which, together with the massive handles, would also place its date about 1765. The case is divided into three sections, the sides of the lower part being devoted to drawers. The lower middle section has four drawers, above which is a wide flap which lets down, disclosing a desk with drawers and pigeonholes.

A bookcase owned by J. J. Gilbert, Esq., of Baltimore, is shown in Illustration 111. It is made after Chippendale designs, and is richly carved. The base and feet are very elaborate, and the cornice and pediment, are wonderfully fine. The broken

Illus. 111.— Chippendale Bookcase, 1770.

Illus. 112. — Hepplewhite Bookcase, 1789.

arch has delicate sprays of carved wood, projecting beyond the edge, and laid over the open fretwork, and the crowning ornament in the centre is a carved urn with a large spray of flowers. The ornaments and mouldings separating the sections of glass in the doors are as fine as the other rich carving upon this bookcase.

A wonderful Hepplewhite bookcase is shown in Illustration 112. It is owned by George W. Holmes, Esq., of Charleston, South Carolina, and carries with it an impression of the wealth and luxury in Charleston, before the Civil War and the other disasters that befell that city in the latter half of the nineteenth century.

This bookcase is nearly nine feet in length, and is made of unusually fine mahogany. The lower part is designed in a series of curves which prevents the plain look that a straight front would give in such length. The doors form one curve and a part of the other two, which are completed by the drawers at each side; a skilful management of a long space. The curves at the top of the pediment follow the same lines, and the bookcase was evidently designed by a master hand. It was probably brought from England, together with a secretary to match it. Above the doors and drawers, shelves pull out, on which to rest books. A fine line of holly runs around each door and drawer, with a star inlaid at the corners of the doors, while a very beautiful design is inlaid in light and dark woods, in the space on the pediment, which is finished with the broken arch, of the high, slender type, with carved rosettes. The centre orna-

L

ment, between the rosettes, is a basket of flowers carved in wood.

After the publication of the designs of Shearer, Hepplewhite, and Sheraton, the heavy desks were

Illus. 113.—Maple Desk, about 1795.

superseded by those of lighter design, and the slant-top bureau desk was seldom made after 1790. Sheraton says: "Bureau in France is a small chest of drawers. It has generally been applied to common desks with drawers made under them. These pieces of furniture are nearly obsolete in London." Slant-top desks do not appear in cabinet-makers'

Illus. 114.— Hepplewhite Desk, Cabinet Top. 1790.

books published after 1800, and it is safe to assign a date previous to the nineteenth century to any such desk.

Illustration 113 shows the latest type of a slant-top desk, made in 1790–1795. The frame is of maple, the drawers being of curly maple edged with ebony. The lid is of curly maple framed in bird's-eye maple with ebony lines, and in the centre is a star made of mahogany and ebony. The small drawers inside are of bird's-eye maple, three of the drawers having an ebony and mahogany star. The base is what Hepplewhite calls a French base, and the desk, which measures only thirty-six inches in length, is a good example of the artistic use of the different varieties of maple with their golden hues. This desk belongs to the writer.

Illustration 114 shows a Hepplewhite desk with cabinet top owned by the writer, and made about 1790. The drawers are veneered with satinwood, with a row of fine inlaying of holly and ebony around each drawer front. The base is after Hepplewhite's design, and has a row of ebony and holly inlaying across it. The slightly slanting lid turns back and rests upon two pulls to form a writing-table. The pigeonholes and small drawers are behind the glass doors, which are made like two Gothic arches, with three little pillars, and panels of satinwood between the bases of the pillars. The pediment at the top of the cabinet is quite characteristic of the period.

Illustration 115 shows a charming little Sheraton desk owned by W. S. G. Kennedy, Esq., of Worcester. It is made of bird's-eye maple with trimming of mahogany veneer, and a row of ebony and holly inlaying below the drawers. The upper part has one maple door in the centre, with a tambour door

Illus. 115.— Sheraton Desk, 1795.

of mahogany at each side, behind which are pigeon-holes and small drawers. The lid shuts back upon itself, and, when open, rests upon the two pulls at each side of the upper drawer. The wood of this desk is beautifully marked, and the whole effect is very light and well adapted to a lady's use.

The word "tambour" is thus defined by Sheraton: "Tambour tables among cabinet-makers are of two sorts; one for a lady or gentleman to write at, and another for the former to execute needlework by. The Writing Tambour Tables are almost out of use at present, being both insecure and liable to injury. They are called Tambour from the cylindrical forms of their tops, which are glued up in narrow strips of mahogany and laid upon canvas, which binds them together, and suffers them at the same time to yield to the motion that their ends

Illus. 116.— Tambour Secretary, about 1800.

make in the curved groove in which they run. Tambour tables are often introduced in small pieces where no strength or security is desired."

In his will, George Washington left to Dr. Craik "my beaureau (or as cabinet-makers call it, tambour secretary)." Illustration 116 shows what might be called a tambour secretary. It is made of mahogany with lines of light wood inlaid. The lid of the lower part is folded back upon itself. Above it are two tambour doors, behind which are drawers and pigeonholes and a door in the centre with an oval inlay of satinwood. Above these doors is a cabinet with glass doors. The pediment is like the one in Illustration 114. This secretary was made about 1800, and belongs to Francis H. Bigelow, Esq., of Cambridge.

Illustration 117 shows a small Sheraton writing table for a lady's use, also owned by Mr. Bigelow. It is of simple construction, having one drawer, and when

Illus. 117.—Sheraton Desk, 1800.

the desk is closed, the effect is that of a small table with a flat top.

Illustration 118 shows a desk which was copied from one of Sheraton's designs, published in 1793, and described as "a lady's cabinet and writing table." The legs in Sheraton's drawing are slender and straight, while these are twisted and carved, and the

Illus. 118. — Sheraton Desk, about 1810.

space, which in the design is left open for books, in this desk is closed with a tambour door. The slide which shows above the compartment pulls out, with a mechanism described by Sheraton, and when fully

Desks 153

out, it drops to form the cover for the compartments. The Empire brasses upon the top are original, but the handles to the drawers are not. They should be brass knobs. This beautiful little desk was made about 1810 for William T. Lane, Esq., of Boston, and is owned by his daughter, Mrs. Thomas H. Gage of Worcester.

Illus. 119.—Desk, about 1820.

Illustration 119 shows a bureau and desk, belonging to Mrs. J. H. Henry of Winchendon. The lid of the desk turns back like the lid of a piano. The carved pillars at the side are like the ones upon the bureau in Illustration 37, and upon other pieces of furniture of the same date, about 1820.

CHAPTER VI

CHAIRS

CHAIRS are seldom mentioned in the earliest colonial inventories, and few were in use in either England or America at that time. Forms and stools were used for seats in the sixteenth and early seventeenth centuries, and inventories of that period, even those of wealthy men, do not often contain more than one or two chairs. The chair was the seat of honor given to the guest, others sitting upon forms and stools. This custom was followed by the American colonists, and forms or benches and joint or joined stools constituted the common seats during the first part of the seventeenth century.

The chairs in use during that period were

"thrown" or turned chairs; wainscot chairs, sometimes described as "scrowled" or carved chairs; and later, chairs covered with leather, or "Turkey work," and other fabrics.

The best-known turned chair in this country is the "President's Chair" at Harvard University. Dr. Holmes has written of it in "Parson Turell's Legacy": —

Illus. 120. — Turned Chair, Sixteenth Century.

> "— a chair of oak, —
> Funny old chair, with seat like wedge,
> Sharp behind and broad front edge, —
> One of the oddest of human things,
> Turned all over with knobs and rings, —
> But heavy, and wide, and deep, and grand, —
> Fit for the worthies of the land, —
> Chief Justice Sewall a cause to try in,
> Or Cotton Mather, to sit — and lie, — in."

In the Bolles collection is a chair similar to the Harvard chair, and one is shown in Illustration 120, owned by Henry F. Waters, Esq., of Salem. A turned chair of the same period with a square seat is owned by the Connecticut Historical Society.

Provision was made for the youngest of the large family of children, with which the colonist was usually blessed, in the high chair, which is found in almost every type. A turned high chair is shown in Illustration 121, brought by Richard Mather to America in 1635, and used to hold the successive babies of that famous family, — Samuel, Increase, Cotton, and the others. The rod is missing which was fastened across the front to hold the child in, and only the holes show where the pegs were placed to support the foot-rest. This quaint little chair is owned by the American Antiquarian Society of Worcester.

A style of turned chair more commonly in use is shown in Illustration 122, said to have been brought on the *Mayflower* by Governor Carver. The chair in Illustration 123, originally owned by Elder Brewster, is of a rarer type, the spindles being greater in number and more finely turned. Both of these chairs are in Pilgrim Hall, in Plymouth. Turned chairs are not infrequently found of the type of Illustration 122, but rarely like the Brewster chair or the turned chair in Illustration 120.

Illus. 121. — Turned Highchair, Sixteenth Century.

The wainscot chair was made entirely of wood, usually oak, with a panelled back, from which came the name "wainscot." Its valuation in inventories was two or three times that of the turned chair, which is probably the reason why wainscot chairs are seldom found.

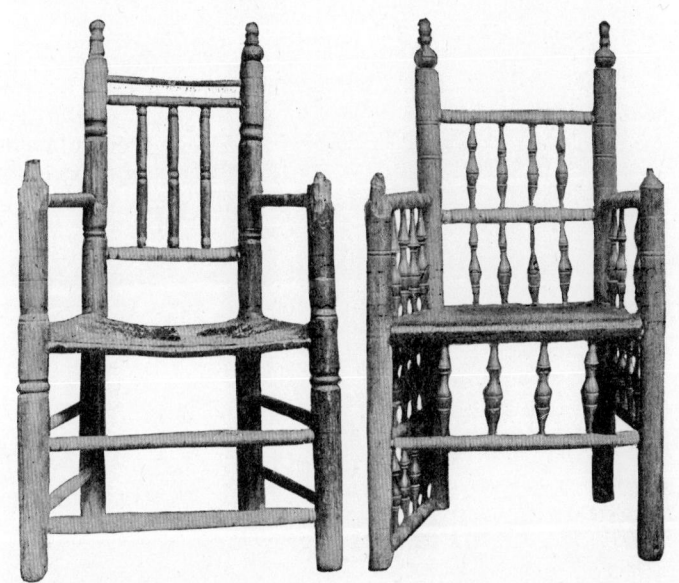

Illus. 122 and Illus. 123.—Turned Chairs, about 1600.

The finest wainscot chair in this country is shown in Illustration 124. It belongs to the Essex Institute of Salem, having been given to that society in 1821 by a descendant of the original owner, Sarah Dennis of Ipswich, who possessed two of these chairs; the other is now the President's chair at Bowdoin College.

A plainer form of the wainscot chair is shown in Illustration 125. It was brought to Newbury in the ship *Hector*, in 1633, and is now in the collection of the late Major Ben: Perley Poore, at Indian Hill.

By the middle of the seventeenth century chairs had become more common, and inventories of that period had frequent mention of leather or leather-backed chairs. Some of the earliest leather chairs have the under part of the frame similar to that of the wainscot chair, with plain legs and stretchers, while others have the legs and back posts turned. Illustration 126 shows a leather chair made about 1660, in the Waters collection. The seat and back have been covered with leather in the same manner as they were originally, as enough remained of the old cover to copy.

Illus. 124.—Wainscot Chair, about 1600.

A chair of some later date, about 1680, is shown in Illustration 127, also from the Waters collection, the back and seat of which were originally of Turkey

Chairs

work. The frame is similar to that in Illustration 126, with the exception of the carved brace across the front, which feature leads one to give the chair a later date than the one in Illustration 126. The feet have been sawed off. Other coverings beside Turkey work were used, — velvet, camlett, plush, or cloth, as well as an occasional cover "wrought by hir owne hand." Until the latter part of the seventeenth century a somewhat architectural style prevailed in chairs, settles, and tables. This was succeeded by the graceful lines and carving of the cane furniture which came into fashion during the last quarter of that century. It is called Jacobean furniture, although that name would not seem to be strictly accurate, for the Jacobean period was ended before cane furniture was introduced into England, about 1678. The cane chairs form a complete contrast to the heavy wainscot or turned

Illus. 125. — Wainscot Chair, about 1600.

chairs in use previously, the light effect coming not only from the cane seat and back, but also from the frame, which was usually carved in a graceful design.

Illustration 128 shows a chair which belonged to Sir William Pepperell, made possibly for his father,

Illus. 126.— Leather Chair, about 1660.   Illus. 127.— Chair originally covered with Turkey work, about 1680.

for Sir William was not born until 1697. The front legs, carved with the scroll foot turning forward, are in the pure Flemish style. The brace in front, carved to correspond with the top of the back, appears in cane chairs with a carved frame. The seat was originally of cane. This chair is now in the Alexander Ladd house in Portsmouth.

A chair of similar effect, but with turned legs, and carved in a different design, with the crown as the central figure of

Illus. 128. — Flemish Chair, about 1690.

Illus. 129. — Flemish Chair, about 1690.

the underbrace and top, is shown in Illustration 129. It belongs to Miss Mary Coates of Philadelphia, to whom it has descended from Josiah Langdale, in

M

whose inventory this chair, with its mates, was mentioned. Josiah Langdale took ship with his family and belongings, from England for America, in 1723. Before sailing he became very ill and prayed that he might die and be buried in the old graveyard, but his wish was not granted, and he was carried on board, taking his coffin with him. Three days out (but not far from land) he died, and was buried in his coffin, at sea. The coffin was not sufficiently weighted, however, and it drifted back to land, where it was opened, and its occupant identified, and Josiah Langdale was buried from the old Quaker meeting-house, as he had prayed. His widow came safely to America with her furniture, among which was this chair. Both Flemish and Spanish characteristics appear

Illus. 130.—Cane Chair, 1680–1690.

in the chair in Illustration 130. The front legs are in the Flemish style, the scroll foot turning back as it often does. The twisted stretchers and back

Illus. 131.—Cane High-chair and Arm-chair, 1680-1690.

posts show the influence of Spanish or Portuguese fashions. This chair is in the Poore collection at Indian Hill, Newburyport.

Illustration 131 shows two beautiful chairs owned by Dwight Blaney, Esq., of Boston. The Portuguese twist has an unusually graceful effect in the

Illus. 132.—Cane Chair, 1680-1690.

tall legs of the little high chair. It will be noticed that, instead of being twisted, the upper part of the front legs is turned in balls to provide a stronger hold for the pegs which support the foot-rest. There are four holes for these pegs, at different heights, in order that the rest might be lowered as the infantile legs lengthened. The crown appears in the top of the high chair, while the arm-chair has a child's figure carved in the centre of the top. The arms of both chairs are carved with the acanthus leaf.

An example of the finest carving attained in cane furniture is shown in Illustration 132. This exquisite chair is owned by Harry Harkness Flagler, Esq., of Millbrook. The design of the top is repeated in the front brace, but much enlarged. The frame of the seat and the arms are carved like those in Illustration 131. The legs end in a curious form of the Spanish foot.

The popularity of the cane chair, as well as its strength, is attested by the number which have survived the centuries, in fair condition for chairs so light in appearance.

The cane chair in Illustration 133 is owned by Dwight M. Prouty, Esq., of Boston. The top of the under brace is carved in a crescent-shaped design, which is used again in the top rail. The front leg is a Flemish scroll with a ball beneath it. The cane back is unusual in design, the carved wood on each side making a diamond-shaped effect.

The chair in Illustration 134 belongs to the writer. The cane extends up into the curve made in the top rail of the back, which is, like the underbrace and the sides of the back, more elaborately carved than the chairs in Illustrations 128 and 129.

Illus. 133 and Illus. 134.—Cane Chairs, 1680–1690.

Stools were not common, but are occasionally found, following the styles in chairs. With the wainscot chairs were joined or joint stools.

The stool in Illustration 135 was used with the turned chair, like the one in Illustration 126.

Illustration 136 shows a very rare piece, a Flemish stool, with a carved underbrace, probably like the ones upon the cane-back chairs used with it. These two fine stools are in the collection of Dwight M. Prouty, Esq., of Boston.

A chair once owned by General Henry Dearborn of Revolutionary fame is shown in Illustration 137.

Illus. 135.—Turned Stool, 1660.

The back and seat were originally cane, and it has a perfect Spanish foot.

The chair in Illustration 138 is of the style called Queen Anne. It has Spanish feet but the back shows the first use of the Dutch splat, afterward developed and elaborated by Chippendale and others. This chair and the one in Illustration 137 belong to the writer.

Illus. 136.—Flemish Stool, 1680.

A chair which retained some characteristics of the cane chair was the banister-back chair, which appears in inventories of the first half of the eighteenth century.

Two banister-back chairs owned by the writer are shown in Illustration 139 and Illustration 140. It will be seen that the tops and one carved under-brace are similar to those upon cane chairs, while

Illus. 137. — Cane Chair, 1690–1700.

Illus. 138. — Queen Anne Chair, 1710–1720.

the legs of one chair end in a clumsy Spanish foot. The banisters which form the back are turned on one side and flat on the other. These chairs have the flat side in front, but either side was used in banister chairs, plainer types of which are found, sometimes with the slats not turned, but straight and flat. The chair in Illustration 140 was used for the deacon's chair in the old meeting-house in Westborough, Massachusetts, built in 1724, and it stood in "the deacon's pue," in front of the pulpit, for

Illus. 139 and Illus. 140. — Banister-back Chairs, 1710–1720.

the deacon to sit upon, as was the custom. The deacon must have longed for the two hours' sermon to end, if he had to sit upon this chair with its high, narrow seat. There are several kinds of wood in these chairs, and when found they were painted black.

An unusually fine banister chair, from the Poore collection at Indian Hill, Newburyport, is shown in Illustration 141, with carved top and underbrace and Spanish feet. The seat is rush, as it usually is in banister chairs.

"Roundabout" chairs are met with in inventories from 1738 under various names,—"three-cornered chair," "half round chair," "round about chair," — but they are now

Illus. 142.—Roundabout Chair, about 1740.

Illus. 141.—Banister-back Chair, 1710–1740.

known as roundabout or corner chairs. They were made in different styles, like other chairs, from the turned or the Dutch bandy-leg, down to the carved Chippendale leg with claw-and-ball foot.

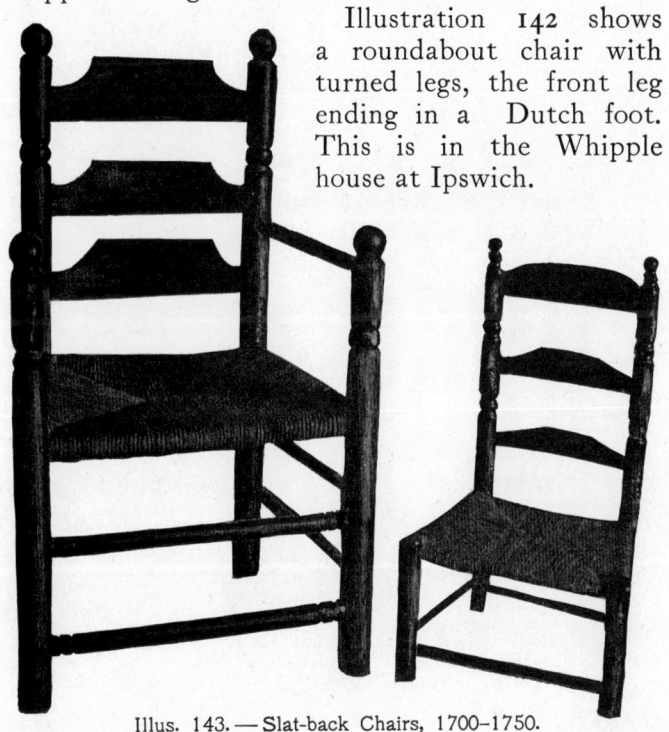

Illustration 142 shows a roundabout chair with turned legs, the front leg ending in a Dutch foot. This is in the Whipple house at Ipswich.

Illus. 143.— Slat-back Chairs, 1700–1750.

The most common chair during the first half of the eighteenth century was the "slat back," with a rush seat. The number of slats varied; three, four, and five slats being used. The slats were also made in different designs, those made in Pennsylvania being curved.

Two slat-back chairs are shown in Illustration 143 from the Whipple house in Ipswich. The large chair was found in the country, stuffed and covered with many layers of wadding and various materials. When they were removed, this frame was disclosed, but the tops of the posts had been sawed off. The back posts should terminate in a turned knob, like the Carver chair in Illustration 122, which this chair strongly resembles, the slats taking the place of the turned spindles of the Carver chair. The small chair is probably of later date, and was evidently intended for a child's use. Chairs with three-slat backs are in Illustrations 54 and 201.

Illus. 144.—Five-slat Chair, about 1750.

Chairs

Illustration 144 shows a five-slat or five-back chair owned by the writer. It was made about 1750, and the rockers were probably added twenty-five or thirty years later. They project as far in front as in the back, which is evidence of their age. Later rockers were made longer, probably for safety, the short rocker at the back proving dangerous to the equilibrium of a too vigorous occupant of the rocking chair. This chair has never been restored and is a very good example of the slat-back chair. It is painted black with lines of yellow.

Illustration 145 shows an armchair with a five-slat back which is now the property of the Historical Society of Pennsylvania.

Illus. 145.—Pennsylvania Slat-back Chair, 1740–1750.

The slats are the typical Pennsylvania ones, made to fit the back, with a deeper curve than some, and, as may be seen by comparing them with others illustrated, with a more decided curve to both the upper and lower edges of the slats. The stretcher across the front is turned and is unusually heavy.

The type of chair succeeding the slat-back in popularity was the Windsor, which was made for

Illus. 146. — Windsor Chairs, 1750–1775.

years in large numbers both in England and America.

Windsor chairs made their first appearance in this country about 1730, in Philadelphia, and "Philadelphia made" Windsor chairs soon became very popular. Advertisements of them abound in newspapers up to 1800, and they may be found with the

Chairs

slat-back chairs in almost any country house, frequently upon the piazza, whence many a one has been bought by the keen-eyed collector driving along the road. The original Philadelphia fashion was to paint the chairs green, but after they were made all over the country they were probably painted to suit the taste of the buyer.

There is a story that the name Windsor was derived from the English town, where one of the royal Georges found in a shepherd's cottage a chair of this style, which he bought and had others made from, — thereby setting the fashion.

Windsor chairs are found in several styles, two of which are shown in Illustration 146, owned by the writer. Side-chairs like the arm-chair were made with the dividing strip which connects the arms left out, and the rounding top rail continuing down to the seat. The other chair in the illustration is known as a "fan back" from its shape with the flaring top.

Illus. 147.—Comb-back Windsor Rocking-chair, 1750–1775.

Illustration 147 shows a "comb-back" Windsor rocking-chair, owned by Mrs. Clarence R. Hyde, of

Brooklyn, N. Y. The middle spindles are extended to form the little head-rest, from which the name is derived.

A fine, high-backed arm-chair, and a child's chair are shown in Illustration 148, owned by Miss Mary Coates of Philadelphia. These chairs may have been some of the original Philadelphia-made Windsor chairs, as they were

Illus. 148.— High-back Windsor Arm-chair, and Child's Chair, 1750–1775.

bought in that town by Benjamin Horner, who was born in 1737.

Windsor writing-chairs are occasionally found, and one is shown in Illustration 149, possessing more than common interest, for it is said to have belonged to Thomas Jefferson, and upon its table may have been written the Declaration of Independence. It now belongs to the American Philosophical Society of Philadelphia. The seat is double, the top one revolving. The legs have been shortened.

Illus. 149. — Windsor Writing-chair, 1750–1775.

Illustration 150 shows two late Windsor rocking-chairs, the one of curly maple being several years later than the other, as the rockers, short in front and long behind, bear evidence. These chairs are owned by the writer.

The Dutch chair with bandy or cabriole legs and a splat in the back made its appearance with the early years of the eighteenth century, and was the forerunner of the Chippendale chair. The first Dutch chairs have a back similar in form to the Queen Anne chair in Illustration 108, slightly higher and narrower than later backs. They are sometimes called Queen Anne chairs, and sometimes

Illus. 150. — Windsor Rocking-chairs, 1820–1830.

parrot-back, from the shape of the opening each side of the solid splat. The stretchers or underbraces of earlier chairs are retained in the first Dutch chairs, one of which is shown in Illustration 151, owned by Mrs. Charles H. Prentice, of Worcester.

The first mention found of claw-and-ball feet is in 1737, when "six Crowfoot chairs" appear in an in-

Chairs

ventory. In one of 1750, "chairs with Eagle's foot and shell on the Knee" are entered.

A chair is shown in Illustration 152, still retaining the stretchers, but with the claw-and-ball foot and a shell at the top of the back. This chair was made about 1720–1730. It belongs to Walter Hosmer, Esq.

Illustration 153 shows a chair also belonging to Mr. Hosmer. It is made without stretchers, and the splat is pierced at the top.

A chair which retains the form of the Dutch chair, with "Eagle's foot and shell on the Knee," is shown in Illustration 154, but the splat is cut in an elaborate design, with the centre opening heart-shaped, which was the shape of the earliest piercing made in the plain splat.

Illus. 151.—Dutch Chair (back stretcher missing), 1710-1720.

This chair and the one in Illustration 155 are in the Poore collection at Indian Hill, Newburyport. They show the development from the Dutch to the Chippendale style. The legs in

Illustration 155 are carved upon the knee with an elaborate form of shell and a scroll. The splat is not pierced, but has a curious design of ropes with tassels carved at the top. These chairs were made about 1740-1750. The backs of the last four

Illus. 152 and Illus. 153. — Dutch Chairs, about 1740.

chairs are made with the characteristic Dutch top, curving down into the side-posts with rounded ends, with the effect of back and sides being in one piece.

A style of chair common during the first half

of the eighteenth century is shown in Illustration 156; one chair having turned legs while the other ends in a Spanish foot. The tops are in the bow shape, and the splats are pierced, showing the influence of Chippendale fashions. The splat is alike in both, but the country cabinet-maker who probably

Illus. 154 and Illus 155. — Dutch Chairs, 1740–1750.

made these chairs may have thought the splat would look as well one way as the other, and so put one in upside down. They are in the Deerfield Museum, and were made about 1750.

A roundabout chair in the Dutch style is shown in Illustration 157. The bandy legs end in a foot with a slight carving in grooves, and the seat is rounding upon the corners like that in the ordinary

Dutch chair. This very graceful chair is owned by Francis H. Bigelow, Esq., of Cambridge.

Easy-chairs formed a part of the bedroom furniture inventoried during the eighteenth century, and

Illus. 156. — Dutch Chairs, 1750–1760.

they were made in various styles, with Dutch, Chippendale, and Hepplewhite legs. Hepplewhite gives a design in 1787 for what he calls "an easy-chair," and also a "saddle-check chair," while upon the same page, with intentional suggestion, is a design for a "gouty-stool."

Illustration 158 shows an easy-chair with the Dutch bandy leg and foot, owned by the writer. Such chairs were inventoried very high, from one pound to ten, and when one considers the amount of material required to stuff and cover the chair, the reason for the high valuation is understood. In the days when the fireplace gave what heat there was in the room, these great chairs must have been most comfortable, with the high back and sides to keep out draughts.

An easy-chair with claw-and-ball feet is shown in Illustration 159. It is owned by Francis H. Bigelow, Esq., of Cambridge. A beautiful easy-chair with carved cabriole legs, owned by Harry Harkness Flagler, Esq., is shown in Illustration 248.

We now come to the most important period in the consideration of chairs, — the last half of the eighteenth century. During this period many books of designs were published, which probably came to this country within a year or two of their publication, and which afforded American cabinet-makers an opportunity for copying the best English examples.

Illus. 157. — Dutch Roundabout Chair, 1740.

Chippendale's designs were published in 1753, Hepplewhite's in 1789, Sheraton's in 1791. Besides these three chief chair-makers, there were Ince

Illus. 158. — Easy-Chair with Dutch Legs, 1750.

and Mayhew, 1765; Robert Manwaring, 1765; R. and J. Adam, 1773; and others of less note.

Chippendale drew most of his ideas from the French, notably in the way of ornamentation, but the form of his chairs was developed chiefly from the Dutch style, with the bandy leg and splat in the back. His straight-legged chairs were suggested by the Chinese furniture, which was fashionable about the middle of the eighteenth century. These vari-

Illus. 159.—Claw-and-ball-foot Easy-chair, 1750.

ous styles Chippendale adapted, and employed with such success that his was the strongest influence of the century upon furniture, and for a period of over thirty years it was supreme.

The claw-and-ball foot does not appear upon any

186   Furniture of the Olden Time

of Chippendale's designs in "The Gentleman's and Cabinet-Maker's Director." His preference was plainly for the French scroll foot, shown upon the sofa in Illustration 209 and the candle-stand in Illustration 333. Doubtless, however, he made furniture

Illus. 160.—Chippendale Chair.

with the claw-and-ball foot, which was the foot used by the majority of his imitators and followers.

An early Chippendale chair is shown in Illustration 160, from the Poore collection at Indian Hill, with stretchers, which are unusual in a Chip-

Illus. 161 — Chippendale Chair.

Chairs

pendale chair. The cabriole legs are carved upon the knee and end in a claw-and-ball foot. The top of the back has the bow form, which is a distinguishing characteristic of Chippendale. This chair-seat and the one following are very large and broad.

The lines in the back of the chair in Illustration 161 form a series of

Illus. 162. — Chippendale Chair.

curves, extremely graceful in effect, and the carving upon the back and legs is very fine. This chair is one of a set of six owned by Harry Harkness Flagler, Esq.

Illustration 162 shows a chair owned by Miss Mary Coates of Philadelphia. The design of the back,

Illus. 163. — Chippendale Chair.

Illus. 165.—Chippendale Chairs.

with some variations, is often seen. The top forms a complete bow with the ends turning up, and a shell is carved in the centre.

A variation of this back is shown in Illustration 163. The top has a fan instead of a shell, and the ends of the bow top are grooved. This chair is one of a set formerly owned by Miss Rebecca Shaw of Wickford, Rhode Island, who died in 1900, over ninety years of age. They are now in the possession of Mrs. Alice Morse Earle of Brooklyn, New York.

A fine arm-chair owned by Miss Mary Coates is shown in Illustration 164.

Two very beautiful and unusual Chippendale arm-chairs are shown in Illustration 165. They are owned by Harry Harkness Flagler, Esq., and the larger chair, which was formerly in the Pendleton collection, is undoubtedly an original Chippendale. Its proportions are perfect, and the elaborate carving is finely done. The other chair presents some Dutch characteristics, in the shape of the seat and back,

Illus. 164.—Chippendale Chair.

but the details of the carving indicate it to be after the school of Chippendale.

Illustration 166 shows a graceful chair with carving upon the back and knees. It belonged formerly to Governor Strong of Massachusetts, and is now owned by W. S. G. Kennedy, Esq., of Worcester.

Illus. 167.—Roundabout Chair.

Illus. 166.—Chippendale Chair.

The roundabout chair in Illustration 167 was originally owned by the Rev. Daniel Bliss, the Congregational minister in Concord, Massachusetts, from 1739 to 1766. He was succeeded by William Emerson, who married his daughter, and who was the grandfather of Ralph Waldo Emerson.

William Emerson died in 1777, and Dr. Ezra Ripley succeeded to the pastorate and the widow, and took possession of the manse and of this chair, which must have served the successive ministers at the desk, while many hundreds of sound sermons were written. It now belongs to the Concord Antiquarian Society.

An unusually fine example of a Dutch corner chair with an extension top, is shown in Illustration 168, owned by the Metropolitan Museum of Art.

Illus. 168.—Extension-top Roundabout Chair.

The finest type of roundabout chair is shown in Illustration 169. It is of mahogany and has but one cabriole leg, the others being uncompromisingly straight, but the cabriole leg, and the top rail and arms are carved finely with the acanthus design, worn almost smooth on the arms. It belongs to Dwight M. Prouty, Esq.

Illustration 170 shows a chair owned by Albert

Illus. 169. — Roundabout Chair.

Illus. 170. — Chippendale Chair.

S. Rines, Esq., of Portland, Maine.

It is extraordinarily good in design and carving, fine in every detail. The gadrooned edge upon this and the roundabout chair is found only upon the best pieces.

Illustration 171 shows one of six chairs owned by the writer.

The design of the chair-back in Illustration 172 is one that was quite common. The chair belongs to the writer.

The chair in Illustration 173 is owned by Mrs. E. A. Morse of Worcester; the one in Illustration

Illus. 171 and Illus. 172.—Chippendale Chairs.

174 is in the Waters collection, in Salem, and is one of a set of six. The legs and the rail around the seat of the last chair are carved in a rosette design in low relief.

About the middle of the eighteenth century it was fashionable to decorate houses and gardens in "Chinese taste," and furniture was designed for

o

"Chinese temples" by various cabinet-makers. That the American colonies followed English fashions closely is shown by the advertisement in 1758 of Theophilus Hardenbrook, surveyor, who with unfettered fancy modestly announced that he "designs all sorts of Buildings, Pavilions, Summer Rooms, Seats for Gardens"; also "all sorts of

Illus. 173 and Illus. 174.—Chippendale Chairs.

rooms after the taste of the Arabian, Chinese, Persian, Gothic, Muscovite, Paladian, Roman, Vitruvian, and Egyptian."

Illustration 175 shows a Chippendale chair in "Chinese taste" owned by Harry Harkness Flagler, Esq., of Millbrook. The legs and stretchers are straight, like those of Chinese chairs, and the outline of the back is Chinese, but the delicate carving is English. A sofa and a chair in "Chinese taste" are shown in Illustration 211.

Illustration 176 and Illustration 177 show two Chippendale chairs with backs of entirely different design from the splat-back chairs previously illustrated. Their form was probably suggested by that of the slat-back chair. Illustration 176 is one of a set of six, originally owned by Joseph Brown, one of the four famous brothers of Providence, whose dignified names, John, Joseph, Nicholas, and Moses, have been familiarly rhymed as "John and Josey, Nick and Mosey." The six chairs are now owned by their kinswoman, Mrs. David Thomas Moore of Westbury, Long Island. Each slat is delicately carved, and the chairs represent the finest of this type of Chippendale chairs. Illustration 177 shows a chair owned by Charles R. Waters, Esq., of

Illus. 175.—Chippendale Chair in "Chinese Taste."

Salem, with carved slats in the back. Chairs with this back but with plain slats are not unusual.

Hepplewhite's designs were published in 1789, and his light and attractive furniture soon became fashion-

Illus. 176.—Chippendale Chair.

able, superseding that of Chippendale, which was pronounced "obsolete." Hepplewhite's aim was to produce a light effect, and to this he often sacrificed considerations of strength and durability. While

Illus. 177.—Chippendale Chair.

Chippendale used no inlaying, Hepplewhite's furniture is ornamented with both carving and inlay, as well as painting. His chairs may be distinguished by the shape and construction of the back, which was usually of oval, shield, or heart shape. The carving in Hepplewhite's chairs is of quite a different character from that of Chippendale. The three feathers of the Prince of Wales often form a part of the back, for Hepplewhite was of the Prince's party when feeling ran strong during the illness of George III. Carved drapery, wheat, and the bell-flower, sometimes called husks, are other characteristics of Hepplewhite's chairs, two of which are shown in Illustration 178, belonging to Dwight Blaney, Esq., of Boston. The Prince's feathers appear in the middle of one chair-back and upon the top rail of the other.

Illustration 179 shows an arm-chair from a set of Hepplewhite dining-chairs owned by Francis H. Bigelow, Esq., of Cambridge. The back is carved with a design of drapery and ears of wheat.

Illus. 179.—Hepplewhite Chair.

A chair is shown in Illustration 180, which has features of several styles. The legs are French and

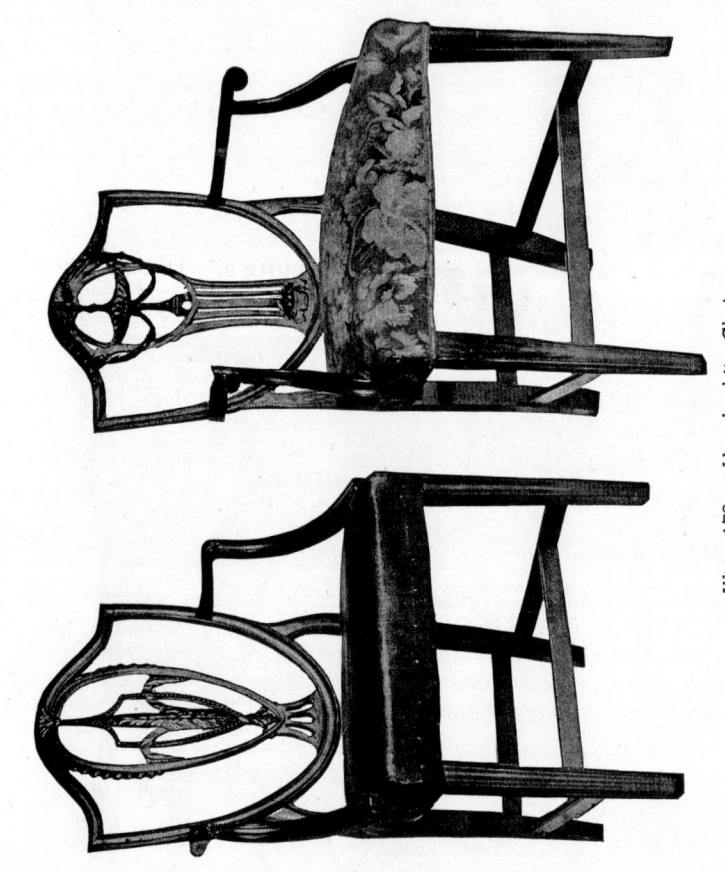

Illus. 178. — Hepplewhite Chairs.

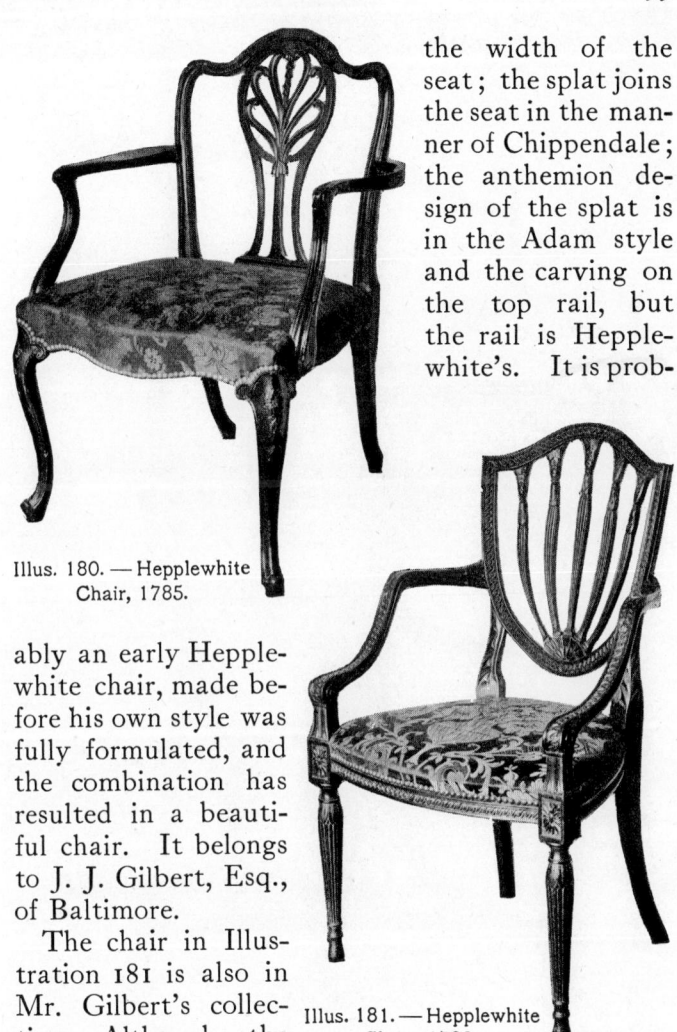

Chairs

the width of the seat; the splat joins the seat in the manner of Chippendale; the anthemion design of the splat is in the Adam style and the carving on the top rail, but the rail is Hepplewhite's. It is prob-

Illus. 180. — Hepplewhite Chair, 1785.

ably an early Hepplewhite chair, made before his own style was fully formulated, and the combination has resulted in a beautiful chair. It belongs to J. J. Gilbert, Esq., of Baltimore.

The chair in Illustration 181 is also in Mr. Gilbert's collection. Although the

Illus. 181. — Hepplewhite Chair, 1789.

shield back is generally accredited to Hepplewhite, Adam made it before him and it was used by the other chair-makers of his time. This chair shows very strongly the Adam influence in the carved and reeded legs and the fine carving, which is called guilloche, upon the arms and around the back and the frame of the seat. The entire chair is beautifully carved.

The arm-chair shown in Illustration 182 has stood since 1835 in front of the pulpit in the Unitarian church in Leicester, Massachusetts, but of its history nothing is known for the years before that date, when it was probably given to the new church, then just starting with its young pastor, Rev. Samuel May. This chair, like the one in Illustration 181, which it resembles, has characteristics of different styles. It is probable that both Hepplewhite and Sheraton had practised their trade some years, and had made much furniture before their books were published in 1789 and 1791, and had adopted and adapted many ideas from the cabinet-makers and designers of the day, as well as from each other.

Illus. 182.—Hepplewhite Chair, 1789.

Chairs

The chair in Illustration 183 was used by Washington in the house occupied as the Presidential mansion in Philadelphia. It is now owned by the Historical Society of Pennsylvania. This chair has the same guilloche carving as the chair in Illustration 181, extending entirely around the back. The legs are

Illus. 183.—French Chair, 1790.   Illus. 184.—Hepplewhite Chair, 1790.

short and the chair low and wide, and this with the stuffed back indicates that the chair is French.

The chair in Illustration 184 is also in the rooms of the Historical Society, and is one of the set owned by Washington. The urn and festoons in the back show a marked Adam influence, but the three feathers above the urn are Hepplewhite's.

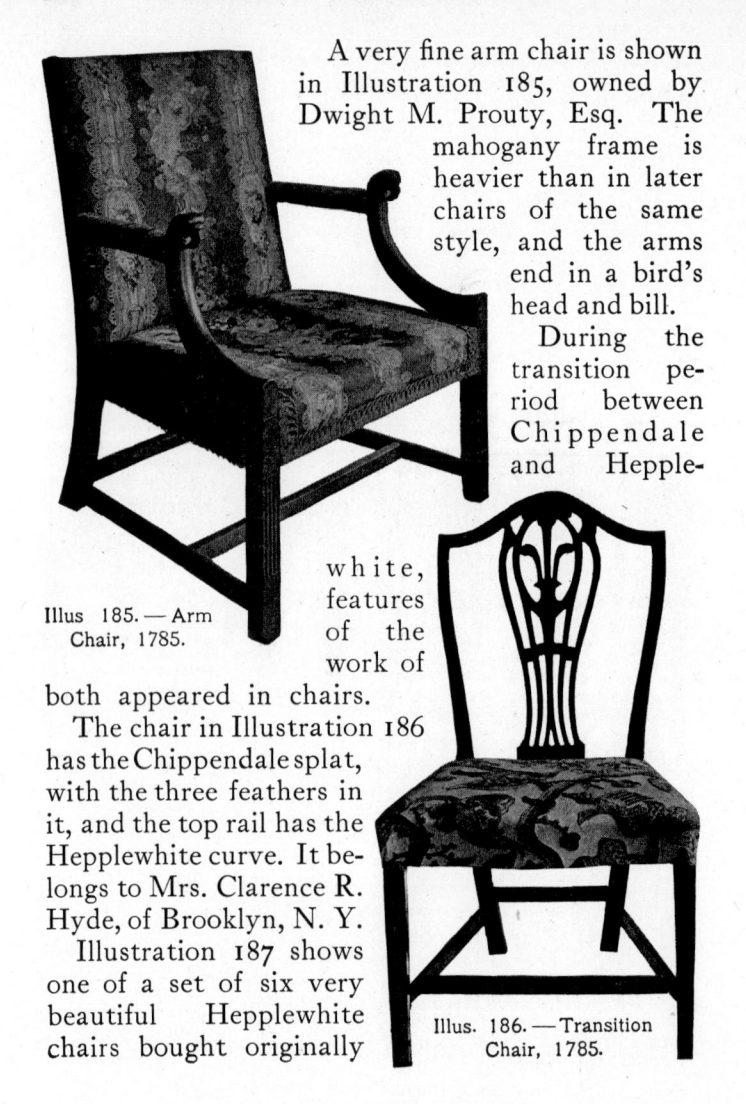

A very fine arm chair is shown in Illustration 185, owned by Dwight M. Prouty, Esq. The mahogany frame is heavier than in later chairs of the same style, and the arms end in a bird's head and bill.

During the transition period between Chippendale and Hepplewhite, features of the work of both appeared in chairs.

Illus 185. — Arm Chair, 1785.

The chair in Illustration 186 has the Chippendale splat, with the three feathers in it, and the top rail has the Hepplewhite curve. It belongs to Mrs. Clarence R. Hyde, of Brooklyn, N. Y.

Illustration 187 shows one of a set of six very beautiful Hepplewhite chairs bought originally

Illus. 186. — Transition Chair, 1785.

by the grandfather of their present owner, Charles R. Waters, Esq., of Salem. This chair is carved upon the legs with the bell-flower, and the three middle rails of the back are exquisitely carved. Chairs of

Illus. 187 and 188. — Hepplewhite Chairs.

this design, with the ornament of inlay instead of carving, are also found.

The chair in Illustration 188 belongs to W. S. G. Kennedy, Esq., of Worcester. The rails are not carved or inlaid, but the fan-shaped ornament at the lower point of the shield back is of holly and ebony, inlaid. This design of Hepplewhite chair is more frequently found than any other.

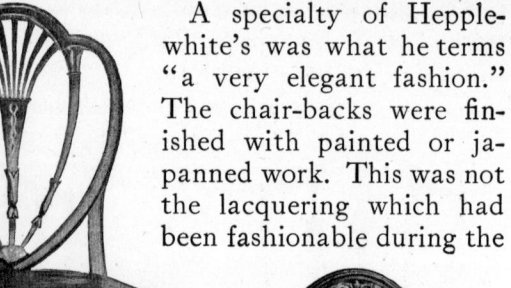

A specialty of Hepplewhite's was what he terms "a very elegant fashion." The chair-backs were finished with painted or japanned work. This was not the lacquering which had been fashionable during the

Illus. 189. — Hepplewhite Chair.

Illus. 190. — Hepplewhite Chair.

first half of the eighteenth century, with Chinese figures, but it was a process of coating the chairs with a sort of lacquer varnish, and then painting them in gold or colors upon a black ground.

Haircloth was used for the seats of chairs; the edges were finished with brass-headed nails, arranged sometimes to simulate festoons, as in Illustration 191.

A Hepplewhite chair with a back of quite a different design from the examples described previously, is shown in Illustration 189. The back is heart-shaped, and the ornamentation is of inlaying in light and dark wood. This chair is one of four in the Poore collection at Indian Hill. They formed a part of the set bought by Washington for Mount Vernon, and were in use there at the time of his death.

A chair owned by Miss Mary Coates of Philadelphia is shown in Illustration 190. The characteristic bell-flower is carved in the middle of the back of this chair.

Hepplewhite in turn was superseded by Sheraton, whose book of designs was published in 1791, only two years later than Hepplewhite's; but that short time sufficed for Sheraton to say that "this book [Hepplewhite's] has already caught the decline"; while he asserted of Chippendale's designs, that "they are now wholly antiquated and laid aside, though possessed of great merit, according to the times in which they were executed."

Sheraton's chairs retained many of Hepplewhite's

Illus. 191.—Sheraton Chair.

characteristics, but the great difference between them lay in the construction of the back, which it was Sheraton's aim to strengthen. His chairs, except in rare cases, do not have the heart or shield shaped back, which distinctly marks Hepplewhite chairs, but the back is rectangular in shape, the top rail being

Illus. 192.—Sheraton Chairs.

curved, straight, or with a raised piece in the centre, corresponding to the piece in the middle of the back. A rail extends across the back a few inches above the seat, and the splat or spindles end in this rail, and never extend to the seat.

Sheraton's designs show chairs with carved, twisted, reeded, or plain legs. The best Sheraton chairs found

Chairs

in this country usually have straight legs, slightly smaller than those upon the straight-legged Chippendale chairs. The tapering, reeded leg, which is characteristic of Sheraton, is not found so often upon his chairs as upon other pieces of furniture.

The chair in Illustration 191 is owned by the Misses Nichols of Salem, and it was brought with its mates to furnish the house built by McIntire in 1783. The chairs were imported, and as the back is precisely like one of Sheraton's designs in his book, they may have been made by him, before the book was published in 1791. The impression given by this chair is of strength combined with lightness, the

Illus. 193.—Sheraton Chair.   Illus. 194.—Sheraton Chair.

effect which Sheraton strove to attain, while at the same time he made the chairs strong not only in effect but in reality, an end which Hepplewhite did not accomplish. The legs of the chair are plainly turned, but in the original design they are reeded.

Illus. 195. — Sheraton Chair.

Illus. 196. — Sheraton Chair.

Illustration 192 shows two Sheraton chairs owned by Francis H. Bigelow, Esq. It will be seen that the carving in the back is similar in design to that of Hepplewhite chairs, and the carving and shape of the upper part of the chair-back with the curved top rail is often seen upon Hepplewhite's "bar-back" chairs.

Mr. Bigelow also owns the upholstered arm-chair in Illustration 193, sometimes called a Martha Washington easy-chair, from a similar chair at Mount Vernon. This chair and one in Illustration 194, which belongs to Mr. Bigelow, are after the Sheraton style, although these designs do not appear in Sheraton's books. The arm-chair in Illustration 194 is said to

Illus. 197.—Sheraton Chair.

have belonged to Jerome Bonaparte, but as Lucien and Joseph Bonaparte both had residences in this country, it would more probably have been owned by one of them rather than by Jerome, whose career in America was short and meteoric. The wood of this chair is cherry, said to have grown upon the island of Corsica, and the

Illus. 198.—Painted Sheraton Chair, 1810–1815.

P

style of the back, while upon the Sheraton order, differs from any of Sheraton's designs.

The chair in Illustration 195 belongs to Walter Bowne Lawrence, Esq., of Flushing, Long Island. It is one of the finest types of a Sheraton chair. The front legs end in what Hepplewhite called a

Illus. 199.—Late Mahogany Chairs, 1830–1845.

"spade foot," which was frequently employed by him and occasionally by Sheraton.

Illustration 196 shows a Sheraton chair owned by Mrs. E. A. Morse of Worcester. The top bar is carved with graceful festoons of drapery, and the back is in a design which is often seen.

A chair after Sheraton's later designs is shown in Illustration 197. It is one which was popular in the first decade of the nineteenth century. This chair is part of a set inherited by Waldo Lincoln, Esq., of Worcester.

The chair shown in Illustration 198 is owned by Mrs. J. C. Cutter of Worcester. It has a rush seat, and the back is painted in the manner called japanning, with gilt flowers upon a black ground. These chairs, which were called "Fancy chairs," were very popular during the first part of the nineteenth century, together with settees decorated in the same fashion.

Illustration 199 shows two mahogany chairs owned by Waldo Lincoln, Esq., of the styles which were fashionable from 1840 to 1850, examples of which may be found in almost every household, along with heavy sofas and tables of mahogany, solid or veneered.

In the first half of the nineteenth century and in the last quarter of the eighteenth, furniture was fashionable made of the light-colored woods; maple, curly and bird's-eye, and in the more expensive pieces, satinwood, which was used chiefly as a veneer on account of its cost. The two varieties of maple, being a native wood and plentiful, were always used lavishly, and rarely as a veneer. The thick maple drawers in old bureaus have been sawed into many thicknesses to use in violins, for which their seasoned wood is especially valuable. The parlor in John Hancock's house, in Boston, was "furnished in bird's-eye maple covered with damask brocade." As Governor Hancock was a man of inherited wealth and probably of fashion as well, his parlor would be furnished according to the mode of the day.

The three maple chairs in Illustration 200 belong to the writer. They were probably made about

Illus. 200. — Maple Chairs, 1820–1830.

1820 to 1830. The wood in all is beautifully marked curly maple, and in the upper rail of two is set a strip of bird's-eye maple. The design of the carved piece across the back is one that was used at this time in both maple and mahogany chairs.

CHAPTER VII

SETTLES, SETTEES, AND SOFAS

THE first form of the long seat, afterward developed into the sofa, was the settle, which is found in the earliest inventories in this country, and still earlier in England. The settle oftenest seen in America is of simple construction, usually of pine, and painted; probably the work of a country cabinet-maker, or even a carpenter. It was made to stand by the great fireplace, to keep the draughts out and the heat in, with its tall back, and the front of the seat coming down to the floor; and sadly was it needed in those days when the ink froze in the standish, as the minister sat by the fire to write his sermon. Illustration 201 shows a settle in the Deerfield Museum, in the kitchen. In front of the settle stands a flax-wheel, which kept the housewife busy on winter evenings, spinning by the firelight. Beside the settle is a rudely made light-stand, with a tin lamp, and a brass candlestick with the extinguisher on its top, and snuffers and tray beside it. Upon one side of the settle is fastened a candle-

Illus. 201.—Pine Settle, Eighteenth Century.

stick with an extension frame. Behind the flax-wheel is a banister-back chair, the plain type of the chairs in Illustration 139, and at the right of the picture is a slat-back, flag-bottomed chair such as may be seen in Illustration 143.

Illustration 202 shows a settle of oak, which has

upon the back the carved date 1708. The front of the seat has four panels, while the back has five lower panels, with a row of small panels above. The top rail is carved in five groups, the middle design of each group being a crown, and between each small panel is a turned ornament. The arms are

Illus. 202.—Oak Settle, 1708.

like the arms of the wainscot chairs in Illustration 124 and Illustration 125. The top of the seat does not lift up, as was often the case, disclosing a box below, but is fastened to the frame, and probably there were provided for this settle the articles often mentioned in inventories, "chusshings," "quysyns," or cushions, which the hard seat made so necessary. This settle belongs to Dwight Blaney, Esq., of Boston.

The word "settee" is the diminutive of "settle," and the long seat which corresponded to the chairs with the frame of turned wood was called a settee or small settle, being of so much lighter build than the settle.

Illustration 203 shows a settee owned by the Essex Institute of Salem, and said to have been

Illus. 203. — Settee covered with Turkey work, 1670–1680.

brought to this country by a Huguenot family about 1686. It is upholstered, like the chairs of the same style, in Turkey work, the colors in which are still bright. Turkey work was very fashionable at that time, rugs being imported from Turkey in shapes to fit the seat and back of chairs or settees.

Another form of the long seat was one which was

intended to serve as a couch, or "day-bed." It was really what its French name implies, *chaise longue*, or long chair, the back being an enlarged chair-back, and the body of the couch equalling three chair-seats. Illustration 204 shows a couch owned by the Concord Antiquarian Society, which formerly belonged to the descendants of the Rev. Peter

Illus. 204. — Flemish Couch, 1680–1690.

Bulkeley. It had originally a cane seat, and evidently formed part of a set of furniture, for a chair of the same style is with it, which also belonged to the Bulkeley family. Both couch and chair are Flemish in design, with the scroll foot turning backward. The braces between the legs are carved in the same design as the top of the back.

Illustration 205 shows a walnut couch made in the Dutch style about 1720–1730, with bandy legs and

Dutch feet. The splat in the back is Dutch, but instead of the side-posts curving into the top rail like the

Illus. 205.— Dutch Couch, 1720–1730.

Dutch chairs, in which the top and the side-posts apparently form one piece, these posts run up, with a finish at the top like the Flemish chairs, and like the posts in the back of the couch in Illustration 204. It is interesting to compare this couch, which is owned by the Misses Hosmer of Concord, Massachusetts, with the

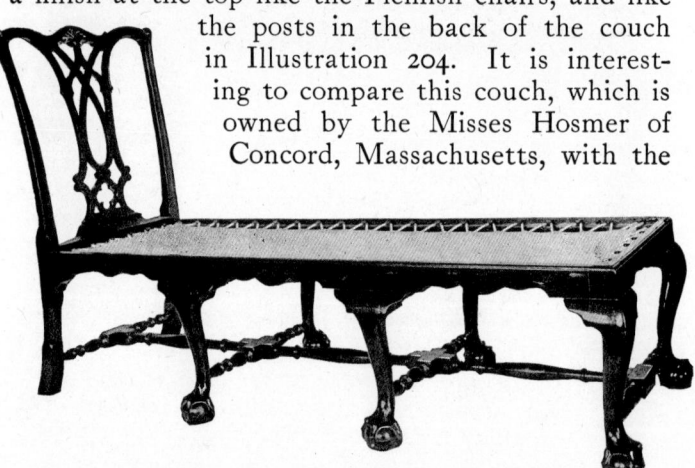

Illus. 206.— Chippendale Couch, 1760–1770.

following one, Illustration 206, which belongs to Mr. Walter Hosmer of Wethersfield, Connecticut, and was made about 1770. This couch, of mahogany, has a back like one of the familiar Chippendale chairs, somewhat higher than the back of the couch

Illus. 207.—Chippendale Settee, 1760.

in Illustration 205, which is longer than this Chippendale couch. The bandy legs with claw-and-ball feet are unusually well proportioned, and the effect of the piece of furniture is extremely elegant. The canvas seat is drawn tight by ropes laced over wooden knobs.

A double chair owned by Dwight M. Prouty, Esq., of Boston, is shown in Illustration 207. The splats are cut in an early design, with the heart-shaped opening in the lower part. The settee is not so wide as some, and the back is not equal to two chair backs,

Illus. 208. — Sofa, 1740.

lacking the side rails which are usually carried down in the middle between the splats. The front legs have the acanthus carving upon the knees, and end in a Dutch foot. This settee is what was called a "Darby and Joan" seat, just wide enough for two.

A sofa is shown in Illustration 208 from "Stenton," the fine old house in Philadelphia, now occupied by the Colonial Dames. The back and arms are upholstered, and the shape of the arms, and the curved

Illus. 209. — Chippendale Settee, 1765–1770.

outline of the back are like early Chippendale pieces. A distinction was made between the "sopha" and the settee, the sofa being a long seat with the back and arms entirely upholstered, like the sofa in Illustration 208.

Illustration 209 shows a Chippendale settee with beautifully carved cabriole legs, owned by Harry

Harkness Flagler, Esq. The three front legs are carved with the scroll foot turned to the front. This foot was called the French foot by the cabinet-makers of that period, about 1765–1770.

Illustration 210 shows a double chair, also owned by Mr. Flagler. It has characteristics of various

Illus. 210.—Double Chair, 1760.

nationalities and styles, mainly Chippendale. The back consists of two chair backs, wider than arm-chair backs, which is almost always true of the double chair. The corners of the seat, and the ends of the top rails are rounding after the Dutch style, but the splats are Chippendale. The three front legs end in a small claw-and-ball, and the knees are carved. The most noticeable feature of this graceful piece is the rococo design at the top of the back and upon the front of the seat.

Illustration 211 shows a Chippendale double chair and one of four arm-chairs, formerly owned by Governor John Wentworth, whose household goods were confiscated and sold at auction by the Federal government, in 1776. Since that time these pieces have been in the Alexander Ladd house at Portsmouth, New Hampshire, where they now stand. They are a perfect exemplification of Chippendale's furniture in the Chinese style, and are probably the finest examples of that style in this country. They are of mahogany, with cane seats. The design of the backs is more elaborate than any of the Chinese designs for furniture of either Chippendale, Manwaring, Ince, or Mayhew; an unusual thing, for a majority of the designs in the old cabinet-makers' books are far more elaborate than the furniture which has come down to us. Chippendale says that these "Chinese chairs are very suitable for a lady's boudoir, and will likewise suit a Chinese temple." One wonders if Governor Wentworth had a Chinese temple for these beautiful pieces of furniture. He had, we know, splendid gardens, which were famous in those days, and possibly a Chinese temple may have been one of the adornments, with these chairs for its furniture.

Illustration 212 shows a double chair, which is well known from representations of it in various books.

Illus. 211.—Chippendale Double Chair and Chair, in "Chinese Taste," 1760–1765.

Settles, Settees, and Sofas

It is one of the finest examples existing of the Chippendale period, and was undoubtedly, like the double chair in Illustration 211, made in England. The carving upon the three front legs is unusually good. The feet are carved with lions' claws, and the knees with grotesque faces, while the arms end in dragons' heads.

Illus. 212.—Chippendale Double Chair, 1750–1760.

The corners of the back are finished with a scroll, turning to the back. The wood of this double chair is walnut, and it is covered in gray horsehair. This chair formerly belonged to John Hancock, and was presented to the American Antiquarian Society in 1838, with other pieces bought from the Hancock house, by John Chandler, of Petersham, Massachusetts.

The little settee in Illustration 213 is owned by Albert S. Rines, Esq., of Portland, Maine. It was evidently made from the same design as a long settee in the Pendleton collection in Providence, which has the same Chippendale carvings on the back at the centre and ends, and the same effect of the leg

Illus. 213.—Chippendale Settee, 1770.

being continued up into the frame of the seat. This settee has the middle leg unevenly placed.

The settee in Illustration 214 is entirely unlike any shown. It is French, of the time of Louis the Sixteenth, and with the six chairs like it, was part of the cargo upon the ship *Sally*, which sailed from France in 1792, and landed at Wiscasset, Maine, with a load of fine furniture and rich belongings intended to furnish a home of refuge for Marie

Antoinette, who did not live to sail upon the *Sally*. The sideboard in Illustration 75 has the same history and it can be traced directly to the *Sally*. The settee and chairs came from Bath, Maine, where there are also other chairs from the *Sally*, which are, however, like the sideboard, English in style.

Illus. 214.—French Settee, 1790.

The settee is of solid rosewood, with the short legs of the Louis XVI period, and a very deep seat. The wood of the back is elaborately carved in a design distinctly French, of roses, with a bow of ribbon in the centre. The settee and chairs are now owned by Mrs. William J. Hogg, of Worcester.

A double chair owned by Francis H. Bigelow, Esq., is shown in Illustration 215. The back is made of two Hepplewhite chair-backs, which combine the outline of the shield back and the middle of the interlaced heart back shown in the chair in Illustration 189.

Illus. 215. — Hepplewhite Settee, 1790.

The three front legs are inlaid with fine lines and the bell flower, and the backs are very finely inlaid, with lines in the urn-shaped piece in the centre, and a fan above, while a fine line of holly runs around the edge of each piece. The stretchers between the legs are a very unusual feature in such settees.

Illustration 216 shows a Sheraton settee, now in Girard College, Philadelphia. It was a part of the furniture belonging to Stephen Girard, the founder of that college. It has eight legs, the four in front being the typical reeded Sheraton legs. The back has five posts dividing it into four chair-backs. The seat is upholstered.

The Sheraton sofa in Illustration 217 was probably made in England about 1790–1800. It is

Illus. 216.— Sheraton Settee, 1790–1795.

owned by Francis H. Bigelow, Esq., of Cambridge. The frame is of mahogany, and the rail at the top of the back is exquisitely carved with festoons and flowers. The front of the seat is slightly rounding at the ends, and the arm, which is carved upon the upper side, extends beyond the upholstered frame, and rests upon a pillar which continues up from the corner leg. This style of arm is quite characteristic of Sheraton. The legs of the sofa are

Illus. 217. — Sheraton Sofa, 1790–1800.

plainly turned, not reeded, as is usual upon Sheraton sofas.

The sofa in Illustration 218 is a typical Sheraton piece, of a style which must have been very fashionable about 1800, for such sofas are often found in this country. The frame is of mahogany, with

Illus. 218. — Sheraton Sofa, about 1800.

pieces of satinwood inlaid at the top of the end legs. The arms are like the arms of the sofa in Illustration 217, and they, the pillars supporting them, and the four front legs are all reeded. This sofa is owned by W. S. G. Kennedy, Esq., of Worcester.

Illustration 219 shows a Sheraton settee which came from the Flint mansion in Leicester, Massachusetts, and is now owned by the writer. It has

Illus. 219.—Sheraton Settee, about 1805.

a rush seat, and the frame was originally painted black, with gilt flowers. It is very long, settees of this style usually equalling three chairs, while this equals four. It measures seventy-six inches in length, and from front to back the seat measures seventeen inches. It makes an admirable hall settee, and seems to be substantial, although extremely light in effect.

Another settee is shown in Illustration 220, with a cane seat, and painted in the "japanning" of the period in black with gold figures. It is owned by Mrs. Clarence R. Hyde, of Brooklyn, N. Y.

An Empire settee of graceful shape, owned by Barton Myers, Esq., of Norfolk, Virginia, is shown in

Illus. 220. — Sheraton Settee, about 1805.

Illustration 221. The lines of the many curves are all unusually good. The wood of the settee is mahog-

Illus. 221. — Empire Settee, about 1805.

any, and the seat is rush. The ornaments upon the front and the rosettes at the tip of each curve are brass.

In 1816 there was launched in Salem the yacht called *Cleopatra's Barge*, built and owned by Capt. George Crowninshield, who had been a partner with his brothers in the East India trade and had lived from a boy upon his father's ships. Finally retiring from business, he built this splendid yacht with the intention of spending years in travel, but he died after the first long voyage to the Mediterranean. The yacht was the wonder of the day and was visited

Illlus. 222. — Empire Settee, 1816.

by thousands, not alone in Salem but in every foreign port. She was furnished with great magnificence, in the Empire style, the woods used in the saloon being mahogany and bird's-eye maple, and the two settees in the saloon were each eleven feet in length. One is shown in Illustration 222, now owned by Frederic B. Crowninshield, Esq., of Marblehead. The backs are lyre-shaped, and when new the seats were covered with crimson velvet and edged with wide gold lace. The hook upon the back leg was probably to hold the settee to the wall in bad weather.

Illustration 223 shows the influence of the fashion for heavier and more elaborate frames, which came in with the nineteenth century. The arms are made after the Sheraton type shown in Illustration 217 and Illustration 218, but where a simple pillar was employed before, this settee has a carved pineapple forming the support to the arm, which ends in a scroll. Instead of four front legs either plain or fluted, there are two of larger size carved with the same leaves which sheathe the pineapple. The covering is horsehair, which was probably the original cover.

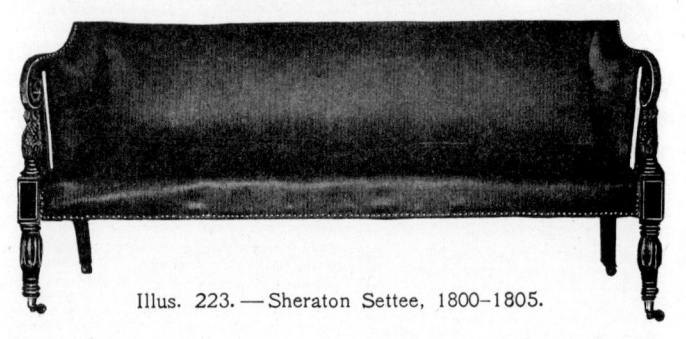

Illus. 223. — Sheraton Settee, 1800-1805.

This settee now belongs to the Concord Antiquarian Society, and was owned by Dr. Ezra Ripley, who was minister of the old Congregational Church of Concord from 1777 to 1840, and who lived in the Old Manse, afterward occupied by Hawthorne. The settee remained in the manse until comparatively recent years.

The sofa in Illustration 224 belongs to the Misses Hosmer of Concord, and stands in their old house, filled with the furniture of generations past, and interesting with memories of the Concord philosophers. The lines of this sofa are extremely elegant and graceful, and its effect quite classic. The legs are what is known as the Adam leg, which was designed by the Adam brothers, and which Sheraton used frequently. The style of the sofa is that of the Adam brothers, and it was probably made from their designs about 1800–1810. The writer has seen a window seat which belonged to Charles Carroll of Carrollton, after exactly this design, without the back.

Illus. 225. — Sofa in Adam Style, 1800-1810.

The back of the sofa in Illustration 225 follows the same graceful curves as the one in Illustration 224. This sofa was found by the writer in the shed of a farmhouse, on top of a woodpile, which made it evident what its fate would be eventually, a fate which has robbed us of many a fine piece of old furniture. After climbing upon a chair, then a table, the sight of these carved feet protruding from the woodpile was almost enough to make the antique hunter lose her insecure footing; but with the duplicity learned in years of collecting, all emotion was concealed until the sofa had been secured. The writer knows of four sofas, all found near Worcester,

Illus. 224. — Sofa, 1815-1820.

measuring the same, seven feet in length, and with the same carving of oak leaves upon the legs and ends, but this is the only one of the four which has the carved oak leaves across the front of the seat, and the rows of incised carving upon the back rail. The sofa was covered with black haircloth, woven in an elaborate design, and around the edge of the covering ran the brass beading which may be seen

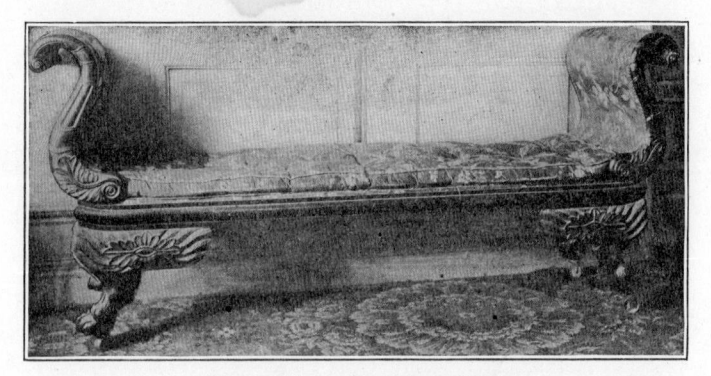

Illus. 226.—Sofa, about 1820.

in the illustration. This beading is three-eighths of an inch wide, and is of pressed brass, filled with lead, so that it is pliable and may be bent to go around a curve. Such beading or trimming was used in the place of brass-headed tacks or nails, and is found upon chairs and sofas of about this date, 1815–1820.

Illustration 226 shows one of a pair of sofas without backs. The frame is of mahogany with legs and arms carved rather coarsely. The covering is of stiff old brocade, probably the original cover when these sofas were made, about 1820, for the Warner house in Portsmouth, where they still stand. The panelling of the old room, built in 1716, shows behind the sofa, and on the floor is the Brussels carpet upon which is a stain from wine spilt by Lafayette, when he visited the house in 1824.

The sofa in Illustration 227, known as a cornucopia sofa, from the design of the carving, shows the most ornate type of this style. The frame is of mahogany, and the ends of the arms are carved

Illus. 227.—Cornucopia Sofa, about 1820.

in large horns of plenty, the same design being repeated in the carving of the top rail of the back and in the legs, which end in a lion's claw. The round hard pillows, called "squabs," at each end, were always provided for sofas of this shape, to fit into the hollow made by the curves of the cornucopia. This sofa is owned by Dr. Charles Schoeffer of Philadelphia.

Illustration 228 shows a sofa and miniature sofa made about 1820 for William T. Lane, Esq., of Boston, and now owned by his daughter, Mrs. Thomas

H. Gage of Worcester. Mr. Lane had two little daughters, and for them he had two little sofas

Illus. 228. — Sofa and Miniature Sofa, about 1820.

made, that they might sit one each side of the large sofa. This fashion of making miniature pieces of

Illus. 229. — Sofa, about 1820.

furniture like the larger ones was much in vogue during the first quarter of the nineteenth century.

A sofa of similar lines is shown in Illustration 229. The back and legs are different, and reeding takes the place of the twist in Illustration 228.

The sofa and chair in Illustration 230 are part of a set of furniture bought by the father and mother of the late Major Ben: Perley Poore, for their house at Indian Hill, about 1840. These pieces are interesting not only for the design of the mahogany frames, carved with swans' necks and heads, but for the covering, which is of colored haircloth, woven in a large figure in red and blue upon a gray ground. The seat of the sofa is worn and has a

Illus. 230.— Sofa and Chair, about 1840.

rug spread upon it, but the back and pillows and the chair-seat are perfect.

From 1844 to 1848 a cabinet-maker named John H. Belter had a shop in New York, where he manufactured furniture, chiefly from rosewood. The backs of the chairs and sofas were deeply curved, and in order to obtain the strength necessary, thin pieces of rosewood were pressed into the desired curve, and the several thicknesses glued together, and pressed again. The strong back made in this way was then elaborately carved, in an openwork pattern of vines and leaves. The sofas of these sets were usually in the shape shown in Illustration 231,

Illus. 231.—Rosewood Sofa, 1844-1848.

which belongs to Mrs. M. Newman of New York. Many of the wealthy families of New York had this Belter furniture, which was always covered with a rich silk brocade. It is eagerly sought for now and brings large prices.

CHAPTER VIII

TABLES

THE earliest form of table in use in this country was inventoried in 1642 as a "table bord," and the name occurs in English inventories one hundred years earlier. The name "board" was given quite literally from the table top, which was a board made separately from the supporting trestles, and which, after a meal, was taken off the trestles, and both board and trestles were put away, thus leaving the room free. These tables were long and narrow, and had in earliest times a long bench or form at one side only, the other side of the board being left free for serving. In the Bolles collection is a veritable "borde" rescued from the attic of a deserted house, where it had stood for scores of years. The board is about twelve feet long and two feet one inch wide, and bears the mark of many a knife. It rests upon three rude trestles, presenting a wonderfully interesting example of the "table borde" of the sixteenth and early seventeenth centuries, and one which is extremely rare.

It will be easily seen how the expression "the festive board" originated. Presently it became the custom to leave the board upon its trestles, instead of removing both, and in time the piece was called a table, which name covered both board and trestles. Some of the different forms of the table mentioned in inventories are framed and joined tables, chair tables, long tables, drawing-tables, square, oval, and round tables. The framed and joined tables refer

Illus. 232.— Chair Table, Eighteenth Century.

to the frame beneath the board. The other tables derive their names from the shape or construction of the tops. A drawing-table was one made with extension pieces at each end, supported when out by wooden braces, and folding back under or over the table top when not in use.

A chair table is shown in Illustration 232. The table top is put back in the illustration, so that the piece can be pushed against the wall and used as a chair. Chair tables always had the drawer beneath the seat. They are inventoried as early as 1644.

Illus. 233.—Oak Table, 1650–1675.

This chair table belongs to Dwight Blaney, Esq., of Boston.

The framed or joined table had turned legs, with stretchers between, and a drawer under the table top. Illustration 233 shows an oak table formerly owned in the Coffin family, and now in the building of the Newburyport Historical Society. The table is a good example of the framed or joined table early in the seventeenth century. The legs and stretchers are of the same style as those upon wainscot chairs, which belong to the same period as the table.

Illustration 234 shows a table with slate top, owned by the American Antiquarian Society of Worcester. The slate top originally filled the eight-sided space in the centre of the

Illus. 234.—Slate-top Table, 1670–1680.

table, but only the middle section is now left. Beside the piece of slate is a paper written by the late John Preston of New Ipswich, New Hampshire, in 1847, when he gave the table to the Antiquarian Society, detailing the history of the table from the time it was given to his ancestor, the Rev. Nehemiah Walter, who graduated from Harvard University in 1682. The table was used by generation after generation of ministers and lawyers, whose

Illus. 235.—"Butterfly Table," about 1700.

ink-stains cover the marquetry border around the top, and whose feet have worn the stretchers. Slate-top tables are very rare, and there are but few known to exist. The turned legs and stretchers and the drawer in the table are features which appear in

Illus. 236. — "Hundred-legged Table," 1675–1700.

tables of the same date with wooden tops. There is one drop handle left upon the drawer, the frame around which has the early single moulding.

Illustration 235 shows a curious little table, several of which have been found in Connecticut, and which were probably made there. It has the turned legs, with plain stretchers, of the tables in Illustration 233. The oval top has drop leaves which are held up by

Illus. 237. — "Hundred-legged Table," 1680–1700.

wing-shaped braces, from which comes the modern name for this table, of "butterfly table."

The table in Illustration 236 is an unusually fine example of what is now called a "hundred-legged" or "forty-legged" table, evidently from the bewildering number of legs beneath it, which are wofully in the way of the legs of the persons seated around it. This table is made of oak, with twisted legs, and measures four feet by five and a half. The supporting legs, when not in use, swing around under the middle leaf. The table is owned by Dwight Blaney, Esq.

Illus. 238. — Gate-legged Table, 1680–1700.

Illustration 237 shows a superb walnut dining-table, now in the rooms of the Albany Historical Society. It measures six and a half feet by six feet. It belonged to Sir William Johnson and when confiscated in 1776 from that Royalist, it was bought by Hon. John Taylor, whose descendants loan it to the Society. These tables are also called "gate-legged," from the leg which swings under the leaf, like a gate.

Illustration 238 shows a very small, and very rare

gate-legged table with trestle feet upon the middle section, enabling it to stand firmly with the leaves dropped. It belongs to Dwight M. Prouty, Esq.

Illustration 239 shows a spindle-legged, gate-legged table, a type exceedingly rare like all spindle-legged furniture. The slender legs have Dutch feet. This dainty table has descended to Mrs. Edward W. Rankin of Albany, from Katherine Livingstone, who brought it with her when she came to Albany in 1764, as the bride of Stephen Van Rensselaer, the Patroon. It must then have been an inherited piece.

Illus. 239.—Spindle-legged Table, 1710–1720.

Illustration 240 shows a forty-legged table, such as is not uncommonly found. It measures four feet in length. The large Sheffield plate tray on feet was made in the early part of the nineteenth century, when trays of various sizes upon feet were fashionable. The tea-set upon the tray is one made about 1835, and is extremely graceful in shape. The table and silver are owned by the writer.

The little Dutch table in Illustration 241 has the

next style of leg used upon tables, which were made in all sizes, and were presumably very popular, for such tables are often found. One leg slides around on

Illus. 240. — "Hundred-legged Table," 1680–1700.

each side to support the leaves. This table was made about 1740, and belongs to Francis H. Bigelow, Esq.

The same Dutch leg is seen in Illustration 242 upon a dainty little mahogany card-table, with slides at each end to hold the candlesticks. This table belongs to Miss Tilton of Newburyport.

Tables

Illustration 243 shows a mahogany table with claw-and-ball feet owned by the writer. The top measures four feet four inches across, and its date is about 1750. The double coaster upon wheels, filled with violets, was made to hold decanters of wine, and one can imagine these wheels rattling down the mahogany table as the evening grew late and the decanters empty.

Illus. 241.— Dutch Table, 1720–1740.

As early as 1676 stands are spoken of in inventories, and during the eighteenth century they were a common article of furniture. The tops were square, oval, or round, and the base consisted of a pillar with three spreading feet. Illustration 244 shows the early foot used for these stands, about 1740. This table is owned by Miss Mary Coates of Philadelphia, and the silver pieces upon it are heirlooms in her family.

Illus. 242.— Dutch Card-table, 1730–1740.

These stands came to be known as "Dutch Tea-

Tables," and the bases were often elaborately carved. The tops of the handsomest tables were carved out of a thick piece of wood, so as to leave a rim, to keep the china from sliding off. This carved rim was in different forms, the finest being what is now called

Ilius. 243. — Claw-and-ball-foot Table, about 1750.

"pie-crust," with an ogee scallop. The plain rim is now known as the "dish-top." Illustration 245 shows a pie-crust table owned by Dwight Blaney, Esq.

Illustration 246 shows a dish-top table belonging to Francis H. Bigelow, Esq. Both tables have claw-and-ball feet, and they are made, like all of the Dutch tea-tables, with the top revolving upon

Tables 253

the pillar. When not in use the top could be "tipped," and the table put back against the wall; and when the top was to be used, it fastened down with a snap.

Illustration 247 shows two of the finest type of tea-tables. They are owned by Harry

Illus. 244.—Dutch Stand, about 1740.

Harkness Flagler, Esq. One has the pie-crust edge, and the other a scalloped edge. The pillars of both are reeded, and the legs are carved. A great difference can be noted between

Illus. 245.—"Pie-crust Table," 1750.

these two bases, in the sweep of the spreading legs, and in the claw-and-ball feet, which are especially fine upon the pie-crust table. The proportions of this table are unusually good, the central pillar being slender, and the finely carved legs having a spread which gives a very graceful and light effect.

Illustration 248 shows another fine table and chair owned by Mr. Flagler. The chair is described upon page 183. The table has an oval top, carved,

Illus. 246.—"Dish-top Table," 1750.

Illus. 247.—Tea-tables, 1750–1760.

not in a regular scallop, but in rococo scrolls. It has a heavier pillar than the pie-crust table in the last

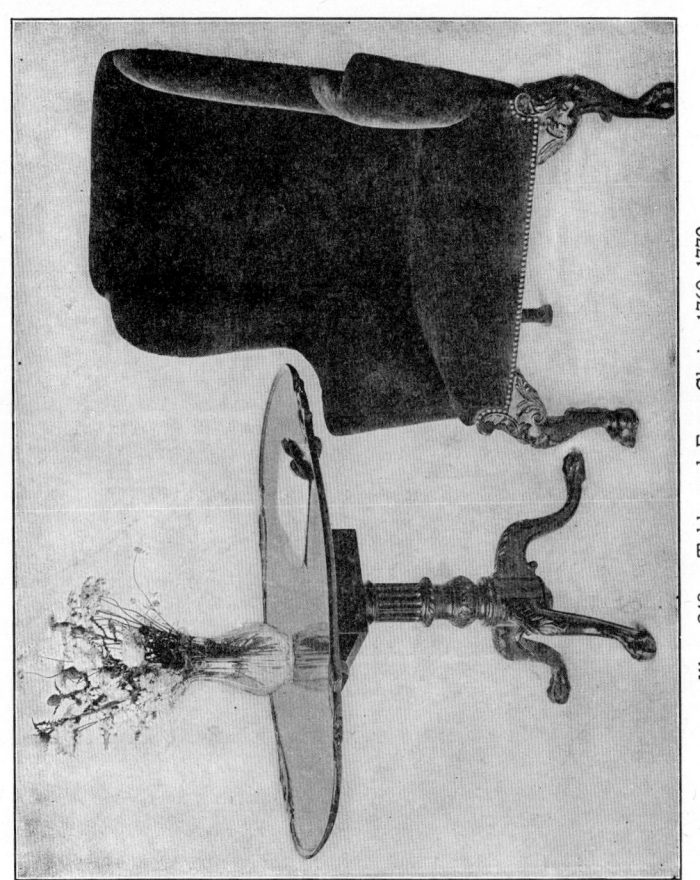

Illus. 248.—Table and Easy Chair, 1760–1770.

illustration, and the legs have a smaller spread.

A tripod table with a remarkable top is shown in Illustration 249. It belongs to J. J. Gilbert, Esq., of Baltimore. The rim is carved and

Illus. 249.— Tripod Table, 1760–1770.

pierced like the mahogany trays of the time.

Illustration 250 shows a Chinese fretwork table owned by Harry Harkness Flagler, Esq. Such tables were designed by Ince and Mayhew and Chippendale, and were called show tables, the

Illus. 250.— Chinese Fret-work Table, 1760–1770.

pierced gallery serving to keep small curios on the table from falling off. Both of these tables were used as tea-tables, the raised rims protecting the tea-cups, more precious then than now.

Stands were made in different sizes, one being intended for a "light-stand" to hold the candlestick, and the smallest for a tea-kettle stand, to accompany the tea-table. Illustration 251 shows three sizes of stands, all smaller than those illustrated previously, and giving somewhat the effect of the three bears of the nursery tale. The middle stand, which has a dish-top, has a base which is exquisitely carved. The tiny kettle-stand is only eighteen and one-half inches high. These three stands also belong to Mr. Flagler.

Illustration 252 shows a small tea-table belonging to Mrs. C. M. Dyer of Worcester. A star is inlaid upon the top, the edge of which has a row of fine inlaying. The base has three fanlike carvings where the legs join the pillar.

The exquisite Chippendale card-table shown in Illustration 253 is not only beautiful in itself, but it frames what is a monument to the industry of the frail young girls who embroidered the top, and to the good housekeeping of its owners for one hundred and twenty odd years. The colors in this embroidery are as brilliant as when new, and never a moth has been suffered to even sniff at its stitches, which are the smallest I have ever seen. The work is done upon very fine linen, and each thread is covered with a stitch of embroidery, done with the slenderest possible strands of crewel, in designs of playing-cards, and of round and fish-shaped counters, in

Illus. 251.—Stands, 1760–1770.

mother-of-pearl shades, copied from the original pearl counters, which still lie in the little oval pools hollowed out for them in the mahogany frame. The fashionable game at that date was quadrille, which was played with these round and fish-shaped counters.

Dr. William Samuel Johnson, the first president of Columbia University, had four daughters, all of whom died in early youth, from comsumption. This embroidery was wrought by them, one taking the task as the

Illus. 252.—Tea-table, about 1770.

Tables 259

other gave it up with her life. The same young girls embroidered the screen in Illustration 328. Small wonder they died young! Far better the

Illus. 253. — Chippendale Card-table, about 1765.

golf and tennis which would occupy the daughters of a modern college president, if he were so fortunate as to have four.

The frame of this table is very beautiful, though

it is cast in the shade by the extraordinary needlework. It is after the finest Chippendale design,

Illus. 254.—Chippendale Card-table, about 1765.

and of the best workmanship. The wood is mahogany, and the table is owned by Mrs. Johnson-Hudson of Stratford, Connecticut.

A Chippendale card-table, owned by the writer, is shown in Illustration 254. The mahogany top is shaped in deep curves, with square corners and is an inch thick to allow the depth of the pools for counters. The lower edge of the table is gadrooned, and the two front legs are finely carved. The two back legs, which are stationary, are carved

Illus. 255. — Chippendale Card-table, about 1765.

on the front side only, while the fifth leg, which swings under the leaf to hold it up, is plain, with simply the claw-and-ball foot.

Illustration 255 shows another Chippendale table with a baize-covered top. It has the pools

Illus. 256.— Pembroke Table, 1760–1770.

for counters, and the corners of the top are shaped in square pieces to stand the candlesticks upon. The knees of the cabriole legs are finely carved, and the edge of the front is finished with gadrooning. It will be noticed that there is a leg at each corner with the table open; in closing, two legs turn in accordion fashion, and a leg is still at each corner of the closed table, with the top half the size. This card-table is owned by Harry Harkness Flagler, Esq., of Millbrook, N. Y.

A style of table popular during the eighteenth century was called a Pembroke table, according to Sheraton, from the name of the lady who first ordered one, and who probably

Illus. 257.— Pembroke Table, 1780–1790.

gave the idea to the workman. Illustration 256 shows a Pembroke table in the Chippendale style, with rather unusual stretchers between the legs. The characteristic which gives a table the name of Pembroke consists in the drop leaves, which are held up, when the table is open, by brackets which turn under the top. The shape of the top varies, being square, round, oval, or with leaves shaped like the table in the illustration. They are always small, and were designed for breakfast tables. This table belongs to the Concord Antiquarian Society.

A beautiful Pembroke table owned by the Metropolitan Museum of Art is shown in Illustration 257. It is made of mahogany entirely veneered with curly sycamore, with a band of tulip wood around the top and leaves, which are exquisitely inlaid in a circular design, and upon the legs are lines of holly with an oval inlay at the top.

Illus. 258.—Lacquer Tea-tables, Eighteenth Century.

Illustration 258 shows a set or "nest" of Chinese tea tables owned by Dwight M. Prouty, Esq. They and the tea caddy case are lacquered in black with Chinese scenes in gold. These sets of tables were brought by ships in the Chinese trade, and were fashionable among the tea drinkers of early times.

From about 1786 the designs of Shearer, Hepplewhite, and Sheraton entirely superseded the fashions of the fifty years preceding, and the slender tapering leg took the place of the cabriole leg. Illustration 259 shows a Hepplewhite card-table, of about 1789, with inlaid legs, one of which swings around to support half of the top, which is circular when open. Upon this table is a mahogany tea tray with handles at each side and a raised rim with a scalloped edge to keep the cups and saucers from slipping off. Oval trays of this style are not uncommon, of mahogany with inlaying, but this tray is shaped to fit the table top. This table and tray are owned by the Concord Antiquarian Society. The china upon the tray is Lowestoft, so called.

Illus. 259.— Hepplewhite Card-table with Tea-tray, 1785–1790.

Illustration 260 shows two typical Hepplewhite card-tables owned by the writer. They are of mahogany, the square, tapering legs being inlaid with a fine line of holly. The front of one table has an oval inlay of lighter mahogany, and small oval

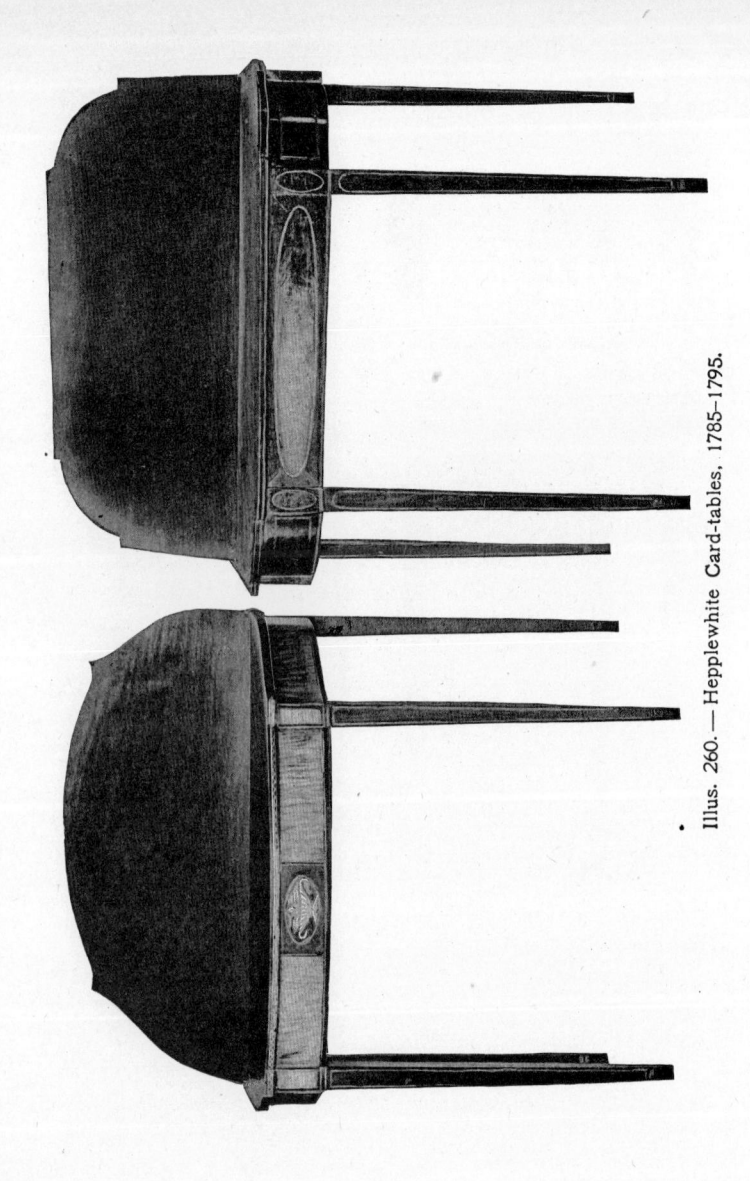

Illus. 260. — Hepplewhite Card-tables, 1785-1795.

pieces above each leg. The edge of this table is inlaid with lines of holly. The front of the other table is veneered with curly maple, and has a panel in the centre inlaid with an urn in colored woods. There is a row of fine inlaying in holly and ebony upon the edge of the top. This table was rescued by the writer from an ignominious existence in a kitchen, where it was covered with oilcloth and used for kitchen purposes. The leaf of each of these tables is supported by one of the legs, which swings around.

Illus. 261 — Sheraton Card-table, 1800.

Illustration 261 shows a Sheraton card-table of the best style, with reeded legs and the front veneered in satinwood. It is owned by Irving Bigelow, Esq., of Worcester.

Illus. 262. — Sheraton Card-table, 1800–1810.

The Sheraton card-table in Illustration 262 is of a few years later date than the one in Illustration 261, with slightly heavier legs, reeded and carved. The curves of the front of the table are extremely graceful. It belongs to Dwight Blaney, Esq.

Illustration 263 shows a Sheraton stand, called a "what-not," made of mahogany, with reeded legs. The posts above the legs are veneered in bird's-eye maple, and the two drawers are veneered in satinwood. The handles are of bone or ivory. The effect of this little stand is most airy and light. It belongs to Mr. Blaney.

Illustration 264 shows a mahogany dining-table and one of eight chairs which came from the John Hancock house in Boston. They are now owned by Clinton M. Dyer, Esq., of

Illus. 263.—Sheraton "What-not," 1800–1810.

Illus. 264.—Sheraton Dining-table and Chair, about 1810.

Worcester. They were made probably about 1810. The legs of the table end in the Adam foot. The table which has both leaves dropped shows the position of the legs when the table is not in use; each leg swings around to support the leaves when in use. The table with slightly rounded corners can be taken apart, and the extra table put between the two sections, the leaves being fastened together by a curious brass spring. Each leaf measures five and one-half feet in length. The drop leaves are twenty-six inches wide, and the table, when all the top is spread out, measures five and a half by twelve feet.

Illus. 265.—Sheraton Work-table, about 1800.

The chair is made after the style of the late Sheraton chairs, with carved drapery upon the back.

Illustration 265 shows a circular work-table of very graceful design. The wood is mahogany, and the little feet are of bronze. There are three drawers, the two upper

Illus. 266.—Sheraton Work-table 1810–1815.

ones opening with a spring and revolving upon a pivot. In these little drawers may still be seen the beads remaining from the time, about 1800, when it was fashionable for young ladies to make bead bags. The table top has an opening in the centre, which originally had a wooden cover, and the space below the top was utilized to hold the work. At

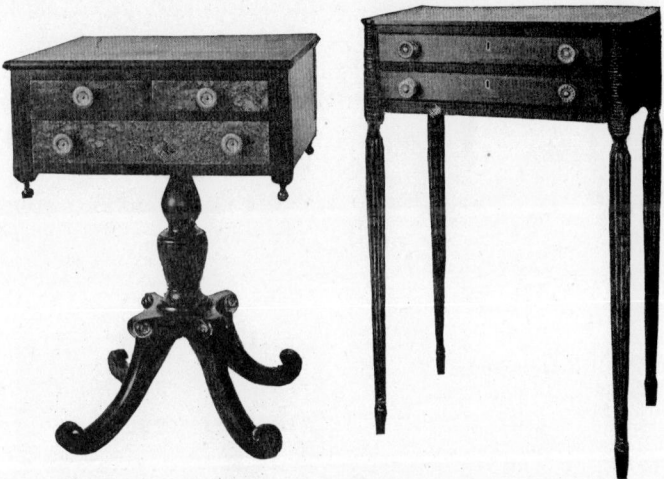

Illus. 267.— Maple and Mahogany Work-tables, 1810–1820.

the back of the top are two short turned posts supporting a little shelf, to hold a candlestick, or to have fastened upon its edge the silver bird which was used by needlewomen of those days to hold one end of the work. This little table is owned by the Misses Hosmer of Concord.

Illustration 266 shows a Sheraton work-table, owned by Mrs. Samuel B. Woodward of Worcester.

The carving at the top of the reeded legs is very fine, and the little table is quite dainty enough to serve the purpose for which it was bought,—a wedding gift to a bride. The brass fixtures for the casters are unusually good, but the handles are not original. The top drawer contains a sort of writing desk, besides compartments for sewing materials, and at the side of the table a slide pulls out, which had originally a silk bag attached, to hang below the table.

Illus. 268.—Work-table, 1810.

Illustration 267 shows two work-tables of mahogany and bird's-eye maple belonging to Francis H. Bigelow, Esq. Similar tables were common about 1810–1820.

Illustrations 268 and 269 show two work-tables owned by Dwight M. Prouty, Esq. The legs and frame of the upper table are of mahogany, the box being made of pine and covered with

Illus. 269.—Work-table, 1810.

pleated silk. The lower table is more elegant in shape, with a slide, the front of which simulates a drawer, and to this is attached the work bag or box, in this table made of wood, silk-covered, but sometimes made of silk alone.

Illus. 270. — Hepplewhite Dining-table, 1790.

Illustration 270 shows a Hepplewhite dining table, the drop leaf serving to increase the length of the table, when raised and held up by the extra leg, which swings under it. Up to 1800 the dining-table had been made in various styles, in all of which the table legs were more or less in the way of those around the table. In the "hundred-legged" table there seemed to be a table leg for each person. Then came the cabriole leg, also in the way, and finally the Hepplewhite dining-table, which was made in sections, with rounded ends, and four legs on each end.

About 1800 the pillar-and-claw table was invented, which made it possible for several persons to sit around a dining-table without a part of the guests encircling the table legs with their own. These

Illus. 271.—Pillar-and-claw Dining-table, 1800.

tables were made in pairs or in threes, one after another being added as more room was required.

Illustration 271 shows a pillar-and-claw extension dining-table, of mahogany, owned by L. J. Shapiro, Esq. of Norfolk, Virginia. The telescope extension (the same method in use at present) was invented by Richard Gillow, of London, about 1800. The end tables pull apart upon a slide, and extra leaves may be inserted between the ends, held in place by wooden pins.

Tables

The pillar and claw design was most popular and was used for centre tables, bases of piano stools, and even for piano legs (see Illustration 292). A pillar-and-claw mahogany centre table with drop leaves is shown in Illustration 272. The feet are lion's claws, and from this date the lion's or bear's

Illus. 272.—Pillar-and-claw Dining-table, about 1800.

claw foot was used for furniture with carved feet, instead of the bird's claw-and-ball which had been so largely used during the previous century.

A splendid dining-table of mahogany is shown in Illustration 273. It is in three sections, each with a base. The legs have a bold spread, and are simply carved in grooves, ending in lion's claws. This fine table is owned by Barton Myers, Esq., of Norfolk, Virginia.

Illustration 274 shows a mahogany dining-table

T

now in the Worcester Art Museum, inherited from the late Stephen Salisbury, Esq. The method of

Illus. 273. — Extension Dining-table, 1810.

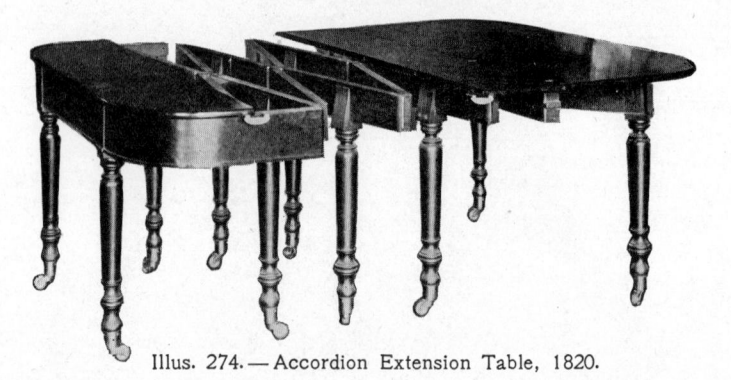

Illus. 274. — Accordion Extension Table, 1820.

extension is after that of an accordion, and necessitates an astonishing number of legs when not extended, ten in all. When the leaves are all in use the table is fourteen feet long, and stands very firmly, the leaves being held together by a brass clamp, seen in the illustration.

A very fine card table owned by Mrs. Clarence R. Hyde of Brooklyn is shown in Illustration 275.

Illus. 275.—Card-table, 1805–1810.

It is made of mahogany, with a band of satinwood around the box top. When open, the whole top revolves upon a pivot. The legs are slender and well carved, with lion's feet.

One of the finest of American cabinet-makers was Duncan Phyfe, whose address in the New York directory of 1802 is 35 Partition Street (now Fulton Street). He pursued his business until 1850, employing one hundred workmen. Much of his furniture still exists, notably chairs with lyre backs.

Illus. 276.—Phyfe Card-table, 1810–1820.

A Phyfe card-table owned by Miss H. P. F. Burnside of Worcester is shown in Illustration 276. The strings of the lyre are of brass, like the lion's feet in which the legs end.

Illus. 277.—Phyfe Card-table, 1810–1820.

A specialty of Phyfe's was a card-table, one of which is shown in Illustration 277. In the illustration the table apparently lacks a fourth leg, as it stands against the wall. But when the top is open, by an interesting mechanism the three legs spread and a brace comes out to support the other half of the top, so that it forms a perfectly proportioned table. Mr. Hagen of New York has an old bill, dated 1816, for

Illus. 278.—Phyfe Sofa Table, 1810.

two of these tables at sixty dollars apiece. The table in the illustration is owned by Dwight Blaney, Esq.

A Phyfe sofa table is shown in Illustration 278, from the Metropolitan Museum of Art. It is very narrow, and was designed, as the name implies, to stand beside a sofa, to hold books, papers, or other articles. The legs end in small lion's feet and are carved, like the posts, with the typical Phyfe leaf. This leaf, so much used by Phyfe, is seen, like the lyre, upon Adam pieces, and apparently the Scotchman,

Illus. 279. — Pier-table, 1820–1830.

Duncan Phyfe, took the Scotchman, Robert Adam, for his model.

The fashion of heavy furniture elaborately carved was more popular in the South than in the North, and the most ornate pieces are found in the South, of later date than the rich carving done in Philadelphia, upon pie-crust tables and high-boys. Heavy posts carved with the acanthus and pineapple and other Empire features found favor. It is probable that during the first quarter of the nineteenth century the wealthy Southern planters refurnished their homes in the prevailing Empire style. The pier-table in Illustration 279 is one of a pair found in Virginia, which were made about 1830. The chief motif in the design seems to be dolphins' heads, which form the feet, and the base of the front supports to the top.

Illustration 280 shows a small work-table of curious shape, with the octagon-shaped interior divided into little boxes for sewing-materials. The middle compartment extends down into the eight-sided pillar. The work-boxes are covered by the

Illus. 280. — Work-table, 1810–1820.

top of the table, which lifts upon hinges. This table belongs to Mrs. E. A. Morse of Worcester.

CHAPTER IX

MUSICAL INSTRUMENTS

SPINETS, virginals, and harpsichords were brought to the American colonies in English ships as early as 1645, when "An old pair of virginalls" appears in an inventory; and another, in 1654. In 1667 a pair of virginals is valued at two pounds. In his diary of 1699 Judge Samuel Sewall alludes to his wife's virginals. In 1712 the Boston *News Letter* contained an advertisement that "the spinet would be taught," and in 1716 the public were requested to "Note, that any Persons may have all Instruments of Music mended, or Virginals or Spinets strung & tun'd, at a Reasonable Rate, and likewise may be taught to play on any of the Instruments above mentioned." From the wording of this advertisement it is evident that these instruments were no novelty.

I have not been able to learn of an existing virginal which was in use in this country, but occasionally a spinet is found. The expression a "pair" or "set" of virginals was used in the same manner as a "pair" or "set" of steps or stairs, and in England an oblong spinet was called a virginal, in distinction from the spinet of triangular shape, which superseded the rectangular, oblong form in which the earliest spinets were made. Both virginal and spinet had but one string to a key, and the tone of both was produced by a sort of plectrum which picked the string. This plectrum usually consisted of a crow quill, set in an upright piece of wood, called a "jack," which was fastened to the back of the key. The depressing of the key by the finger caused the quill to rise, and as it passed the string, the vibration produced the musical tone, which is described by Dr. Burney as "A scratch with a sound at the end of it." The name of the spinet is by some supposed to be derived from these quills, — from *spina*, a thorn. According to other authorities the name came from a maker of the instrument, named Spinetti. The virginal was so called because young maids were wont to play upon it, among them that perennial young girl, Queen Elizabeth. The most famous makers of spinets in England were Charles Haward or Haywood, Thomas and John Hitchcock, and Stephen Keene. In Pepys's diary are the following entries: —

"April 4, 1668. Called upon one Haward that makes virginalls, and there did like of a little espinette and will have him finish it for me; for I had a mind to a small harpsichon, but this takes up less room."

"July 15, 1668. At noon is brought home the espinette I bought the other day of Haward; cost me 5£."

Illustration 281 shows a spinet in the Deerfield Museum, which formerly belonged to Miss Sukey Barker of Hingham, who must have been a much envied damsel. It is marked Stephanus Keene, which places the date of its make about 1690. The

Illus. 281.—Stephen Keene Spinet, about 1690.

body of the spinet stands twenty-four inches from the floor. Its extreme length is fifty-six inches, and the keyboard of four and one-half octaves measures twenty-nine inches. There are but six keys left, but they are enough to show that the naturals were black and the sharps white. There is a row of fine inlaying above the keyboard, and the maker's name is surrounded with painted flowers.

The spinet, as may be seen, was a tiny instrument,

in shape similar to our modern grand piano. The body of the spinet was entirely separate from the stand, which was made with stretchers between the legs, of which there were three and sometimes four, so placed that one leg came under the narrow back end of the spinet, one under the right end of the front, and one or sometimes two at the left of the front. The instrument rested upon this table or trestle.

The name upon the majority of spinets found in this country is that of Thomas Hitchcock. His spinets are numbered and occasionally dated. There is a Thomas Hitchcock spinet owned by the Concord Antiquarian Society, numbered 1455, and one owned in Worcester, numbered 1519.

Illustration 282 shows a spinet which was owned by Elizabeth Hunt Wendell of Boston. It was probably an old instrument when she took it with her from Boston to Portland in 1766 upon her marriage to the Rev. Thomas Smith, known as Parson Smith of Portland. It is now owned by her great-great-granddaughter in Gorham, Maine. The board above the keys has two lines of inlaying around it, and is marked "Thomas Hitchcock Londoni fecit, 1390." The front of the white keys is cut with curved lines, and the black keys have a line of white ivory down the centre. The parrot-back chair in the illustration is described upon page 168. Authorities seem to vary upon dates when the Hitchcocks made spinets. Mr. A. J. Hipkins of London, the well-known authority upon pianos, harpsichords, and spinets, writes me that he dates the Thomas Hitchcock spinets from 1664 to 1703, and those of John Hitchcock, the son of Thomas, from 1676 to about 1715. Mr. Hipkins says that the highest number he has met with upon Thomas Hitchcock's spinets is 1547, so it is safe to date this spinet in Illustration 282, which numbers 1390, to about 1690.

Illus. 282.—Thomas Hitchcock Spinet, about 1690.

By the latter half of the eighteenth century proficiency upon various musical instruments was not uncommon. John Adams in 1771 speaks of a young man of twenty-six, as "a great proficient in music, plays upon the flute, fife, harpsichord, spinet, etc.; a very fine Connecticut young gentleman." In 1768 in the *Boston Chronicle* appears the advertise-

Illus. 283. — Broadwood Harpsichord, 1789.

ment of John Harris, recently from England, "that he makes and sells all sorts of Harpsichords and Spinets," and in 1769 the *Boston Gazette* says, "A few days since was shipped for Newport a very curious Spinet, being the first one ever made in America, the performance of the ingenious Mr. John Harris." In 1770 the same paper praises an excellent "spinet" made by a Bostonian, "which for goodness of workmanship and harmony of sound is esteemed by the best judges to be superior to any that has been imported from Europe." This would seem to indicate that a tone of superiority in musical matters was assumed by Boston at an early date. The statement with regard to the first spinet made in America is incorrect, for over twenty years earlier, in 1742, Hasselinck had made spinets in Philadelphia.

In the Essex Institute of Salem is a spinet made by Samuel Blythe of Salem, the bill for which, dated 1786, amounts to eighteen pounds.

The harpsichord, so named from its shape, was the most important of the group of contemporary instruments, the virginal, spinet, and harpsichord, the tone of which was produced with the quill and jack. The harpsichord had two strings to each key, and the instrument occupied the relative position that the grand piano does to-day, being much larger and having more tone than the spinet. Like the spinet, its manufacture ceased with the eighteenth century. Illustration 283 shows a harpsichord formerly owned by Charles Carroll, who was so eager to identify himself as a patriot, that he signed his name to the Declaration of Independence as Charles Carroll of Carrollton. This harpsichord was discovered twenty-five years ago in the loft of an old college building in Annapolis, where it had lain for fifty years. The Carroll coat of arms, painted upon porcelain and framed in gold, is fastened above the keyboard. The inscription upon this instrument is "Burkat Shudi et Johannes Broadwood, patent No. 955 Londini, Fecerant 1789, Great Poulteney Street, Golden Square."

There are two banks of keys, with a range of five octaves, and three stops, which were intended to change the tone, two of them being marked harp and lute. The case is quite plain, of mahogany, with a few lines of inlaying above the keyboard and a line around the body and top. It is owned by William Knabe & Co. of Baltimore, and is one of fourteen Broadwood harpsichords known to exist.

That the harpsichord was not an uncommon instrument in this country during the latter half of the eighteenth century is shown by the number of advertisements of the harpsichord and its teachers.

Illustration 284 shows a clavichord or clavier, made about 1745. It is owned by Mr. John Orth of Boston. The clavichord, like its successor, the square piano, was of oblong shape. The musical tone was produced in a different manner from that of either the spinet or piano. Each key had at the back an upright "tangent" or wedge-shaped piece of brass, which, as the front of the key was depressed, rose and set the string of twisted brass wire in vibration, by pressing upon it, instead of picking it like the quill of the spinet and harpsichord. This pressure divided the string into two different lengths, the shorter length being prevented from vibrating by a band of cloth interlaced with the strings. The same interlaced cloth stopped the vibration of the longer division of the string, as soon as the pressure was taken from the key, thus allowing the tangent to fall. In the earlier clavichords

Illus. 284. — Clavichord. 1745.

one string had to serve to produce the tone for two or three different keys. These instruments were called "gebunden," or fretted. Later instruments are "bund frei" or free, having a string for each key. The clavichord player could feel the elasticity of the wire string, and could produce a sort of vibration of tone by employing the same method as that used in playing the violin, a pressure and vibration of the fleshy end of the finger while the note was held.

The tone of the clavichord was very delicate, and it afforded far more power of expression than the spinet or harpsichord, which, however, were more brilliant, and entirely superseded the weaker clavichord in England. In Germany the clavichord has always been a favorite instrument, even into the nineteenth century. It is probable that but few clavichords came to this country.

The *piano e forte* — soft and loud — was invented about 1720. The strings of the piano are struck by hammers instead of being picked by quills, and the force of the hammer strokes made a stronger frame necessary than that of the spinet or harpsichord, in order to hold the heavier strings.

Brissot de Warville wrote in 1788 that in Boston "one sometimes hears the forte piano, though the art is in its infancy." He then soulfully bursts forth, "God grant that the Bostonian women may never, like those of France, acquire the malady of perfection in this art. It is never attained but at the expense of the domestic virtues." According to this the domestic virtues must be a scarce quality in Boston at the present time.

In 1792 Messrs. Dodd & Claus, musical instrument manufacturers, 66 Queen Street, New York, announced that "the forte piano is become so fashionable in Europe that few polite families are without it." As this country kept pace with Europe in the fashions, we can assume that the forte piano formed at the close of the eighteenth century a part of the furniture of the polite families of the United States.

The date of a piano can be approximately determined by its legs. The earliest pianos had four slender legs similar to the legs of the spinet or harpsichord. The next instruments had six legs, increased in size and fluted or carved. Then the number was reduced to four, and the legs were still

Illus. 285. — Clementi Piano, 1805.

larger, and more elaborately carved, until by 1840 the ugly legs found commonly upon the square piano were the only styles employed.

Illustration 285 is a fine example of an early pianoforte. Like the spinet and clavichord, the body of the instrument is separate from the lower frame, which is fastened together at the corners with large screws like a bedstead. This may have been for convenience in transportation, and it is possible that while the top containing the works was imported, the supporting frame may have been made in this country. There are four slender inlaid legs, and one pedal, and under the body of the piano runs a most convenient shelf for music. The case is of mahogany, with rows of fine inlaying in colors, having two rows of different width around the top of the lid. The board above the keys is of satinwood, and it has, beside the delicate frets at each side, charmingly painted garlands of sweet peas, a flower very popular in England at that time, about 1805. The name plate has the inscription "Muzio Clementi & Co., Cheapside, London," and the number of the piano is 3653. It measures sixty-seven inches in length, and has a compass of five and one-half octaves. There is a line of inlaying around the inside of this piano, which is finished carefully in every detail. The music-rack is of simple form like the rack in Illustration 286. The music may also rest, as in the illustration, upon the edge of the lid, when put back. This piano is owned by the writer, who bought it in Falmouth, Massachusetts. It was said to be the first piano brought into Falmouth, or upon the "Cape," and in looking at this dainty instrument, which had never left the room in which it found its home, a hundred years ago, one can imagine the wonder and envy of the little seaport village when a whaling captain, after a successful voyage, gave the piano to his daughter. Nothing could sound more quaint than a Glück or Mozart minuet played upon its tinkling keys.

The founder of the Astor family about 1790 to 1800 made one branch of his business the importing of pianos, which were labelled with his name and which are quite commonly met with. Illustration 286 shows an Astor piano owned by Mrs. Sanford Tappan of Newburyport. The style of this piano is similar to that of the "Clementi" in

Illus. 286. — Astor Piano, 1790–1800.

Illustration 285, but it lacks the delicate ornamentation of the Clementi piano. In the *Columbian Centinel* of 1806 is an advertisement with a woodcut of an instrument very like this.

There is an Astor piano in Salem, described as having four legs in the front, indicating that it was made as late as 1815. It had two pedals, one being used to prolong the tones. The other pedal served

Illus. 287.— Clementi Piano, about 1820.

to produce a novel and taking effect, by lifting a section of the top of the piano lid, which was then allowed to fall suddenly, the slamming serving to imitate the firing of cannon. The young lady who owned the piano created a great sensation by playing battle pieces with this startling accompaniment.

Illustration 287 shows the change in the legs, this piano having six legs, which are considerably larger. The piano was made by Clementi, and is numbered 10522. It is of light mahogany, and has a row of dark mahogany veneer around its frame. The feet and tops of the six legs are of brass, like the handles to the three drawers, and a brass moulding goes around the frame. The piano stool, also of mahogany, is of a somewhat later date. This piano and stool are owned by W. S. G. Kennedy, Esq., of Worcester. This style of piano was in use from 1820 to 1830.

Illus. 288.— Combination Piano, Desk, and Toilet-table, about 1800.

Illustration 288 shows one of the curious combinations which the cabinet-makers of about 1800 seemed to be so fond of designing. Their books have complicated drawings of tables and desks with mechanical devices for transforming the simple-looking piece of furniture into one full of compartments, drawers, and boxes, with contrivances which allow surprising combinations to spring out. Sheraton, who was a shrewd observer, said, "A fancifulness seems most peculiar to the taste of females"; and this piece of furniture was made, apparently, to appeal to that "fancifulness." Between the works

Illus. 289.—Piano, about 1830.

of the piano and the cover is a tray divided into compartments to hold toilet and writing utensils, ink-bottle, sand-sifter, stationery, pins, and sewing-implements, and over the keyboard rests a long tray for similar articles. These trays can be removed when the piano is to be used. There is a front panel which lets down, forming a writing-table,

Illus. 290.— Peter Erben Piano, 1826-1827.

and a mirror is set in the face of the rest that supports the lid when raised. Thus the lady for whom all this was designed, after using it as a dressing-table, could play the piano and look at her own pretty face in the mirror while she played and sang. This combination of piano, dressing-table, and writing-desk is owned by the Rev. James H. Darlington, D.D., of Brooklyn, New York.

In 1829 the manufacture of pianofortes had increased so that during that year twenty-five hundred pianos were made in the United States, chiefly in New York, Philadelphia, and Boston.

The piano in Illustration 289 belongs to Mrs. Ada Grisier of Auburn, Indiana, and is an unusually fine specimen of the six-legged piano fashionable about 1830. The case is of mahogany and is inlaid with lines of brass, while around the body run two rows, of different width, of brass moulding. The legs are large, and elaborately carved, and are set in brass standards. On each corner of the frame is a design in gilt. There is one wooden pedal, and the range of the piano is five and one-half octaves. The name of the maker has been obliterated.

The piano in Illustration 290 is owned by Mrs. Louis M. Priest of Salem, New York. The body is of rosewood inlaid with brass, the lid being of mahogany, like the elaborately carved trestle-shaped supports. It has two drawers for holding music, and one pedal, the standard for which is a carved lyre with a mirror behind its strings. The keyboard has a range of six octaves. The name upon the front is Peter Erben, 103 Pump St., New York.

Peter Erben was a music-teacher whose address from 1826 to 1827 was 103 Pump Street, which determines the date of this piano. The writer knows of four pianos with the carved mahogany trestle-supports, all with the name of Peter Erben as maker, though it is probable that, like modern pianos, the works were bought, and whoever wished might have his name upon the name-plate, since Peter Erben is in the New York directories for thirty years as "Musick teacher" or "Professor of musick" only.

The piano-stool in Illustration 291 was made to use with the piano in Illustration 290. The wide spread to the three feet gives the effect of a table base, but there is no doubt that this was made originally to use for a piano-stool. The little weather-beaten house, in which the piano and stool had always stood, possesses a ghost story of a young girl who was starved to death by her miser brother, and who was said to haunt the house. This piano and stool give the impression of the reverse of a miser, and the poor ghost must have been before their day. The stool is now owned by the writer, but is neither practical nor comfortable, the feet being much in the way.

Illus. 291.—Piano-stool, 1820–1830.

Illustration 292 shows a piano of most elaborate design, made about 1826. There is no maker's name upon the piano. The frame is of mahogany and has a brass moulding around the body, and brass rosette handles to the drawers. Around each

Illus. 292.—Piano, 1826.

square carved panel upon the front legs is a brass beading, and the lions' claws on the front legs and the sockets upon the back legs are of brass. The front legs are elaborately carved like table bases, and the three pedals have a support that is a cross between a lyre and a wreath. The keyboard has six octaves, and the music-rack is very simple.

Illustration 293 shows two piano-stools made between 1825 and 1830. The stool with four fluted legs was sold with a piano made by Wood, Small, & Co., of London, which has six legs fluted in the same manner. The other stool has a base like the claw-and-pillar table, and the sides of the seat are carved dolphins, whose tails turn up and support a

Illus. 293. — Piano-stools, 1825–1830.

carved rail to form a low back for the seat. This stool belongs to the writer.

The "table piano" in Illustration 294 is marked as being made by John Charters, Xenia, Ohio, which alone would attract attention, aside from the curious construction of the base, which places the date of the piano about 1835. The pedals are quite concealed as one stands by this piano, and the whole design is clumsy and poor. The music-rack seems to have remained unchanged for many years, and from the earliest piano shown, made in 1800, until the large square piano of 1840, the music-rack is the same, simply constructed of four pieces of wood which are put together with pivots, so that by pushing

Illus. 294.—Table Piano, about 1835.

one end of the top piece they all slide and fold down together, in order that the piano may be closed.

Illustration 295 shows a Chickering piano made in 1833, of a design entirely different from the other pianos shown, and of great elegance and richness. The mahogany case is inlaid with the heavy bands of plain brass, and the legs are pillars with Ionic capitals.

The music-rack is of the same simple form as the one upon the preceding piano, and the one pedal is fastened into a lyre-shaped support.

Illus. 295.—Chickering Piano, 1833.

Illustration 296 shows a music-stand made about 1835, owned by Mrs. John D. Wing, of Millbrook, New York. The rest for the music is of the favorite lyre shape, which seems especially adapted to this purpose. The stand is of mahogany and is very pretty and graceful.

Musical Instruments 303

Illustration 297 shows a music-stand owned by Dwight Blaney, Esq., of Boston. It is of mahogany, and its date is about 1835. The upper part with the music-rest can be lowered or raised, and is held in place by pins thrust through the small holes in

Illus. 296. — Music-stand, about 1835.

Illus. 297. — Music-stand, about 1835.

the supports. The stand is somewhat heavy in effect, but very firm and secure.

Illustration 298 shows a dulcimer which is in the Deerfield Museum. It has an extremely plain case, and must have been, when new, an inexpensive instrument. The dulcimer of early times was a small, triangular-shaped instrument, to be laid upon a table. Above the sounding-board were stretched wire strings, which were struck with small hammers held in the

Illus. 298.—Dulcimer, 1820-1830.

hand, and doubtless the piano was first suggested by the dulcimer and its hammers. The heads of the hammers were covered with hard and soft leather to give a loud or soft tone. The instrument in the illustration was probably made from 1820 to 1830, during which time the dulcimer was quite popular, especially in the country, where the piano was too costly a luxury. Music-books were published for the dulcimer, and it retained some popularity in country villages until ousted by the melodeon.

Illustration 299 shows a set of musical glasses called a harmonica. The fine ladies in "The Vicar of Wakefield" would talk of nothing but "pictures, taste, Shakespeare, and the musical glasses." This was in 1761, and the musical glasses

Illus. 299.— Harmonica, or Musical Glasses, about 1820.

were fashionable before that, for Glück in 1746 played "a concerto on twenty-six drinking glasses, tuned with spring water." Franklin invented an instrument for the musical glasses, which he called the Armonica, for which famous composers wrote music,

x

and in which the glasses were arranged upon a rod which turned with a crank, while below was a trough of water which moistened the glasses as they dipped into it. There is a Franklin Armonica in the Metropolitan Museum of Art in the Brown collection. In Watson's "Annals" is a description of a visit to Franklin in Paris. It says: "He conducted me across the room to an instrument of his own invention which he called the 'Armonica.' The music was produced by a peculiar combination of hemispherical glasses. He played upon it and performed some Scotch pastorales with great effect. The exhibition was truly striking."

Illus. 300.— Music-stand. 1805.

The box in Illustration 299 holds twenty-four glasses, which, when used, are filled with water, and are tuned by the amount in each glass. The finger is dipped in the water and rubbed on the edge of the glass, producing a sound of penetrating tone. The stand and box in this illustration are of mahogany, and make an ornamental piece of furniture.

A stand for music is shown in Illustration 300, owned by J. J. Gilbert, Esq., of Baltimore. It is elegant in design and possesses also the very desirable merit in a rest for music, of standing firmly upon its four lion's claw feet, with the heavy

Illus. 301. — Music-stand, 1800–1820.

turned and reeded post to support the top and the lyre-shaped music rack.

The mahogany case for music books in Illustration 301 is owned by Dwight M. Prouty, Esq. It has a drawer for sheet music and a shelf below, beside the five compartments for books, with the lyre-shaped divisions of solid wood, and the ends open, with lyre strings of wood.

Illustration 302 shows a harp-shaped piano, made by André Stein, d'Augsburg. It is owned by B. J. Lang, Esq., of Boston, and was made about 1800. Pianos of this style are occasionally found in this country. The shape of the top shows how the strings run, the effect being similar to a grand piano stood upon its end. The silk draperies are the original ones, and are faded from red to a soft dead leaf color, which is most artistic and harmonious. The six pedals are supposed to produce different effects to correspond with the following names: fagotti, piano, forte, pianissimo, triangle, cinelle.

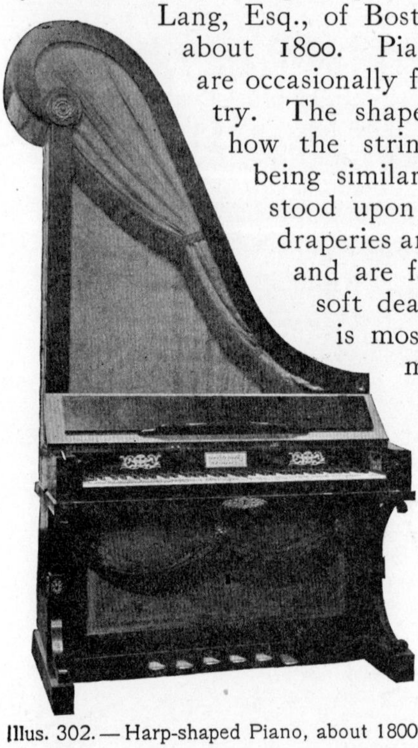

The upright piano, known then as a cottage piano, was invented in 1800. Illustration 303 shows a small upright piano said to have belonged to Lady Morgan, the "wild Irish girl." The case is an exquisite

Illus. 302.— Harp-shaped Piano, about 1800.

example of the work of an English cabinet-maker, from 1800 to 1810, and may have been that of Sheraton himself. The lower panels are of satinwood, with the frame and the oval piece in the centre of

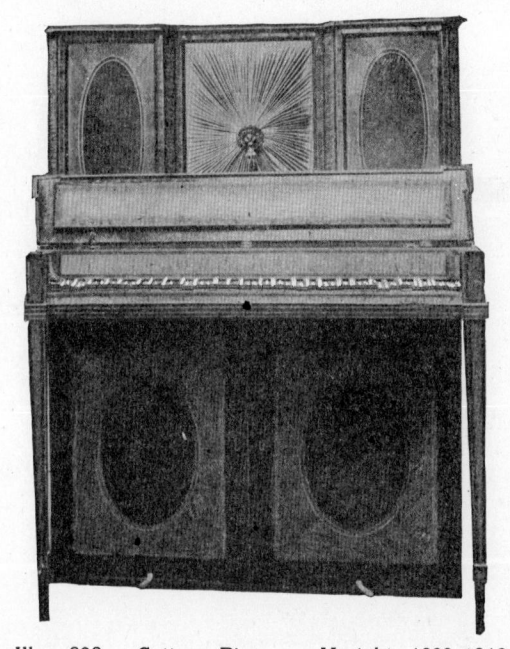

Illus. 303.—Cottage Piano, or Upright, 1800–1810.

mahogany, outlined with ebony and white holly. The upper middle panel is filled with a sunburst made of pleated silk. The side-panels are of satinwood, framed in bird's-eye maple, outlined with mahogany, and the ovals in the centres are of mahogany, with fine lines of ebony and white holly.

Altogether, it is as dainty an instrument as any lady could wish for her boudoir.

Illustration 304 shows a Chickering upright piano made in 1830. The frame is of mahogany, and the front of the upper part is filled with a sunburst made of pleated silk, from which this style of piano was sometimes called a sunburst piano.

A very beautiful and ornamental piano is shown in Illustration 305, owned by James H. Darlington, D.D., of Brooklyn, New York. The body of the piano is made of rosewood. The strings are arranged like those in a grand piano, but the sounding-board extends only the distance of the piano body; above that the strings are exposed like those of a harp. The wooden frame upon which the wires are strung is supported by a post of wood elaborately carved and gilded. The keyboard has a range of seven octaves. Upon the inside of the cover is the inscription "New York Piano Company — Kohn patent."

Illus. 304.—Chickering Upright Piano. 1830.

Illus. 305.—Piano, about 1840.

The story is that a piano-maker in New York vowed he would make the most beautiful piano in the world. One like this was the result, and it was bought by A. T. Stewart, at that time, about 1840, the merchant prince of New York. Six others were made like the original piano, and they are scattered

Illus. 306.— Hawkey Square Piano, about 1845.

over the country, one being in the Brown collection of musical instruments in the Metropolitan Museum of Art.

Illustration 306 shows the form in which the square piano was finally made, and which, with few variations, continued fashionable until the introduction of the present style of upright pianos, since when there have been practically no square pianos manufactured. This piano was made by Henry Hawkey of New York, about 1845, and it is noteworthy because the keys are made of mother-of-pearl, and the scrolls above the keyboard are inlaid in mother-of-pearl. The case is covered with rosewood veneering, and the legs are large and clumsy. The music-rack and pedal support are similar in style to those now in use.

Proficiency upon the piano and spinet would appear to have comprised the chief accomplishments in instrumental music of the young ladies of the eighteenth and early nineteenth centuries, as far as we can judge by mention of such accomplishments. But it seems reasonable to suppose that where a few English ladies employed their fair hands upon the harp, there were not lacking a similar number of Americans who also appreciated the opportunity which that classic instrument affords of dis-

Illus. 307.— Harp, 1780–1790.

playing the grace and beauty of a rounded arm and wrist. Even in our own day, the list of those who play the harp is restricted, and it must have been the same in early days, hence the lack of allusions to the harp. When Lady Morgan, the "wild Irish girl," was creating such a sensation in London with her harp-playing, it is certain that she had imitators in this country.

Christopher Columbus Baldwin, in his diary of 1832, speaks of Madam Papanti, who at that time lived in Worcester with her husband, the famous dancing-teacher. She gave music lessons, possibly upon the harp, for Mr. Baldwin tells of her playing that instrument upon Sundays at Dr. Bancroft's church, while her husband played the French horn, "which, with two flutes, a base viol, and violin, make very good musick."

Illustration 307 shows a very beautiful harp made previous to 1800, belonging to Mrs. Reed Lawton of Worcester. In construction it is not very different from the modern harp, although considerably smaller. It is exquisitely carved, and instead of being gilded is painted in colors, and finished with a varnish like the vernis martin, the general effect being a golden brown. The harp which Marie Antoinette played upon is still preserved, and is very like this one.

CHAPTER X

FIRES AND LIGHTS

WHEN wood was plentiful and easily gathered, the fireplace was built of generous proportions. At the back, lying in the ashes, was the back-log, sometimes so huge that a chain was attached to it, and it was dragged in by a horse. The forestick rested upon the andirons, and small sticks filled the space between backlog and forestick. In the wall beside the fireplace was built the brick oven, in which the baking was done. Upon baking day a wood fire was made inside this oven, and when the oven was thoroughly heated, the coals were removed, and the bread placed upon the oven bottom to bake leisurely. The tin kitchen was set before the fire, and pies and bread

Illus. 308.— Kitchen Fireplace in Lee Mansion, 1760.

Fires and Lights

upon its shelves were cooked by the heat reflected and radiated from the tin hood.

Illustration 308 shows a great kitchen fireplace in the Lee mansion in Marblehead, Massachusetts, with the tin kitchens in front of the fire, and the kettles and pots hanging over it, and the various kitchen utensils around it.

Fire-dogs or andirons are mentioned in the earliest inventories.

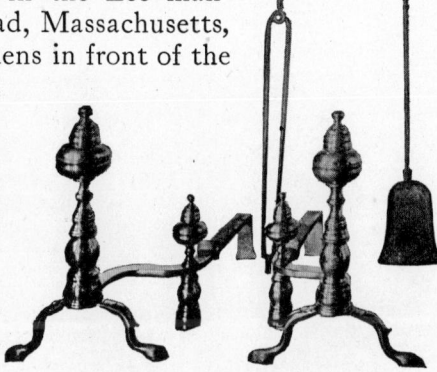

Illus. 309. — Andirons, Eighteenth Century.

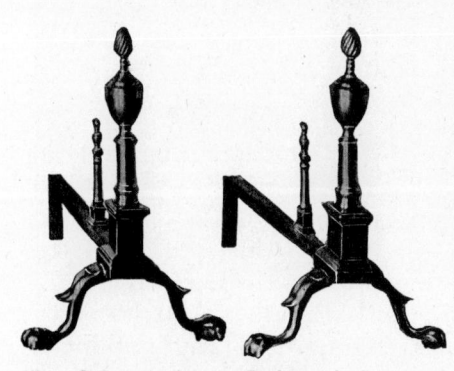

Illus. 310. — Andirons, Eighteenth Century.

The name "fire-dogs" came from the heads of animals with which the irons were ornamented. "Andirons" is a word corrupted from "hand irons," although some inventories speak of end-irons. Kitchen andirons were of iron similar to the ones in Illustration 316, but for the other fireplaces they were made of steel, copper, or brass, and in England even of silver.

Illustration 309 shows a pair of andirons, with shovel and tongs, owned by Francis H. Bigelow, Esq. The andirons are "rights and lefts," and have the brass knobs to prevent the forestick from falling forward. Illustration 310 shows another pair belonging to Mr. Bigelow, with claw-and-ball feet and the twisted flame top. These are given as good examples of the best styles of andirons in use in well-to-do households in America during the seventeenth century.

Illustration 311 shows a pair of "Hessians" made of iron. Andirons of this style were very popular immediately after the Revolutionary War, the figures of the hated allies of the British thus receiving the treatment with flame and ashes that Americans considered the originals to merit, to say nothing of worse indignities cast upon them by the circle of tobacco-smoking patriots.

Illus. 311. — "Hessian" Andirons, 1776.

Andirons were made of different heights, and sometimes two or more sets were used in one fireplace, to hold larger and smaller sticks. Creepers are mentioned in early inventories. They were low irons placed between the andirons, to hold short sticks.

As wood grew less plentiful, and as the forests near by were cleared away, it was not so easy to obtain the huge backlog and the great pile of sticks

Illus. 312. — Fireplace, 1770–1775.

to fill the generous fireplace, and by the middle of the eighteenth century its size had diminished. Many of the larger ones were partially filled in. The fireplace in the Ipswich Whipple house, when the house was bought by the society which now owns it, had been bricked in twice — once to make the space less, and the second time to fill it in entirely and put a fire-frame in its place. Chimneys which did not smoke were the exception until Count Rumford made his researches in heat and light, and by his discoveries and improvements in construction enabled our ancestors to have chimneys which did not smoke, and which did not carry up the greater portion of the heat from the fire.

Illustration 312 shows a fireplace in Salem of about 1775, with ball-topped andirons. The sets for the fireplace comprised the andirons, shovel, and tongs. The poker never accompanied the older sets, which were made before the use of coal as fuel had become common in this country, but a pair of bellows generally formed a part of the equipment of the fireplace.

Illustration 313 shows a fireplace in the residence of Harry Harkness Flagler, Esq., with a brass fender and a pair of "steeple-topped" andirons. Fenders were used in England earlier than in this country, to keep the sticks or coals of fire from rolling or flying out upon the floor in front of the fireplace, and to prevent children from getting into the fire. Their size was adapted to the reduced dimensions of the fireplaces, and they were used more with coal fires than with wood.

Illus. 313.—Steeple-topped Andirons and Fender, 1775–1790.

The design of andirons most commonly found is shown in Illustration 314. The little andirons

Fires and Lights

between the larger ones are "creepers," and are used to hold short pieces of wood. They are of the same design as the larger pair, although they were bought several years, and hundreds of miles, apart.

The fender in Illustration 314 is of wire, painted black, with the top rail and balls of brass. The andirons and fender belong to the writer.

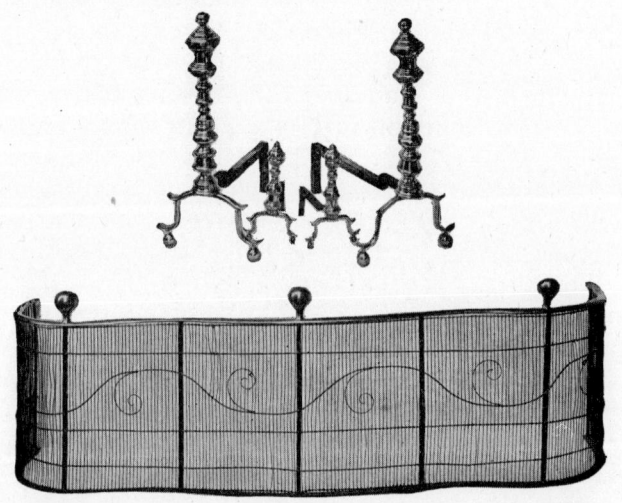

Illus. 314.—Andirons, Creepers, and Fender, 1700–1800.

Judge Sewall ordered in 1719 for his daughter Judith, about to be married, "a bell-metal skillet, a warming pan, four pairs of brass headed iron dogs, a brass hearth for a chamber with dogs, tongs, shovel and fender of the newest fashion (the fire to lie on the iron), a brass mortar, four pairs of brass candlesticks, four brass snuffers with stands, six small brass chafing dishes, two brass basting ladles, a pair of bellows with brass nose, a small hair broom, a dozen pewter porringers, a dozen small glass salt cellars, and a dozen good ivory hafted knives and forks."

The appurtenances for the fireplace in this list comprise the fender, shovel, tongs, broom, bellows, and the "dogs."

Illus. 315. — Brass Andirons, 1700–1800.

Illustration 315 shows a pair of brass andirons and Illustration 316, a set of "brass-headed iron dogs," such as Sewall ordered. Both pairs belong to Dwight M. Prouty, Esq. of Boston.

By 1650 the use of coal had become common in England from the scarcity and expense of wood as a fuel, and from that time fireplaces in that country were con-

Illus. 316. — Brass-headed Iron Dogs, 1700–1800.

structed for coal fires. The books of designs of the eighteenth century show many and elaborate drawings of grates for coal. In this country, however, the lack of wood has never been felt, and the fireplace to burn wood has held its own, with its andirons, not so generous as in the early days, but still of goodly size.

Firebacks were made of iron for fireplaces, sometimes cast with the coat-of-arms of the owner or the date of construction. In Pennsylvania were famous iron workers, and there is a collection of iron firebacks in the museum at Memorial Hall, Philadelphia. At Mount Vernon is a fireback with the Fairfax coat-of-arms which Washington took from Belvoir, the estate of Lord Fairfax, adjoining Mount Vernon.

Illustration 317 shows a chimney piece in the west parlor at Mount Vernon. Washington's coat-of-arms is carved at the top, and his crest and initials are cast in the fireback. In the panel over the mantel is a painting which was sent to Lawrence Washington in 1743, by Admiral Vernon, in acknowledgment of the courtesy shown by Lawrence Washington to his old commander, in naming the estate Mount Vernon. The painting represents Admiral Vernon's fleet at Cartagena.

About 1750 the hob-grate was invented. Illustration 318 shows a mantel and fireplace with a hob-grate in the house of Charles R. Waters, Esq., of Salem. The fireplace was filled in with brick or stone at each side, and the grate set between. The bars, of course, are of iron for holding coal, and the

Illus. 317. — Mantel at Mount Vernon, 1760–1770.

sides of the grate are of brass. These were at first called "cat-stones" to distinguish them from "fire-dogs," but later they were named "hob-grates."

Illus. 318.—Mantel with Hob-grate, 1776.

Below the grate is a small brass fender to prevent the ashes from scattering, and around the fireplace is a fender of iron wire with brass rails and feet.

The hob-grate was more in use in the South than in the North.

In 1745, after many experiments, and goaded to it by the smoking chimneys and wasted heat of the fireplace, Franklin invented the stove in use ever since, called the Franklin stove or grate. Illustration 319 shows a Franklin stove in the Warner house at Portsmouth. The fireplace, faced with tiles, was originally built to burn wood, but when the new-fashioned Franklin stove became popular, one was bought and set into the fireplace, the front of the stove projecting into the room. The stove is made of iron, with the three rosettes, the open-work rail at the top, the large knobs in front and the small knobs at the back, of brass, which every good housekeeper kept as brightly polished as the brass andirons and the handles of the shovel and tongs. At each side of the fireplace are the original brass rests for the shovel and tongs.

Later in the century the fireplace was filled in with a board or bricks, and what was called a fire-frame was used. It was similar to the upper part of a Franklin stove; the back and sides of iron, somewhat larger than those of the Franklin stove, resting directly upon the stone hearth, giving the effect of an iron fireplace in front of the old one. Oftentimes in an old house may be found a large fireplace filled in, with the iron fire-frame in front of it, that in its turn superseded by a stove placed with its pipe passing through the fire-frame. Illustration 320 shows a fire-frame in the Wayside Inn at Sudbury, Massachusetts.

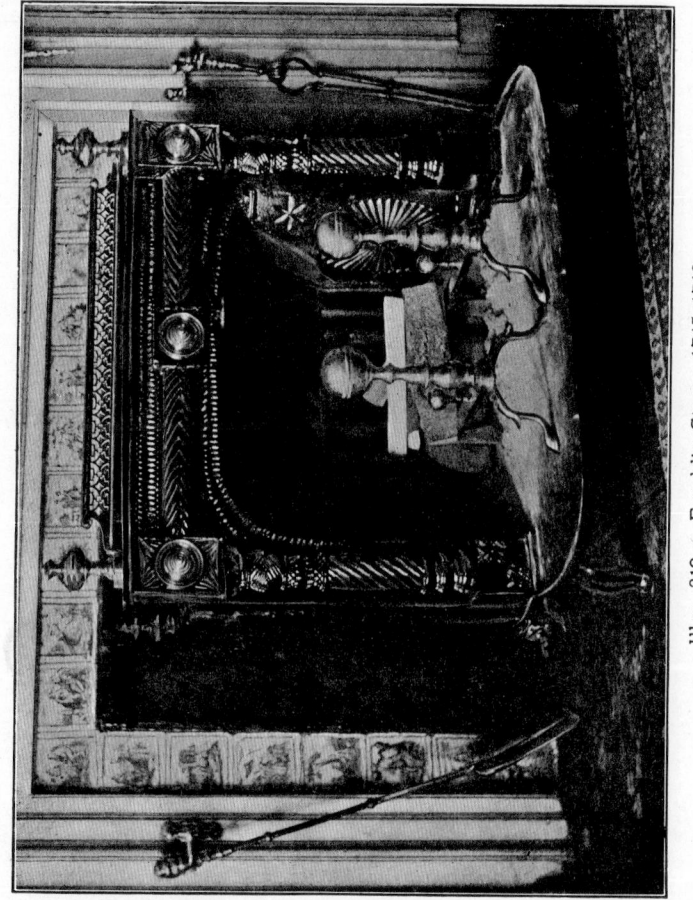

Illus. 319. — Franklin Stove, 1745-1760.

Candles and whale oil, with pine-wood knots, provided the light for the Pilgrim fathers, aside from that thrown out by the great wood fire. Candlesticks formed a necessary part of the furnishings of

Illus. 320. — Iron Fire-frame, 1775-1800.

a house. They were made of brass, iron, tin, pewter, and silver, but candlesticks of brass were the ones in most general use.

The earliest form of lamp in use in the colonies was what is known as a "betty lamp," and it must have been a most untidy little utensil, giving but a meagre light. Illustration 321 shows several betty lamps owned by the writer. The smallest is of iron, two and a half inches in diameter, with a nose

Fires and Lights

projecting one inch and a quarter beyond the receptacle for grease or fat. A chain and hook are attached to the handle, by which the lamp was hung upon a chair-back or a nail. The wick, made of a twisted cotton rag, was placed with its end protruding from the nose of the lamp, and provided a dull, poor flame. Another lamp has the chain and the receptacle for grease made of brass, while the handle, the hook by which it was to hang, and the pin for cleaning the lamp, attached to the chain, are of steel. The bottom of the brass receptacle is of copper. There is a cover to the front part of this lamp, so that the interior

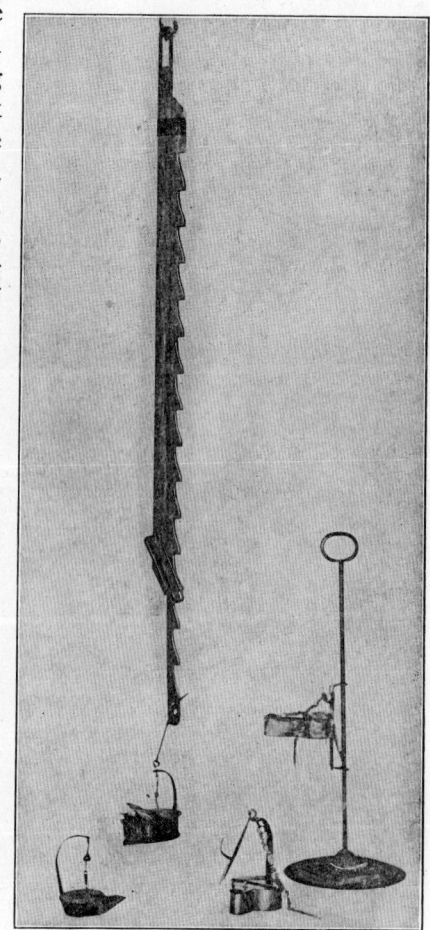

Illus. 321.— Betty Lamps, Seventeenth Century.

Illus. 322. — Candle-stands, first half of Eighteenth Century.

Fires and Lights

can be cleaned, and the piece of steel forming the handle runs through the interior of the lamp, the end providing a nose for the wick just inside of the brass one, thus allowing the drippings from the wick to drain back into the receptacle. The lamp with a standard has an iron rod, upon which the lamp can slide up and down, with a ring at the top of the rod to lift it by. The fourth betty lamp is hung upon an old wooden ratchet intended for that purpose. The ratchet is made of two strips of wood, one cut with saw-teeth edge, which can be raised and lowered to place the lamp at the desired height. Betty lamps were in use during the seventeenth century, and much later than that in the South.

As early as 1696, inventories mention a "Candle-stand for two brass candlesticks." Illustration 322 shows two of these candle-stands in the collection of the late Major Ben: Perley Poore at Indian Hill. The larger stand is made of iron, and was fashioned by the local blacksmith, near Indian Hill. It was taken by the grandfather of Major Poore to Harvard University when he went there a student in 1776. The tongs hanging upon this stand are a smoker's tongs, for lifting a coal from the fire to light the pipe, the curved end on one side of the handle being used to press the tobacco into the pipe, or to clean it out. The three feet of the other stand are of iron, and the pole, candlesticks, and two pairs of snuffers are of brass. These stands probably were made during the first half of the eighteenth century. The room, a corner of which shows in the illustration, is fitted with panels from the "Province House," the home at one time of Agnes Surriage. The pillars showing behind the candle-stands were taken from the old Brattle Street Church in Boston when it was pulled down. One end of a Sheraton

Illus. 323. — Mantel with Candle Shades, 1775–1800.

sofa may be seen in the picture, and several of the illustrations for this book were taken in this fine room.

Illustration 323 shows a mantel in the house of Mrs. Johnson-Hudson at Stratford, Connecticut. The looking-glass frame is made entirely of glass. Upon the shelf are two candlesticks, and over them are large glass shades, called hurricane glasses, used to protect the flame from draughts. These shades are now reproduced, and it is almost impossible to tell the old from the new. The clock upon the shelf is a very old English one, but the reflections upon the glass cover make it difficult to see the clock. The effect of this mantel, with the glass shades, all reflected in the looking-glass, is most brilliant. The candlesticks are of Sheffield plate, about one hundred years old.

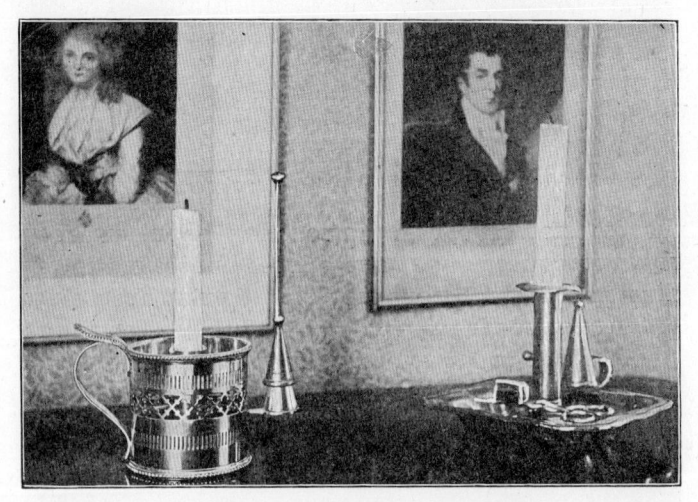

Illus. 324.—Candlesticks, 1775-1800.

Illustration 324 shows two candlesticks owned by the writer. The one shaped like a mug with a handle is of Sheffield plate, and was made for use in a sick-room or any place where it was necessary to burn a light during the entire night. There should be a glass chimney to fit into the candlestick and protect the flame from draughts. The open-work band around the candlestick allowed the passage of air, thus insuring a clear flame. The long-handled extinguisher upon the rest provided for it was to put out the light of a candle which was protected by a chimney or by glass shades such as are in Illustration 323. The other candlestick is of brass, with extinguisher and snuffers which were made to fit the candlestick, the ordinary handleless extinguisher serving to put out the flame of any candle unprotected by a chimney or shade.

In 1784 a Frenchman named Argand invented the lamp still called by his name. The first Argand lamp brought to this country was given by Thomas Jefferson to Charles Thomson. These lamps gave what was then considered to be a brilliant and even dazzling light, but their price placed them beyond the reach of ordinary folk, who continued to use tallow candles. Wax candles were burned by the wealthy, in candlesticks and sconces, and occasionally in chandeliers.

Illus. 325. — Crystal Chandelier, about 1760.

Fires and Lights

Illustration 325 shows a rich chandelier for candles, in the Warner house, at Portsmouth. It was probably brought to this country about 1765, the same date that other handsome furnishings were bought for this house. The metal work of this chandelier is of brass. Chandeliers with glass drops are spoken of in the sixteenth century, coming from Venice.

Illustration 326 shows one of the pair of beautiful lamps which are fastened to the wall above the mantel of the banquet hall at Mount Vernon, and which were in use there during the life of Washington. They are made of silver, with

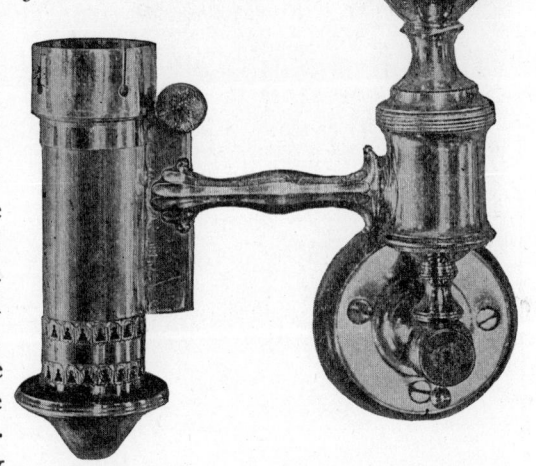

Illus. 326.—Silver Lamp from Mount Vernon, 1770–1800.

the reservoir for oil of a graceful urn shape.

Eliza Susan Morton Quincy gives a description of the house of Ebenezer Storer in Boston, and in it

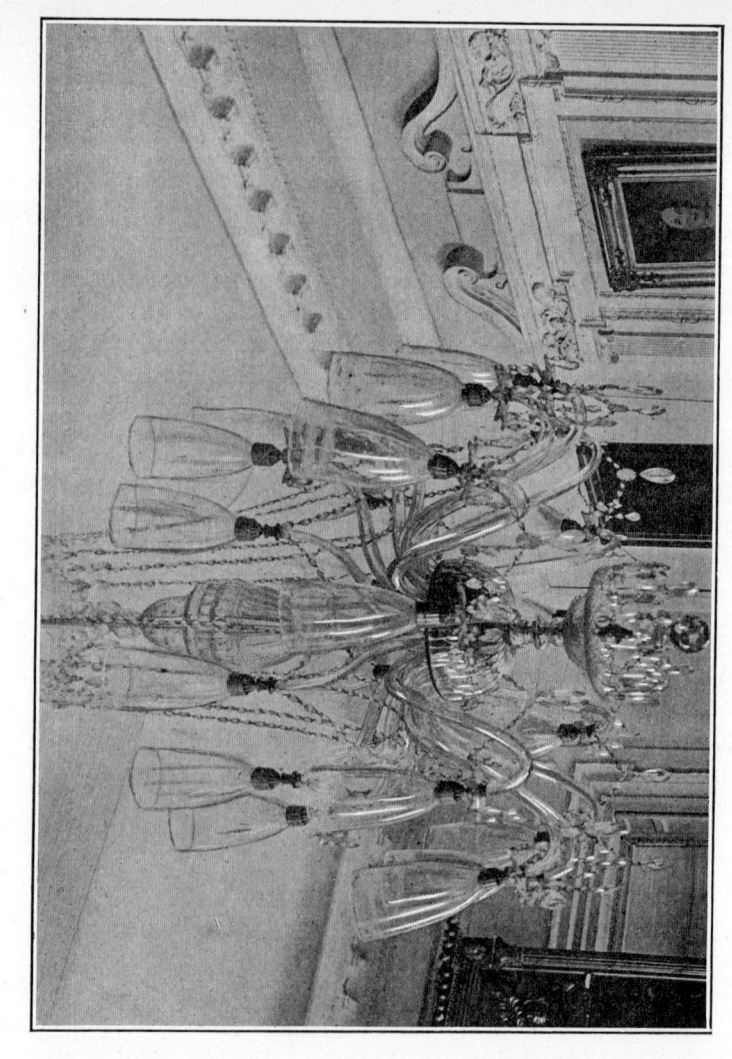

Illus. 327.— Glass Chandelier for Candles, 1760.

she says: "The ceilings were traversed through the length of the rooms, by a large beam cased and finished like the walls; and from the centre of each depended a glass globe, which reflected as a convex mirror, all the objects in the room." These globes also reflected the light from candles in the room.

From the rafters or ceiling in plainer homes hung sometimes a candle beam, a rude chandelier, made of two pieces of metal crossed or a circle of metal, with sockets for candles fixed upon them.

The chandelier in Illustration 327 is for candles, and is without doubt the finest one of its period in this country. It is in the Pringle house in Charleston, South Carolina, and it was probably placed in the house when it was built in 1760, at which time it was furnished with great elegance. It is amazing that so frail a thing as this glass chandelier with all of its shades should have survived the Civil War, and still more, the earthquake which laid low a large part of the city, but not one shade has been shaken down. There are twenty-four branches to the chandelier, twelve in each row, and a large glass shade for each candle, to protect the flame from the draughts. The long chains hang from a bell of glass, from which fall glass drops, and from a large bowl spring the branches with their tall shades, and between them are glass chains with drops. The glass chains are very light and the chandelier is not loaded with heavy drops. It is impossible to imagine anything more light and graceful in effect.

"Skreans" are mentioned in very early inventories, and indeed they must have been a necessity, to

z

338   Furniture of the Olden Time

protect the face from the intense heat of the large open fire. They afforded then, as now, an opportunity for the display of feminine handiwork. The dainty little fire-screen in Illustration 328 was made about 1780, and is owned by Mrs. Johnson-Hudson of Stratford, Connecticut. The frame and stand are of mahogany, and the spreading legs are unusually slender and graceful. The embroidered screen was wrought by the daughters of Dr. William Samuel Johnson, the first president of Columbia University. The same young girls embroidered the top of the card-table in Illustration 199, and

Illus. 328. — Embroidered Screen, 1780.

the work is done with the same patient industry and skill. The vase which is copied in the embroidery is of Delft, and is still owned in the family.

A very curious and interesting piece of work is shown in Illustration 329. It forms the back of a sconce owned by Francis H. Bigelow, Esq., and in his book "Historic Silver of the Colonies," Mr. Bigelow describes the candle bracket, made in 1720 by Knight Leverett, which fits into the socket upon the frame. Benjamin Burt, the silversmith, in his will left to a niece "a sconce of quill work wrought by her aunt." In 1755 a Mrs. Hiller advertised to teach "Wax work, Transparent and Filligree, Quill work and Feather work." "Quill work" is made of paper of various colors, gilt upon one side, rolled tightly, like paper tapers. Some were pulled out into points, others made into leaf and petal-shaped pieces, and when finished they were coated with some waxy substance, and sprinkled with tiny bits of glass, all in gay colors, and when the candles were lighted the quill work glistened and sparkled.

The quill work in this sconce is made into an elaborate design of a vase with flowers, and it is set into a very deep frame, and covered tightly with glass, which accounts for its perfect preservation. The top ornament to the frame is cut in the manner of looking glass frames of the period.

The tripod screen in Illustration 330 is owned by Dwight M. Prouty, Esq. The little shelf for the candlestick drops on a hinge when not in use. The tripod feet have a light springing curve, and end in

Illus. 329. — Sconce of Quill Work, 1720.

Fires and Lights 341

a flattened claw-and-ball. The original embroidery is still in the frame.

Illus. 330.—Tripod Screen, 1770.

Illus. 331.—Tripod Screen, 1765.

Another tripod screen is shown in Illustration 331. It is owned by Cornelius Stevenson, Esq., of Philadelphia. The embroidery and the frame upon it were made in the nineteenth century but the stand is much earlier and is finely carved in the Chippendale style, with the French foot. Three

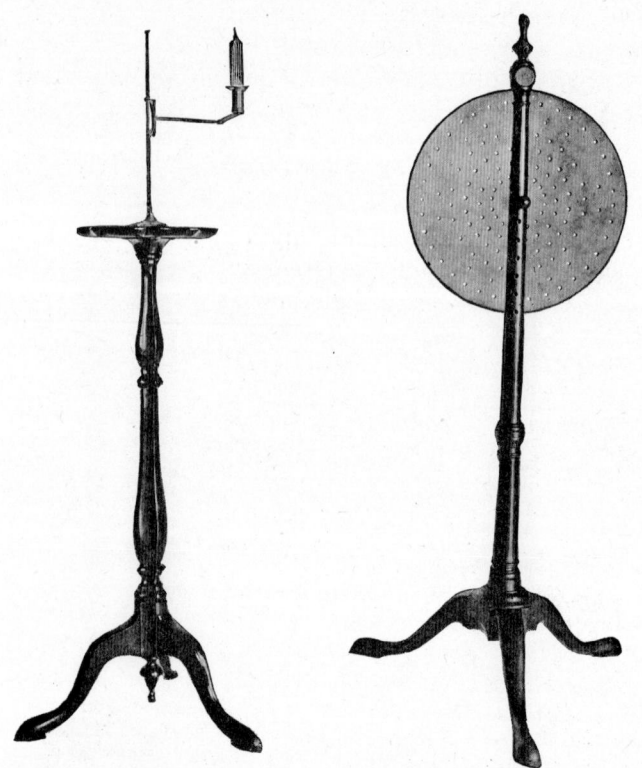

Illus. 332.— Candle-stand and Screen, 1750–1775.

serpents encircle the pole, from which they are completely detached. The wood is mahogany.

Screens were sometimes made of a piece of wood

Fires and Lights 343

perforated, in order that the heat might not be entirely shut off. Illustration 332 shows one of these screens in the collection of the late Major Ben: Perley Poore. Both the screen and the candle-stand in the illustration are made of mahogany. The candlestick upon the stand is a curious one, of brass, with a socket for the candle set upon an adjustable arm, which also slides upon a slender rod, which is fastened into the heavily weighted standard. Both screen and candle-stand were made in the latter half of the eighteenth century. Candle-stands were designed by all the great cabinet-makers, and in those days of candle-light they were a useful piece of furniture.

A candle-stand in the finest Chippendale style is shown in Illustration 333. It is one of a pair owned by Harry Harkness Flagler, Esq. The intention was presumably that a candle-stand with candelabrum should be placed at each side of the mantel. A pair of candle-stands similar to this are in the banquet hall at Mount

Illus. 333.—Chippendale Candle-stand, 1760–1770.

Vernon, and are among the few pieces of furniture there which are authenticated as having been in use during Washington's occupancy of the house. The candle-stand in the illustration is forty-two inches high, and its proportions are beautiful. The legs and the ball at the base of the fluted pillar are very finely carved. The legs end in the French foot, the scroll turning forward, which was such a favorite with Chippendale. The top is carved out

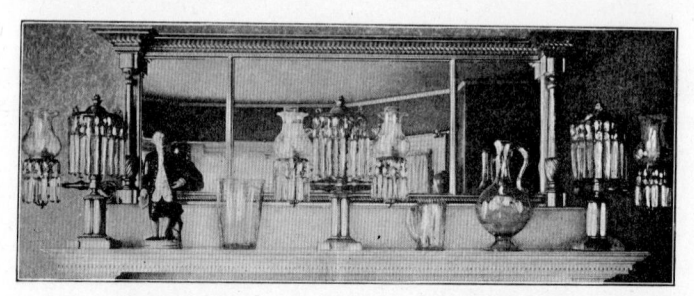

Illus. 334.— Bronze Mantel Lamps, 1815–1840.

so that there is a raised rim, like that upon the "dish-top" table in Illustration 246.

The first recorded instance in this country of lighting by artificial gas is in 1806, when David Melville of Newport, Rhode Island, succeeded in manufacturing gas, and illuminated his house and grounds with it. In 1822 Boston was lighted by gas, but it did not come into general use for lighting until 1840–1850.

During the second quarter of the nineteenth century it was fashionable to use candelabra and lamps which were hung with cut-glass prisms. Sets of candelabra for the mantel were very popular, consisting of a three-branched candelabrum for the middle and a single light for each side. The base was usually of marble, and the gilt standard was cast in different shapes, — of a shepherd and shepherdess, a group of maidens, or a lady clad in the

Illus. 335. — Brass Gilt Candelabra, 1820–1849.

costume of the day. From an ornament at the base of the candle, shaped like an inverted crown, hung sparkling prisms, catching the light as they quivered with every step across the room. A handsome set of these is shown in Illustration 318 upon the mantel.

Illustration 334 shows a set of mantel lamps of bronze, mounted upon marble bases and hung with cut-glass prisms. The reservoir for the oil is beneath the long prisms. This set is owned by Francis H. Bigelow, Esq.

Illustration 335 shows a fine pair of brass gilt candelabra also owned by Mr. Bigelow. They have marble bases, and the five twisted arms are cast in an elaborate design.

Illustration 336 shows a hall lantern which was formerly in use in the John Hancock house. It is

Illus. 336. — Hall Lantern, 1775–1800.

Illus. 337. — Hall Lantern, 1760.

now owned by Harry Harkness Flagler, Esq. Such lanterns were hung in the entry or hall, and were made to burn either a lamp or candle. "Square glass, bell glass, barrel or globe lanthorns for entries or staircases" were advertised as early as 1724 and formed a necessary furnishing for the hall of a handsome house.

Fires and Lights

Illustration 337 shows a hall lantern owned by Dwight M. Prouty, Esq. It is of a globe shape, and very large and handsome, with deep cutting on the glass. The bell-shaped piece of glass above is missing. This bell was to prevent the smoke of the candle from blackening the ceiling. The metal piece below the globe contains the socket and can be removed to change the candle.

Illustration 338 shows one of two lanterns hung in the hall of the house built for the Pendelton Collection, in Providence. It is unusually large, and the glass is red with cuttings of white. Instead of chains the lantern is held by

Illus. 338. — Hall Lantern, 1760.

scrolls of metal like the frame of the glass. Such a lantern as this may have been in the mind of Peter Faneuil of Boston when in 1738 he sent to Europe for "a very handsome Lanthorne to hang in an Entry way."

CHAPTER XI

CLOCKS

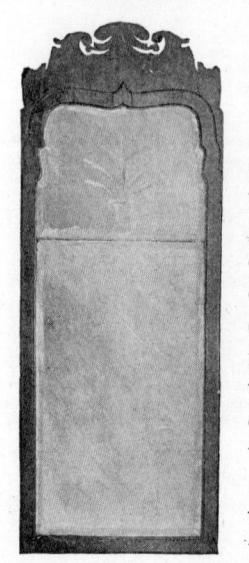

UNTIL about 1600, clocks were made chiefly for public buildings or for the very wealthy, who only could afford to own them; but with the seventeenth century began the manufacture of clocks for ordinary use; these clocks were of brass, and were known as chamber clocks. The earliest form in which they were made was what is now called the "bird-cage" or "lantern" clock. Inventories in this country from 1638 to 1700 speak of clocks with valuations varying from £2 to £20, and occasionally a "brass clock" is specified. This must refer, as some of the others may also have done, to the lantern clock.

The lantern clock in Illustration 339 is owned by William Meggatt, Esq., of Wethersfield. The illustration shows the form of the clock, from which it naturally derived the names "lantern" and "bird-cage." The clock is set upon a bracket, and the weights hang upon cords or chains passing through openings in the shelf; the pendulum also swings through a slit in the shelf. The dial projects beyond the frame of the clock, and is six inches in diameter, and there is but one hand. The dome at the top is partially concealed by the frets above the body of the clock. Different clock-makers had frets of their own, and the design of the fret is often a guide for determining the date of such clocks. The one upon the clock in Illustration 339 is what was called the "heraldic fret" from the small escutcheon in the centre, and it was used upon clocks made from 1600 to 1640. The fret with crossed dolphins was in use from 1650, and is the pattern of fret most frequently found upon these clocks. The long pendulum must have been a later substitution, for it was not commonly used until 1680, clocks up to the time of its invention having the short or "bob" pendulum. There is no maker's name upon this clock.

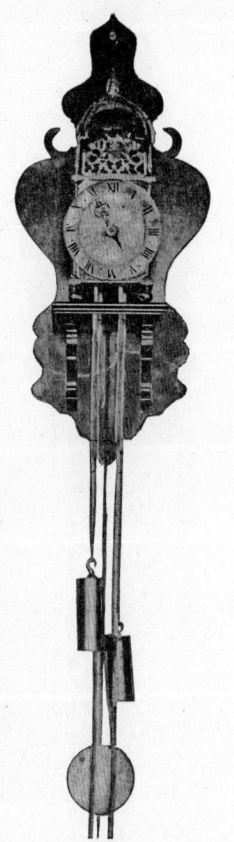

Illus. 339.—Lantern or Bird-cage Clock, First Half of Seventeenth Century.

Illustration 340 shows a "lantern" clock in the house of Charles R. Waters, Esq., which has a fret of a later period, and the long pen-

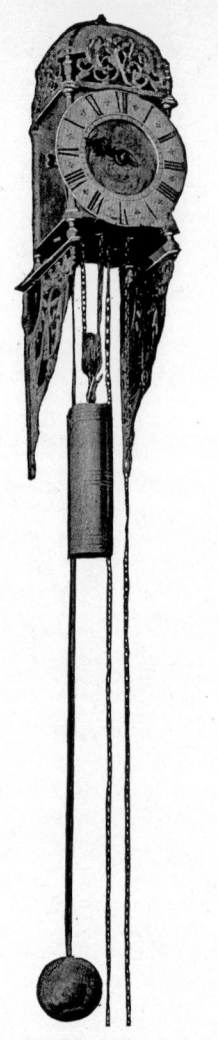

Illus. 340. — Lantern Clock, about 1680.

Illus. 341. — Friesland Clock, Seventeenth Century.

dulum. The dial is slightly larger than the one in Illustration 339, and upon it is engraved the name of the maker, Jno. Snatt, Ashford. This name is not in Britten's list of clock-makers, so it is probable that Jno. Snatt was a country clock-maker. The clock was made about 1680. The brackets are modern.

A clock which was made during the seventeenth century is shown in Illustration 341. It is known as a Friesland clock, from the fact that clocks of this style are common in the north of Holland, having been in use there over two centuries. The pendulum of this clock swings above the shelf. The frame rests upon four wooden feet, and its sides and back are of glass. The face and ornaments are made of lead, the ornaments being gilded, except the parrots at each side, which are painted in vivid parrot greens. The mermaids upon the bracket are painted in colors, and the face also is painted, the whole making a gay bit of decoration. The Friesland clocks generally have mermaids and parrots as part of the decoration of clock and bracket. There is a small brass dial in the centre of the face, which can be set for the alarm. Friesland clocks were in use in the seventeenth century in this country, probably having been brought here by Dutch settlers. This clock is owned by the writer.

Bracket clocks were made during the last years of the seventeenth century with wooden cases, and they were very popular during the eighteenth century. They generally have a brass handle at the top by which they can be carried. A bracket clock with brass face and sides may be seen upon the mantel in Illustration 388. It has the plate of the maker over the dial, with the name Daniel Ray, Sudbury, probably an English clock-maker. This clock was made about 1760.

Illustration 342 shows two bracket clocks in the collection of the late Major Ben: Perley Poore. The larger one has the top made in the arch form instead of the bell top like the clock in Illustration 388, and this would place its date

Illus. 342.—Bracket Clocks, 1780–1800.

about 1780. The name upon this clock, George Beatty, Georgetown, was that of the owner. The smaller clock has an inlaid case, and was evidently made after Sheraton's designs of 1790–1800. Both clock-cases are of mahogany.

The earliest mention of tall clocks in inventories

is in the latter part of the seventeenth century, where they are always spoken of as "clock and case." The use of the long pendulum was probably the cause of the development of the tall clock from the "lantern clock," which had often a wooden hood over it; and when the long pendulum came into use in 1680, the lower part of the tall clock-case was made to enclose the pendulum, and sides and a glass front were added to the hood. The first cases were of oak or walnut, and the dials were square, but early in the eighteenth century the arched top was added to the dial, suggested perhaps by the shape of the dome.

The ornaments which fill in the spandrels, or corners of the face, are somewhat of a guide to the date of a brass-faced clock. The earliest spandrels had cherubs' heads with wings, and this design was used from 1671 until 1700, when more ornaments were added to the cherub's head. Later came a still more elaborate design of two cherubs supporting a crown, until about 1750, when the scrolls were made without the cherubs, but with a shield or head in the centre of the spandrel.

Illustration 343 shows two tall clocks which were owned originally by Thomas Hancock, from whom John Hancock inherited them. Thomas Hancock was a wealthy resident of Boston in 1738 when he wrote thus to London, ordering a clock of "the newest fashion with a good black Walnut Tree Case Veneered work, with Dark, lively branches; on the Top instead of Balls let there be three handsome Carv'd figures. Gilt with burnish'd Gold. I'd have

Illus. 343. — Walnut Case and Lacquered Case Clocks, about 1738.

the Case without the figures to be 10 feet Long, the price is not to exceed 20 Guineas, & as it's for my own use, I beg your particular Care in buying of it at the Cheapest Rate. I'm advised to apply to one Mr. Marmaduke Storr at the foot of Lond^n Bridge."

Which of these two clocks was sent to fill this order we cannot tell. The clock with "Walnut Tree Case Veneered work, with Dark, lively branches" has the name plate of "Bowly, London," probably Devereux Bowley, who lived from 1696 to 1773 and who was master of the Clock-Makers' Company in 1759. The gilt ornaments are missing from the top, so we do not know whether they were the ones so carefully specified in the letter. Both clocks may date to 1738. The clock with the lacquered case has the name "Marm^d Storr, foot of London Bridge," the same to whom Thomas Hancock had "been advised to apply." This clock has the "Balls" at the top to which he objected. Possibly the zealous friend may have sent both clocks. The one with a walnut case is now owned by the American Antiquarian Society, to which it was presented, with other pieces bought from the Hancock house in 1838, by John Chandler of Petersham. The clock with lacquered case was also bought from the Hancock house, and is now in the Boston Museum of Fine Arts, to which it is loaned by Miss Lucy Gray Swett.

A clock-maker well known in and around Boston in the last half of the eighteenth century was Gawen Brown, who had a shop on State Street, and who made the clock upon the Old South Church, in Boston. A letter is still preserved which he wrote asking permission to make a clock for the Society, and he "Promises and Engages that the same shall be put Up and continued there forever." This handsome offer was made in 1768 but not until 1774 did the town act, when they voted to "purchase the Clock of Gawen Brown."

A Gawen Brown clock is shown in Illustration 344, made for his father-in-law, the Rev. Mather Byles. The case is pine painted and the shape of the top and the general appearance would indicate that it was an early effort made before 1768. It is still running in the rooms of the Bostonian Society, in the Old State House in Boston.

Illus. 344.— Gawen Brown Clock, 1765.

Illus. 345.— Tall Clock, 1780.

Illus. 346. — Maple
Clock, 1770.

Illus. 347. — Rittenhouse
Clock, 1770.

The clock in Illustration 345 was made by Gawen Brown, and is in a very handsome mahogany case. It is also owned by the Bostonian Society.

Illustration 346 shows a clock owned by the writer, and is given as an example of the use of curly maple, of which the entire case is made. It is unusually tall, over eight feet in height.

The clock in Illustration 347 was made by David Rittenhouse, in Philadelphia, and is owned by Charles D. Clark, Esq., of Philadelphia. David Rittenhouse was a maker of clocks and mathematical instruments, and an astronomer. He held various positions of importance, and was State Treasurer of Pennsylvania during the Revolutionary war, and President of The American Philosophical Society. This clock has a very handsome case of mahogany with fine inlaying, and possesses seven dials. The large dial has three hands, two for the hours and minutes, and the third to point the day of the month. This is set on the first day of each month. At the two upper corners are two small dials, one of which is set to designate which of the twelve tunes shall be played, and the other has on it "strike" and "silent," also for the tunes. Above, the moon shows its phases and the sun rises and sets every day. Upon the round dial below, the planets revolve around the sun.

Illustration 348 shows a tall clock in a mahogany case made about 1770. The maker's name is Richard Simestere, Birmingham, but I can find no record of him in Britten or elsewhere. The shape of the clock-case, particularly the top, is modelled after a

Chippendale design. The columns at the corners of the case, sometimes fluted and sometimes plain, are characteristic of Chippendale, and appear on the majority of tall clocks made after 1760. This clock is owned by Francis H. Bigelow, Esq., of Cambridge.

After the War of the Revolution enamelled or painted dials took the place of brass dials in this country, to a great extent, the chief reason being, of course, their smaller cost. The works were made by clock-makers who sold them to pedlers, and they took them, four or five at a time, into the country towns to sell; the local cabinet-maker made the case, while the local clock-maker put his own name upon the dial. During the latter years of the eighteenth century, there was a fashion for using moving figures above the dial, a ship heaving upon the waves being the favorite. Many clocks have a painted moon, which rises and sets each month. Miniature tall clocks were made at this time, corresponding in proportions to the tall clocks.

Illus. 348. — Tall Clock, about 1700.

Illustration 349 shows a tall clock and a miniature one, both made about 1800, with painted faces. The tall clock has the name upon its face of Philip Holway, Falmouth. The case is mahogany, and the twisted pillars have brass bases and caps. The brass ornaments upon the top are rather unusual, a ball with three sprays of flowers. The clock was bought in Falmouth by the writer. The small clock has the name of Asa Kenney upon the face. Its case is inlaid with satinwood and ebony. This little clock belonged to the late Sumner Pratt of Worcester, and is now owned by his daughter, Miss E. A. Pratt.

Illustration 350 shows a clock owned by Mrs. E. A. Morse of

Illus. 349. — Miniature Clock and Tall Clock, about 1800.

Worcester. The case is beautifully inlaid with satinwood, holly, ebony, and two varieties of mahogany. It has the painted moon above the dial, and plays seven tunes — one tune being played each hour during the day. The tunes are

    Hob or Knob,
    Heathen Mythology,
    Bank of Flowers,
    Paddy Whack,
    New Jersey,
    Marquis of Granby,
    Amherst.

Amherst is the psalm tune which this pious clock plays upon Sundays, to atone for the rollicking jigs which are tinkled out upon week-days. All of the tall clocks illustrated in this chapter have brass works, but many were made with wooden works, and in buying a clock one should make sure that the works are of brass.

Illustration 351 shows two sizes of a kind of clock occasionally found, which winds by pulling the chain attached to the weights. These clocks were

Illus. 350. — Tall Clock, 1800–1810.

made in Europe; the smaller one, which is owned by the writer, having the label of a Swiss clockmaker. The larger clock belongs to Irving Bigelow, Esq., of Worcester. Both date to the first quarter of the nineteenth century.

Illus. 351.—Wall Clocks, 1800–1825.

The most famous name among American clock-makers is Willard. There were three Willard brothers, — Benjamin, Simon, and Aaron, — clockmakers in Grafton, Massachusetts, in 1765. Benjamin and Simon established a business in Roxbury, and in December, 1771, Benjamin advertised in the *Boston Evening Post* his "removal from Lexington to Roxbury. He will sell house clocks neatly made, cheaper than imported." February 22, 1773, he advertised that he "at his shop in Roxbury Street, pursues the different branches of clock and watch work, and has for sale musical clocks, playing different tunes, a new tune each day, and on Sunday a Psalm tune. These tunes perform every hour. . . . All the branches of the business likewise carried on in Grafton." The third brother, Aaron, may have remained in Grafton, for he went from there later to Roxbury, as fifer of a company of minute-men, in the first days of the War of the Revolution. Simon Willard remained in the same shop in Roxbury for over seventy years, dying in 1848 at the great age of ninety-six years. Aaron Willard built a shop in Boston and made a specialty of tall striking clocks.

Illustration 352 shows a clock owned by Dr. G. Faulkner of Jamaica Plain. Inside the clock is written in a quaint hand, "The first short timepiece made in America, 1784." Dr. Faulkner's father was married at about that date, and the clock was made for him. It has always stood upon a bracket upon the wall, and has been running constantly for one hundred and seventeen years. Upon the

Illus. 352.— Willard Clock, 1784.

scroll under the dial is the inscription "Aaron Willard, Roxbury." The case is of mahogany, and stands twenty-six inches high. Upon the lower part

364　Furniture of the Olden Time

are very beautiful scroll feet, turning back. The upper part stands upon ogee feet, and can be lifted off. The glass door is painted so that it forms a frame for the dial. Mr. Howard, the founder of the

Illus. 353.— Willard Clocks, 1800–1815.

Howard Watch Company, has told me that the Willards invented this style of clock as well as the style known as the banjo clock. Mr. Howard was born in 1813 and when he was sixteen he started to learn his trade in Boston, in the shop of Aaron Willard, Jr. I have not been able to find that clocks of this style were made in England at all, and they seem to be purely American, but in Britten's "Old Clocks and Watches and their Makers" is an illustration of an astronomical clock made by Henry Jenkins, 1760 to 1780, with a case very similar in shape to these clocks, and with a top like the centre one of the three in Illustration 353. Aaron Willard may have obtained his idea from such a clock. The clock in Illustration 352 is the earliest one that I have heard of.

Illustration 353 shows three clocks made some years later, probably about 1800 to 1815. The clock with the ogee feet is a Willard clock, and belongs to W. S. G. Kennedy, Esq. The clock with the door of bird's-eye maple and the inlaid fan-shaped top is owned by Mrs. E. A. Morse. The third clock is owned by the writer.

Another New England clock-maker of long and picturesque life was Stephen Hassam, sometimes called Hasham. He was born in 1761, and is said to have lived to be over one hundred years old. He was a witness, when a boy, of the battle of Bunker Hill from the steeple of a church in Boston, and he lived until after the beginning of the Civil War. He moved from Boston to Grafton and then to Worcester, where he learned the clock-maker's trade, perhaps with the Willards who lived in those towns at about that time. He established himself finally in Charlestown, New Hampshire, where he lived and made clocks, which are highly valued for their excellent qualities, as well as for the associations with the name of the centenarian clock-maker.

A clock similar in size, and also in design, to the last four illustrated is shown in Illustration 354. It was made by Stephen Hassam and bears his name. It is owned by Charles H. Morse, Esq., and has always stood since it was made, about 1800, upon a mahogany bracket in the corner. The case is of very finely grained mahogany.

Simon Willard patented in 1802 an improved timepiece, which Mr. Howard says is the clock now known as the "banjo" clock. Illustration 355 shows a clock bought by the writer in a country town from an old man who called it a timepiece, which is the name given it in the country, "banjo" being suggested to the modern mind by the shape of the upper part. The sides of the clock are of mahogany. The glass door to the face is convex and is framed in brass, and the ornaments at the sides of the clock are also of brass. The long glass in the middle of the case is framed like the door of

Illus. 354.— Hassam Clock, 1800.

Illus. 355. — "Banjo" Clock, 1802–1820.

painted glass in wood gilt. The turned ornament on the top of the clock and the bracket below it are of wood gilt. Plainer clock-cases of this shape were of mahogany without the bracket below.

Aaron Willard, Jr., entered his father's employ in his shop in Boston in 1823, and continued the business for forty years. When one considers that members of this family manufactured clocks for over one hundred years, it does not seem singular that so many clocks are found with the name of Willard upon them.

Occasionally one finds a banjo clock with striking attachment, but they are not common.

Illus. 356.—Presentation Clock.

Illus. 357.—Willard Timepiece.

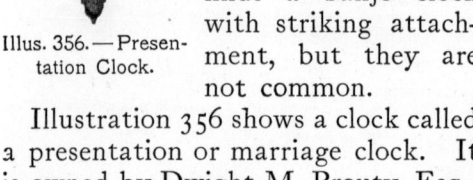

Illustration 356 shows a clock called a presentation or marriage clock. It is owned by Dwight M. Prouty, Esq., of Boston, and it was made for an ancestor of Mr. Prouty, when he was married, as a wedding gift. The decorations are in light colors, pink and blue with gold, very delicate and suitable for a bride. Upon the square glass door, painted above the centre is "S. Willard" and below it "Patent." The bracket is gilt.

Illustration 357 shows another Willard timepiece, with a mahogany case and gilt mouldings and bracket. Upon the door is painted the battle between the *Constitution* and *Guerrière*. The name A. Willard is painted upon the long glass. This clock belongs to Francis H. Bigelow, Esq.

The clock in Illustration 358 has the name Willard upon the face. The case is mahogany, and the mouldings which frame the glass and the bracket beneath the clock are japanned in colors. It belongs to Charles A. Moffett, Esq., of Worcester.

Illus. 358.—Willard Timepiece, 1802–1810.

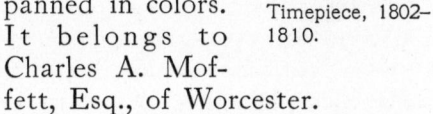

The clock in Illustration 359 is of an entirely different style, and the case, the lower part of which is lyre shaped, is very beautifully carved with scrolls, which are finished in gilt. There

Illus. 359.—Lyre Clock, 1810–1820.

2 B

is no maker's name upon this clock, which belongs to Frank C. Turner, Esq., of Norwich.

The clock in Illustration 360 is in the lyre shape usually seen, which was made as a variation from the banjo. Such clocks are found of wood finished in gilt, or like this clock, in the natural wood, which is mahogany in most cases. The carving is generally in the same design, but some have the lyre strings, made of wood or brass.

Illus. 360.—Lyre-shaped Clock, 1810–1820.

Eli Terry was the first of another famous family of American clock-makers. He started in business in 1793, in Plymouth, near Waterbury, Connecticut, a town well known ever since for its clocks and watches. His first clock was made a year earlier, a wooden clock in a long case with a brass dial, silver washed. He manufactured the works for tall clocks, selling them to pedlers, who took them into the country to dispose of. In 1810 Seth Thomas with Silas Hoadly bought the Terry factory, and continued the manufacture of clocks for long cases. Eli Terry in 1814 invented a wooden shelf-clock, called "The Pillar Scroll Top Case, with pillars 21 inches long resting on a square base, dial 11 inches square, table below dial 7 inches by 11." This clock sold for fifteen dollars, and was made in enormous quantities. Illustration 361 shows two clocks, one an Eli Terry "Pillar Scroll

Top" clock, with carved pillars similar to the ones upon pieces of furniture of that period. The other clock was made by Terry at about the same time. Inside each of these clocks is pasted a paper upon which is printed the following: "Patent Clocks,

Illus. 361.—Eli Terry Shelf Clocks, 1824.

invented by Eli Terry, Plymouth, Connecticut. Warranted if well used. N.B. The public may be assured that this kind of Clock will run as long without repairs and be as durable and accurate for keeping time as any kind of Clock whatever." These clocks are owned by D. Thomas Moore, Esq., of Westbury, Long Island.

Illus. 362.—French Clock, about 1800.

From the time when such mantel clocks were manufactured in great numbers, the fact that they were cheap and good time-keepers put the tall clock out of the market, and its manufacture practically died out soon after, so that but few tall clocks were made later than 1815–1820.

Illustration 362 shows a French clock with onyx pillars, and elaborate Empire brasses. The large ornaments at the side of the dial are of wood gilt. The middle of the dial is occupied by a beautifully wrought design in brass, of an anvil and grindstone, each with a little Cupid. Upon the quarter-hour one Cupid sharpens his arrow at the grindstone, running the grindstone with his foot upon a treadle, and at every hour the other Cupid strikes the anvil with his hammer the necessary number of strokes. A brass figure of a youth with a bow stands below the dial, in front of the mirror in the back of the clock. The base is of black marble. I have seen several clocks similar with the onyx pillars, but none with such beautiful, hand-wrought brass in the face and upon the case.

CHAPTER XII

LOOKING-GLASSES

A STRONG distinction was made in America during the seventeenth and eighteenth centuries between mirrors and looking-glasses; the name "mirror" was applied to a particular kind of glass, either convex or concave, and one old authority states that "a mirror is a circular convex glass in a gilt frame."

Looking-glasses appear in inventories in this country as early as 1650, and in 1658 William Bartlett of Hartford left no less than ten, the dearest valued at one pound.

In 1670 the Duke of Buckingham brought Venetian workmen to England, and established glass works in Lambeth; but up to that date the looking-glasses occasionally mentioned in inventories must have been made in Venice. Some of the records are "a great looking glass," — "looking glass with brasses," — "great looking glass of ebony," — "an olive wood diamond cut looking glass," — and "a looking glass with a walnut tree frame." The glass usually had the edge finished with a slight bevelling about an inch wide, made by hand, of course, which followed the outline of the inside of the frame.

Hungerford Pollen, in "Furniture and Woodwork," says: "The looking-glasses made in the seventeenth and eighteenth centuries . . . had the plates finished by an edge gently bevelled, of an inch in width, following the form of the frame, whether square or shaped in curves. It is of great difficulty in execution, the plate being held by the workman over his head, and the edges cut by grinding. . . . The angle of the" (modern) "bevel is generally too acute, whereby the prismatic light produced by this portion of the mirror is in too violent and showy contrast to the remainder."

Illus. 363.—Looking-glass, 1690.

One can always distinguish an old bevel, by rubbing the finger upon it. The bevel is so slight that it can hardly be felt, where the modern bevel is sharp and distinct.

Looking-glasses of large size were made in two sections, the lower piece with the edge bevelled and lapped over the plain upper piece. This was to avoid the tax upon glass beyond a certain size.

The fashion for japanning or lacquering which obtained vogue at the close of the seventeenth century was followed in looking-glass frames. A London newspaper of 1689 thus advertised: "Several sorts of Screwtores, Tables, Stands and Looking-glasses of Japan and other work."

Illus. 364. — Looking-glass, 1690.

Illustration 363 shows a looking-glass in a japanned frame, owned by Dwight M. Prouty, Esq., of Boston. The wood of the frame is walnut, and it is covered with lacquer in gold and colors. The shape of the frame around the glass is followed by the bevel, and the lower piece of glass laps over the upper.

Illustration 364 shows the top section of a looking-glass with a lacquered frame. In this case the frame was made in sections, the lower section being lost. The curves in the frame are followed in the glass by the old shallow bevelling over an inch in width, and a star is cut in the middle of the glass. The frame is elaborately japanned with gold and bright colors, and is twenty-six inches in height, showing that the looking-glass, when whole, was of generous size. The design of the sawed edge is of a very early style. The glass is owned by the American Antiquarian Society, of Worcester.

The looking-glass at the head of this chapter is owned by E. R. Lemon, Esq., of the Wayside Inn. It is of walnut veneer, and the old bevelled glass is in two sections, the upper one cut in a design, and with the lower edge lapped over the other piece of glass. Another glass of the same period, the first quarter of the eighteenth century, owned by Mr. Lemon, heads Chapter XI. This frame has a top ornament of a piece of walnut sawed in curves which suggest those upon later frames.

Such a looking-glass as this was probably what Judge Sewall meant when he sent for "A True Looking Glass of Black Walnut Frame of the Newest Fashion (if the Fashion be good) as good as can be bought for five or six pounds." This was for wedding furniture for the judge's daughter Judith, married in 1720.

A looking-glass of the same date, with a carved wood frame, silvered, heads Chapter VI. It was originally owned by an ancestor of the late Major Ben: Perley Poore, and was probably made in

Europe. It has always, within the memory of the family, been silvered, and it is safe to say that it was so originally. The carving is rather crudely done, the ornament at the top containing a bird which is sitting upon a cherub's head. This glass is now at Indian Hill, Newburyport.

In nothing is the charm of association more potent than in an old looking-glass, when one considers the faces and scenes that have been reflected in it. Illustration 365 shows a looking-glass which hung in the Schuyler mansion at Stillwater, New York, in which Washington stopped over night; and

Illus. 365. — Looking-glass, about 1730.

although the quicksilver is somewhat worn off the back of the glass, the thought that it must have mirrored the face of Washington preserves it from being restored. The shape is extremely graceful, and the outline of the inside of the frame is followed by little scrolls cut in the glass. The frame is carved in wood, and gilt, and was probably made in Italy about 1730. It is now owned by the writer. The low-boy in the illustration is described upon page 39.

Rococo and Chinese designs were rampantly fashionable in frames for looking-glasses from 1750 to 1780. They present an astonishing combination of Chinese pagodas, shells, flowers, branches, animals, and birds, with occasionally a figure of a man or woman considerably smaller than the flowers and birds upon the same frame.

Some of the famous designers of frames were Matthias Lock, who published "A Book New of Pier Frames, Oval Girandoles, Tables, etc.," in 1765; Edwards and Darley; and Thomas Johnson; besides the better-known cabinet-makers Ince and Mayhew and Chippendale. Lock and Johnson devoted much space to frames for girandoles, pier glasses, ovals, and chimney-pieces, all elaborately carved with scrolls and shells with dripping water, birds, and animals of every sort from a monkey to a cow, the latter unromantic and heavy creature figuring upon a dripping scroll in one of Johnson's frames.

Illustration 366 shows a looking-glass of the size which was called a "pier" glass, which must have been made about 1760. It is carved in walnut, and the natural wood has never been stained or gilt. It

Illus. 366.—Pier Glass in "Chinese Taste," 1760.

presents many of the characteristic designs fashionable at that time, of scrolls and dripping water, while no less than seven pagoda roofs form a part of the frame. The figure, probably a Chinese lady with a parasol, is missing from the pagoda at the top. Below the frame is carved a little monkey sitting in the lower scroll. The frame is rather unusual in having side branches for candles. This looking-glass and the one in the following illustration are owned by Mrs. Charles Barrell of Barrell's Grove, York Corner, Maine, and are in the old Barrell house, which stands with its original furniture, as it stood one hundred and fifty years ago. These looking-glasses were bought by a Barrell ancestor at an auction in London, about 1795. The articles sold at this auction were the furnishings of one of the households of the Prince of Wales, which was, temporarily at least, given up by him upon his marriage, and these glasses have reflected many a gay scene in which the "First gentleman in Europe" figured, while Beau Brummel may have used them to arrange the wonderful toilettes which won him his name. What a change to the little Maine village!

Another looking-glass of carved wood, with the same history, is shown in Illustration 367. This frame is gilded, and possesses none of the Chinese designs of the other frame, but is purely rococo. It has the old glass with bevelled edges. Both of these looking-glasses must have been made at least twenty-five years before the time when they were sold at auction by the royal bridegroom.

382   Furniture of the Olden Time

At the head of Chapter V is shown a looking-glass with a frame of white with gilt ornaments. It formerly belonged to Governor Wentworth, and

Illus. 367.—Looking-glass, about 1760.

is now in the Poore collection at Indian Hill. It is similar in design and decoration to the looking-glasses seen in French palaces, and was probably made in France about 1760.

A charming oval looking-glass which might be of the present latest fashion forms the heading to Chapter III. It has the flowing ribbon bow-knot which Chippendale employed, and which has been fashionable ever since. This looking-glass was made about 1770, and was inherited by Miss H. P. F. Burnside of Worcester from her great-grandmother.

Illustration 368 shows a fine looking-glass with a frame of carved wood. There is a small oval medallion below the frame with emblems of Freemasonry in gilt upon a black ground. A large medallion is above the glass, with Cupids painted upon a black ground, and the frame is surmounted by an eagle. This looking-glass is owned by Mrs. Charles R. Waters of Salem.

Illus. 368. — Looking-glass, 1770–1780.

Another of the same period, with a carved wood frame, is shown at the beginning of Chapter IV. This frame has a classical design of garlands of laurel with an urn at the top. The small oval medallion at the base of both of these frames seems to be a feature of such looking-glasses, together with the garlands of carved wood. This looking-glass is owned by the writer. Upon its back is an oak board which must have been prized highly, for it has been carefully repaired with two patches of wood set into it.

Illustration 369 shows a looking-

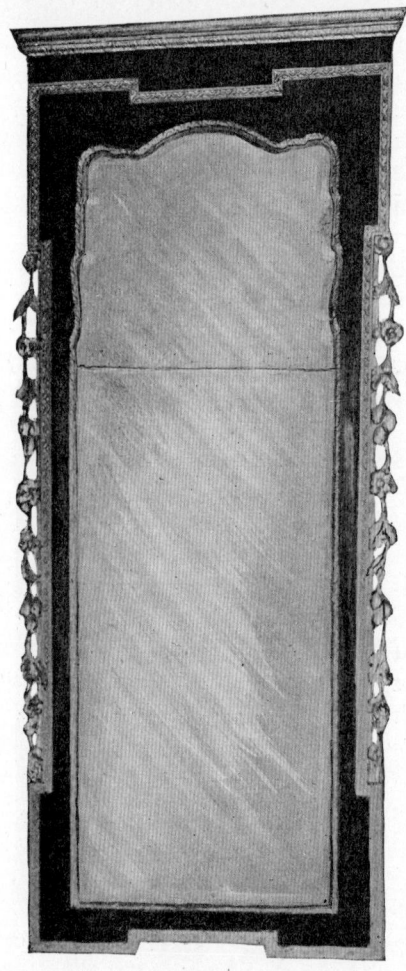

Illus. 369. — Looking-glass, 1725–1750.

glass made in the first half of the eighteenth century, of walnut. The gilt mouldings are carved in wood, as are the gilt leaves and flowers at the side. The waving line of the inside of the frame is followed in the bevelling of the glass. Glasses of this period were usually made in two pieces, to lessen the expense, the edge of one piece of glass being simply lapped over the other. This looking-glass is unusually large, seven and one-half feet high and three feet wide. It is now owned by the Philadelphia Library Association, and was used in 1778 at the famous Mischianza fête, where probably the lovely Peggy Shippen and the beautiful Jewess, Rebecca Frank, and perhaps the ill-fated André, used the glass to put the finishing touches to their toilettes, or to repair the damages wrought during the gay dances of that historic ball.

A looking-glass showing the development from the one in Illustration 369 may be seen in Illustration 26 upon page 39. The frame is more elaborate than the older one in its curves and in the pediment with the broken arch, and its date is about 1770. The original glass is gone, so we cannot tell if it was bevelled, but it probably was. This very fine frame came from the Chase mansion in Annapolis, and is now owned by Harry Harkness Flagler, Esq., of Millbrook, New York.

Another looking-glass owned by Mr. Flagler is shown in Illustration 370. The frame is of walnut veneer, and the shape of the glass without any curves at the top, and the garlands at the side more finely modelled and strung upon a wire, determine it to have been made some years later than the frame in Illustration 369.

A looking-glass with a mahogany and gilt frame, owned by the writer, is shown in the heading to Chapter IX. This looking-glass dates between the last two described; the curved form of the upper edge of the glass in Illustration 26 leaving a slight reminder in the cut-off, upper corners of this glass, which vanishes in the square corners of the one in Illustration 370. The garlands at each side are carved from wood, without wire. These looking-glasses are now reproduced in large numbers and are sometimes called Washington glasses, from the fact that one hangs upon the wall in a room at Mount Vernon.

Illus. 370.—Looking-glass, 1770–1780.

A very unusual looking-glass is shown in Illustration 371, a long mantel looking-glass of very early date, probably not later than 1750. The glass is made in three sections, the two end sections being lapped over the middle one. The glasses are not bevelled. Short garlands carved in wood are upon the sides, and the moulding around the glass is made in curves, while the upper and lower edges of the frame are perfectly straight. A glimpse may be caught above the frame of the two pieces of metal fastened to the back, which are found upon such frames, with a hole for a screw to fasten the heavy frame to the wall. This looking-glass belongs to Dwight M. Prouty, Esq.

The looking-glasses

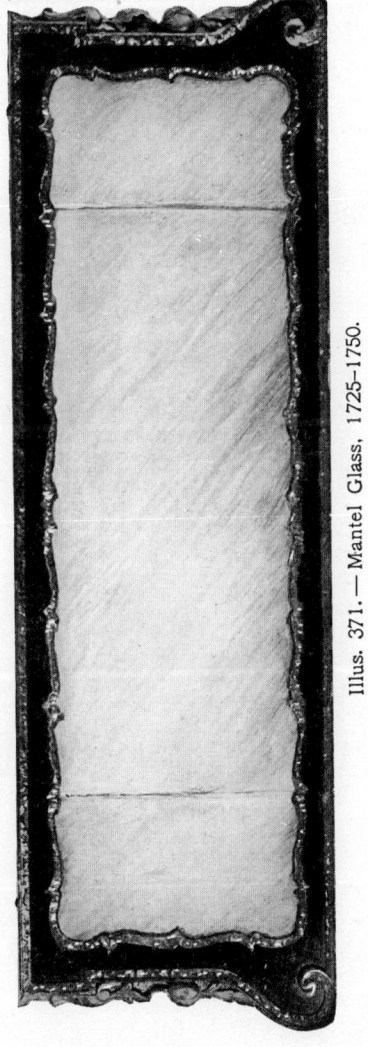

Illus. 371.— Mantel Glass, 1725-1750.

in Illustrations 372 and 373 also belong to Mr. Prouty. Glasses of this style are not uncommon. They are never large, and as they are always about the same size, they must

Illus. 372.—Looking-glass, 1770.

have been made for a certain purpose, or to follow a certain fashion. The decorations vary, but are always applied in gilt upon the high top above the frame, and upon the piece below, while the sides are straight and plain.

Illus. 373.—Looking-glass, 1770.

Illus. 374.—Looking-glass, 1776.

Illustration 374 shows a beautiful looking-glass owned by Bayard Wyman, Washington, D. C. It is carved in wood and gilt, and four pieces of glass are set in the frame, which is surmounted by the eagle holding a shield with stars and stripes.

Illustration 375 shows a very large looking-glass, from the Ogle house in Annapolis. It is finished in white and gold and has the original bevelled glass.

Illus. 375.—Looking-glass, 1780.

The looking-glass which heads Chapter XIII is in the Metropolitan Museum of Art and is of the same period as the glass in Illustration 371.

A looking-glass is shown in the heading to Chapter VIII in which the decoration is produced by both carving and sawing, as well as by gilt ornaments. The sawing of ornamental outlines appears upon the earliest frames, such as Illustration 364, and is found upon frames made during the eighteenth century until its close.

During the last quarter of the eighteenth century frames which are apparently a cheaper form of the mahogany and gilt looking-glasses described, were most popular, and are commonly found. These frames are veneered with mahogany or walnut, and are sawed in outlines similar to those of the richer frames of walnut or mahogany and gilt. The inside of the frame next the glass has a narrow hand-carved gilt moulding, and there is sometimes a gilt bird flying through the opening sawed in the upper part of the frame, while in other frames the opening is partially filled by three feathers, a conventional shell, or a flower in gilt. Occasionally a line of inlaying follows the gilt moulding next the glass. In smaller looking-glasses a gilded plaster eagle was glued upon the frame above the glass. Such frames may be found, or rather might have been found, in almost any old house.

Illustration 376 shows two of these looking-glasses. The larger glass is owned by the writer, the smaller by W. S. G. Kennedy, Esq., of Worcester.

A looking-glass with some variations from those previously shown forms the heading to Chapter X. The lower part of the frame has the sawed outlines which appear upon so many, while the upper part has a broken arch cornice of a high and slender design, showing the influence of the lighter Hepplewhite styles. A colored shell is inlaid in the top of this frame, and there are two rows of fine inlaying around the glass. The frame is surmounted by an

392   Furniture of the Olden Time

urn or vase with flowers and stalks of wheat, upon wires, like the slender garlands at the sides. This

Illus. 376. — Looking-glasses, 1750–1790.

looking-glass belongs to H. H. Kohn, Esq., of Albany.

Illustration 377 shows another looking-glass of the same style, with the wheat and flowers upon wires springing from an urn at the top, and leaves of plaster strung upon wires at the sides.

Looking-glasses

Illustration 378 shows a looking-glass carved and sawed in fantastic outlines, with ribbons at the sides. These two looking-glasses are in the Metropolitan Museum of Art.

Illus. 377.— Looking-glass, 1790.

Illus. 378.— Looking-glass, 1780.

Wooden frames with sawed outlines continued fashionable until the close of the century.

It was customary for these mahogany-framed glasses to rest upon two mirror knobs, which fitted into the lower curves of the frame and were screwed into the wall. These knobs were sometimes made of brass, but the most fashionable mirror knobs were those with a medallion, round or oval, of Battersea enamel upon copper, framed in brass. The design of the medallions varied, heads of historical personages being very popular, while flowers, landscapes, fancy heads, the eagle and thirteen stars, and the ever-favorite design of the monument and weeping willow appear in the bright tints of the enamel. Dwight Blaney, Esq., of Boston, has a collection of over one hundred knobs.

Illus. 379.— Enamelled Mirror Knobs, 1770–1790.

Washington, Lafayette, Franklin, Lord Nelson are some of the heads found upon mirror knobs. Four pairs of enamelled knobs, owned by the writer, appear in Illustration 379. The head of Lord Nelson figures upon one pair.

"A circular convex glass in a gilt frame" is shown in Illustration 380. Such glasses were advertised as "mirrors," in distinction from the looking-glasses which were in ordinary use, and they were sold in pairs, for sconces, the convex or occasionally concave glass precluding the possibility of its use for a literal looking-glass, as any person will agree who has caught in one a glimpse of a distorted reflection of face or figure.

These mirrors were fashionable during the last quarter of the eighteenth century, and were made in various sizes, from twelve inches in diameter to three feet. The eagle formed the

Illus. 380. — Girandole, 1770–1780.

most popular ornament for the top, but many were made with a winged horse, or a sort of dragon, instead of the eagle. These mirrors were called girandoles, like others with branches for candles.

396 Furniture of the Olden Time

The girandole in Illustration 380 is owned by the Albany Historical Society.

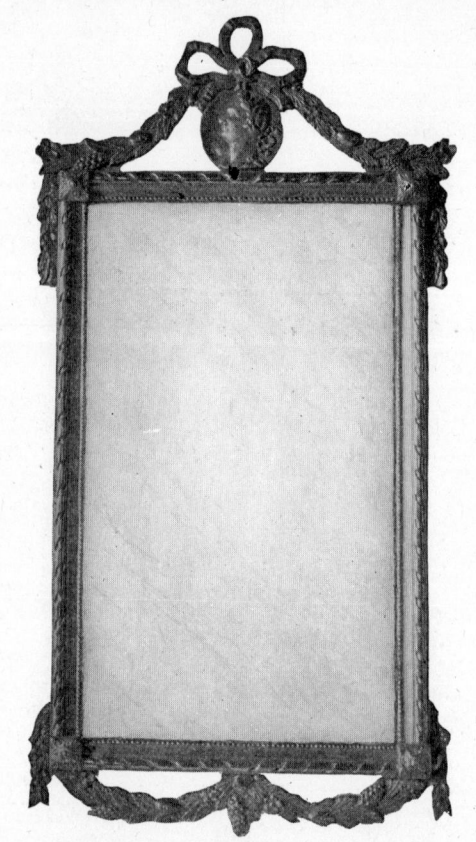

Illus. 381.— Looking-glass, 1780.

The looking-glass in Illustration 381 belongs to the writer, and is in the same style as the glass at the head of Chapter IV, which is described upon page 384. The garlands upon this frame are carved in fruit, grapes and plums with leaves, instead of the laurel which is generally the design, and the medallion above the frame has a classic head in profile, and is surmounted by a ribbon bow-knot of three loops. The glass is of quite a large size.

Illustration 382 shows a looking-glass owned by Mrs. William Preston of Richmond, Virginia. The upper section of the glass is divided from the lower by a gilt moulding, and is delicately painted, in black and gold upon a white ground, with three panels, the middle one having a classical design. The pyramid-shaped pieces at the top

Illus. 382.—Looking-glass, 1790.

are of painted glass and from them go chains, held by an eagle above.

Illustration 383 shows a large and handsome looking-glass made in the fashion of Hepplewhite's designs, the fan-shaped ornament below the glass being quite characteristic of Hepplewhite's frames. The eagle at the top holds in his beak chains which extend to the urns upon the upper corners of the frame.

This looking-glass was made about 1790, and is owned by Mrs. Thomas H. Gage of Worcester.

A looking-glass made to fit the panel over the mantel is shown in Illustration 384. This mantel with the looking-glass is in the Nichols house, in Salem, in a room built in 1783 for a young bride. The upper part of the frame has the lattice and ornaments in gilt upon a white ground, and the overhanging cornice has a row of gilt balls beneath it. The pillars framing the three sections of glass are fluted and bound with garlands.

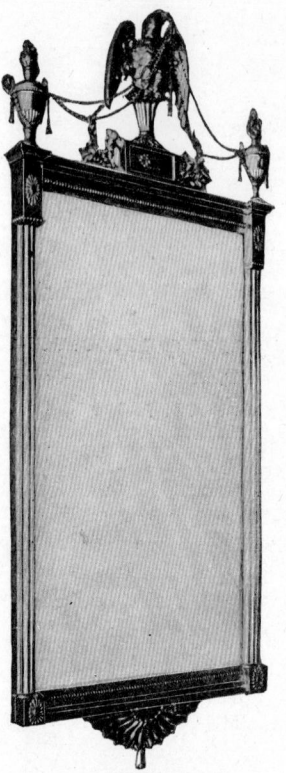

Illus. 383. — Hepplewhite Looking-glass, 1790.

Another large looking-glass of a similar design, but of a few years' later date, is shown in Illustration 385. It is owned by Dwight Blaney, Esq., and was probably made to fit some space, as it is of unusual shape and very large. The three panels at the top are painted upon glass, the middle panel

Illus. 384. — Mantel Glass, 1783.

having one of the mortuary subjects which were so popular with our ancestors, of a monument with a willow carefully trained to weep over the urn, and a despondent female disconsolately gazing upon the ground. The glass may have been ordered by the grief-stricken lady who is depicted in the panel, as evidence that while the looking-glass was a tribute to the vanities of life, the doleful scene in the panel above the glass should serve as a reminder that such

Illus. 385.— Looking-glass, 1790–1800.

vanities are fleeting. The cornice and the capitals of the pillars are very elaborate, and around the top runs a fluted band wound with garlands similar to the pillars in Illustration 384.

Illustration 386 shows a looking-glass in a frame the main portion of which is of salmon-colored marble, which is glued or cemented to the wood in small thin pieces. Upon the edges of this marble is a narrow gilt moulding, and the ornaments at the top and bottom are of gilt, the fine scrolls at the top being made of wire. Such looking-glasses have been found in New England, chiefly in Massachusetts, and the majority that have been traced have Marblehead as their starting-point in this country. In Marblehead they are known as "Bilboa glasses," and the story of the old wives of Marblehead is that these glasses were all brought home by sailors who had been to Bilboa, "In the bay of Biscay, oh," and that the looking-glasses were either given as presents to wives or sweethearts, or more prosaically exchanged for a cargo of Marblehead dried fish. The frames, however, would appear to be of Italian origin, if one wishes to be accurate, and discard the picturesque Marblehead legend.

The looking-glass in Illustration 386 is now in the Boston Art Museum. The "Bilboa glasses" are nearly all similar to this in design, with marble pillars at the side and gilt ornaments at the top and bottom. The glass is the original one with the shallow, wide bevel, and the frame, exclusive of the ornaments at the top and bottom, measures twenty-five inches in height and eighteen in width.

Another "Bilboa glass" is shown in the heading to Chapter VII. This glass is owned by Mrs.

Illus. 386. — "Bilboa Glass," 1770–1780.

M. G. Potter of Worcester, and the story in the family is that this looking-glass was made by Captain John Potter of North Brookfield, a well-known clock-maker and metal-worker, as a present to his bride, about 1790. The glass has always been fastened to the black panel behind it, within the memory of the family. The probability is that the black panel was made by Captain Potter, the frame of

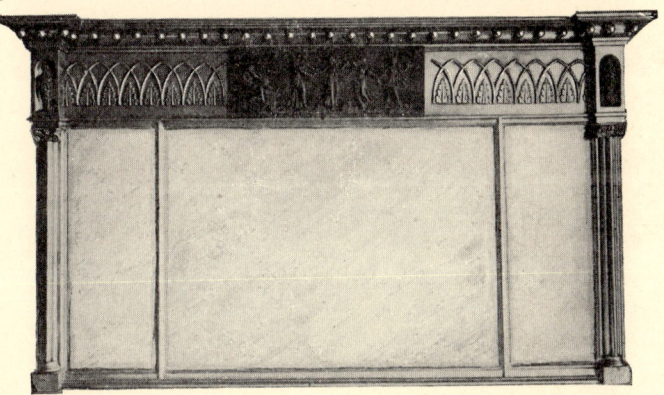

Illus. 387. — Mantel Glass, 1790.

marble with its fine gilt ornamentation having been brought originally with other Bilboa looking-glasses to Marblehead, from Italy or Spain, whichever place they may have been brought from. The top of this glass is distinctly different from the one in Illustration 386, and is on the order of Chippendale or other designers of his day. Several "Bilboa" frames have been found with this little fence at the top. Other Bilboa frames have an oval or round painted panel in the centre of the light, open gilt ornament at the top. Two Bilboa glasses are in the collection of Francis H. Bigelow, Esq., with the marble in the frame dark with white veins, instead of the usual salmon color, but made in the same design with the columns at the sides.

During the eighteenth century, particularly the latter years, it was fashionable to have a looking-glass on the mantel, extending nearly the length

Illus. 388.— Mantel Glass, 1800–1810.

of the shelf, and divided into three sections, the larger section in the middle. The line where the glass was joined was covered by a narrow gilt moulding. Such a looking-glass is shown in Illustration 387. It has the overhanging cornice which was a feature of these glasses, and which was used as early as 1783. A panel of black basalt with a classical design is set into the cornice above the glass, and two small panels above the side columns. Francis H. Bigelow, Esq., owns this looking-glass. It probably was made about 1790, when Wedgwood and Flaxman designs were popular. Another mantel glass of simpler style is shown in Illustration 334. It has the projecting cornice but not the balls beneath. The design of the frame is in the usual classical style, with pillars at the sides. Another similar looking-glass is shown in Illustration 335. Both of these glasses belong to Francis H. Bigelow, Esq., of Cambridge, and they were made from 1800 to 1810.

Illustration 388 shows a very handsome mantel glass owned by Harry Harkness Flagler, Esq., of Millbrook, made about 1810.

Cheval glasses were not common in early times, to judge from the small number of old specimens found. Illustration 389 shows one with a frame and stand of

Illus. 389.—Cheval Glass, 1830–1840.

mahogany, owned by Mrs. N. F. Rogers of Worcester, and made about 1830 to 1840.

Looking-glasses were made from 1810 to 1825, following the heavy designs which were fashionable at that period, and these glasses are commonly found. By this time the shallow bevel upon the glass had disappeared, and the glass in these heavy gilt frames is always plain.

The overhanging cornice, often with acorns or balls beneath, is a feature of these glasses, one of which is shown in Illustration 390, with a classical design below the **cornice**, and with the upper section filled with a

Illus. 390.—Looking-glass, 1810–1825.

gilded panel. It is owned by Francis H. Bigelow, Esq., of Cambridge.

A glass of the same period is shown in Illustration

Illus. 391.—Looking-glass, 1810–1815.

391, with the glass in two sections, separated by a gilt moulding. The sides of the frame are made in a double column, ending at the division in the glass. The frame continues from there in a bracket effect, with a heavy cornice above, and is more classical in design than one with twisted columns. This looking-glass is owned by the writer.

The glass in Illustration 392 is owned by Dwight M. Prouty, Esq. The frame is gilt, and the heavy drapery is carved in wood and gilded.

The richest and largest form of the looking-glass with a projecting cornice is shown in Illustration 393. It is nearly the height of the room as it rests upon a low shelf. The plain surface of the columns at the side is broken by ornaments, and there are no capitals, but the same round moulding with ornaments extends across the frame between the heavy overhanging cornice and the top section, which is very large,

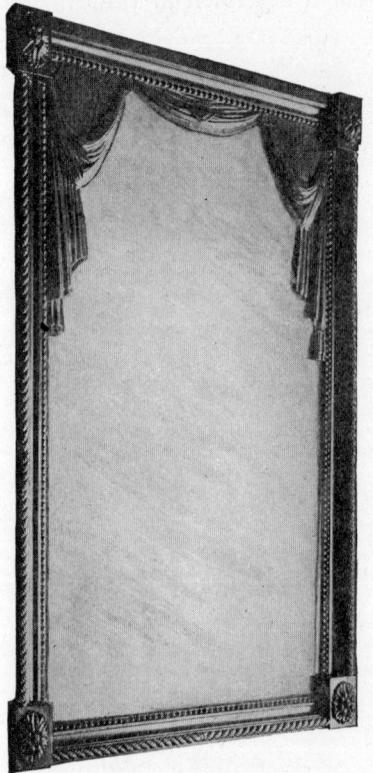

Illus. 392.— Looking-glass, 1810–1828.

Illus. 393. — Looking-glass, 1810–1820.

with scrolls and a basket of flowers in high relief, in gilt. This fine looking-glass belongs to George W. Holmes, Esq., of Charleston, South Carolina.

The glass with a heavy frame in Illustration 394 belongs to the writer. Looking-glasses were made in this style of mahogany also, with pillars twisted, fluted, or carved with the acanthus leaf. The glass was sometimes divided in two sections, separated by a narrow moulding, and the upper section was often filled by a gilded panel, as in Illustration 390. The frame at the head of Chapter II shows a looking-glass owned by Mr. Bigelow. The panel above the glass is gilded, and its design, of a cornucopia, was extremely popular at this period. The upper section was frequently filled with a picture painted upon glass. A looking-glass with such a picture is shown in Illustration 31, and another, owned by Mrs. H. H. Bigelow of Worcester, heads Chapter I.

Illus. 394. — Looking-glass, 1810–1825.

CHAPTER XIII

DOORWAYS, MANTELS, AND STAIRS

NOWHERE in this country can the interiors of the old houses and their woodwork be studied as in Salem. The splendid mansions around Philadelphia and in Maryland and Virginia are detached and not always accessible, but in Salem one may walk through the old streets with a certainty that almost any of the houses passed will prove to contain features of interest to the student. The town was the home of wealthy ship-owners and East India merchants, who built there the houses which we study, for their homes. They did not spare expense—the Derby house cost $80,000; and they were fortunate in having for a fellow citizen a wood-carver, and designer, Samuel McIntire, whose work will bear comparison with that of men whose names have been better known. Within

411

the last few years, however, McIntire's name and work have attracted more attention, and his mantels and doors in Salem have been shown to the reading public in the book "The Woodcarver of Salem," by Frank Cousins and Phil M. Riley.

McIntire built the eighty thousand dollar Derby house, which within a short time of its completion was torn down, owing to the death of Mr. Derby, none of the heirs wishing to keep so costly a mansion. Just at that time, in 1804, Captain Cook was building the house now known as the Cook-Oliver house. McIntire, who was the architect also of this house, persuaded Captain Cook to use much of the fine woodwork which he had made for Mr. Derby, and it was embodied in the Cook house, which was, when finished, given to the daughter of Captain Cook, who married General Oliver, the composer of the hymn, "Federal Street," named for the street upon which this house stands.

Illustration 395 shows a doorway in the hall of the Cook-Oliver house, which was taken from the Derby mansion. The wood is pine, as in most of the Salem houses, painted white, and the ornamentation is all hand-carved. The design is thoroughly classical, with its graceful drapery across the top, and the urns, also ornamented with drapery. Through the doorway may be seen the mantel, which was taken from the Derby mansion, with the fine hob-grate, and a little of the old Zuber paper, which extends around the room, with scenes of the Paris of 1810–1820.

The doorway in Illustration 396 is in a very different style from that of McIntire, with its del-

Illus. 395. — Doorway and Mantel, Cook-Oliver House, Salem, 1804.

414   Furniture of the Olden Time

icate and graceful ornamentation. This doorway is in the house built in 1720 by Michael Dalton, in Newburyport, Massachusetts, and now occupied by the

Illus. 396.— Doorway in Dalton House, Newburyport, 1720.

Dalton Club. It was Michael Dalton who built this house, but its golden years were during the ownership of his son, Tristram Dalton, who married the daughter of "King" Hooper, and who might well be called by the same name as his father-in-law. In evidence of his wealth and lavish manner of life is the story of his splendid coach, lined with white satin, drawn by six white horses, and attended by four outriders, all in white and mounted upon white steeds. In this dazzling equipage the various brides of the family left the house, and the same royal splendor probably attended the arrival at the house of famous guests, of whom there were many. All this display does not agree with the common notion of sober New England, but smacks rather of the aristocratic Virginians who built mansions on the James River. The doorways and mantels in the Dalton house tell of great wealth, for those early years of 1720. They are made of pine, painted white, and all of the woodwork is hand carved. The doorway in Illustration 396 is in the same room with the mantel in Illustration 397 and is designed in the same classical style, with fluted columns and Ionic capitals. The cornice is the same, and the egg and dart moulding upon it extends with the cornice entirely around the room. The immediate frame of the door has the same carved moulding as the lower part of the cornice, and the window frames. The door itself is very fine with eight panels. The knob is new. The original knob was of iron.

Illustration 397 shows the mantel in the room with the doorway, and at one side is a glimpse of the cornice and frame of the window with its deep seat. The fluted square pilasters of the doorway, in the

Illus. 397.— Mantel in Dalton House, 1720.

mantel are changed to round detached columns, and there is a plain panel with simple mouldings over the narrow shelf.

Illustration 398 shows another mantel in the Dalton house, of a plainer form, without columns,

Illus. 398.— Mantel in Dalton House, 1720.

but with a heavy moulding, a variation of the egg and dart, around the fireplace and the plain centre panel.

The narrow shelf is curiously set between the panel and the moulding. There is a panelled door upon each side of the chimney, opening into a cupboard, and below each cupboard may be seen a tinder box, in early days a useful adjunct to a fireplace.

Illus. 399.— Hall and Stairs in Dalton House, 1720.

The stairs in the Dalton house are shown in Illustration 399. The newel is carved with a detached twist around the centre post, and each of the three balusters upon every stair has a different twist, in the fashion of the seaport staircases of the eighteenth century. Two of the Dalton chairs stand at the foot

Illus. 400.—Side of Room, with Mantel; Penny-Hallet House, 1774.

of the stairs, and above them hangs the portrait of Tristram Dalton, a fine gentleman in a white satin waistcoat. Over the stairs hangs a "hall lanthorne" like the one in Illustration 333.

Illustration 400 shows the side of a room in the Penny-Hallett house at 685 Centre St., Jamaica Plain. It dates to 1774, and is all elaborately carved by hand, with scrolls, birds, garlands of flowers and fruit, and a head over each arch at the side of the mantel. All of this woodwork has been removed, and embodied in a Boston house.

Illus. 401. — Parker-Inches-Emery House, Boston, 1818.

The house known by the names of past occupants as the Parker-Inches-Emery house is now occupied by the Women's City Club of Boston, which is fortunate in being able to preserve this house from changes for business purposes. The woodwork is

Illus. 402.— Mantel in Lee Mansion, Marblehead, 1768.

Illus. 403. — Landing and Stairs in Lee Mansion, Marblehead, 1768.

probably the finest in Boston, and is attributed, with the building, to Bulfinch. The doorway in Illustration 401 is from the back parlor of the house. The door is mahogany, and the carved woodwork of the frame is in a severely classical design. The anthemion figures upon the pilasters and in the capital, and the design of the frieze is beautiful in its severity. The house was built in 1818.

In his "Complete Body of Architecture" Isaac Ware says of the chimney-piece: "No common room, plain or elegant, could be constituted without it. No article in a well-finished room is so essential. The eye is immediately cast upon it on entering, and the place of sitting down is naturally near it. By this means it becomes the most eminent thing in the finishing of an apartment."

The mantelpiece in Illustration 402 is in the banquet hall of the house built in 1768, upon generous plans, by Col. Jeremiah Lee in Marblehead. The depth of the chimney is in the rear, and the mantel is almost flush with the panelled walls. It is painted white like the other woodwork, and is richly ornamented with hand carving, in rococo designs, with garlands of fruit and flowers in high relief, after the fashion of the time, and has a plain panel over the narrow shelf, which rests upon carved brackets.

Illustration 403 shows the beautiful landing at the head of the stairway in the Lee mansion, with the large window and Corinthian pilasters, and the wonderful old paper, all in tones of gray. The turn of the stairs is seen, and the finely twisted balusters.

Illustration 404 shows the rear of the stairway, with the front door, in the house built in 1795 by

Illus. 404.— Stairs in Harrison Gray Otis House, Boston, 1795.

Harrison Gray Otis, in Boston. It is now the property and headquarters of the Society for the Preservation of New England Antiquities, having reached that safe haven after the descent from an elegant and fashionable residence to a lodging house. It has now been restored with great care to much of its original appearance. The illustration shows the fine boxing of the stairs and the ornamentation of

Illus. 405.— Mantel in Harrison Gray Otis House, Boston, 1795.

the stair-ends. The balusters are twisted and end in a turn without a newel post.

Illustration 405 shows a mantel in the Otis house of painted wood, with the space above the shelf taken by two sets of doors, one sham, of wood, and the other

426   Furniture of the Olden Time

of iron, which opens into a safe. It is difficult to imagine why this transparent device was placed in such a conspicuous place.

Illus. 406.—Stairs in Robinson House, Saunderstown.

Illustration 406 shows a very good stairway in the Robinson house in Saunderstown, R. I. It has two turns, and the panelling on the side wall has a mahogany rail which turns with the one above the

Illus. 407.—Stairs in Allen House, Salem, 1770.

twisted balusters. The return of the stairs is panelled beneath, and at each corner of the turn of the balusters is a large post like the newel, which extends below the stairs and is finished in a twisted flame-like ornament.

The beautiful stairway with panelled ends and boxing in Illustration 407 is in the Allen house in Salem. The balusters are particularly good.

A section of the fine stairway at "Oak Hill," Peabody, Massachusetts, in Illustration 408, gives the detail of the twisted balusters and newel so often seen in the old seaport towns. Each one of the balusters, of which there are three upon a stair, has a different twist, and the newel is a twist within a twist, the outer spiral being detached from the inner one. The balusters are painted white, and the rail and newel are of mahogany.

Illus. 408. — Balusters and Newel of Stairs at "Oak Hill," Peabody.

Illustration 409 shows the staircase in the

Illus. 409. — Stairs in Sargent-Murray-Gilman House, Gloucester, 1768.

Sargent-Murray-Gilman house in Gloucester, and Illustration 410 shows a mantel in the same house, which was built in 1768, by Winthrop Sargent, for his

Illus. 410.— Mantel in Sargent-Murray-Gilman House, 1768.

Doorways, Mantels, and Stairs 431

daughter when she married Rev. John Murray, who was the founder of the Universalist church in America. Later, the house was occupied by the father of Rev. Samuel Gilman, the author of "Fair Harvard." The mantel is of wood, hand carved, with a broken pediment supported by plain columns with Corinthian capitals, while those below the shelf have Ionic capitals. The stairway is very fine, with panelled boxing and ends, and twisted balusters and newel. There is a good window upon the landing, with fluted pilasters at each side.

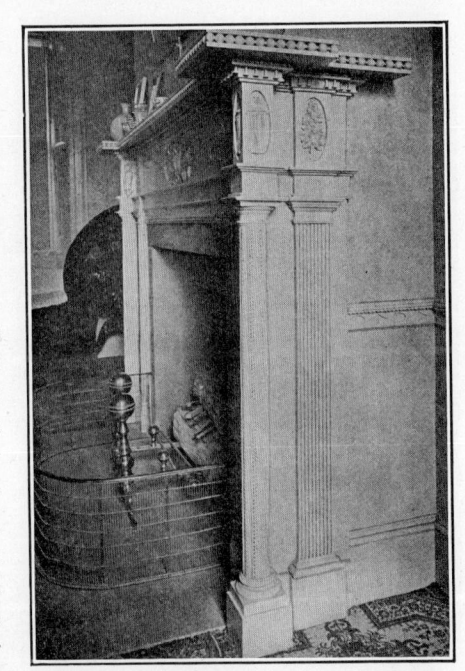

Illus. 411.— Mantel in Kimball House, Salem, 1800.

A McIntire mantel is shown in Illustration 411, from the Kimball house in Salem. The carving is done by hand and is very elaborate, with urns in the corner insets, and a spray in the ones over the fluted pilaster which completes the return of the mantel.

A curious row of little bell-shaped drops is beneath the shelf, the edge of which has a row of small globes set into it, like beads upon a string.

Illus. 412.— Mantel in Lindall-Barnard-Andrews House, Salem, 1800.

Another McIntire mantel is shown in Illustration 412, the parlor mantel in the Lindall-Barnard-Andrews house in Salem. The carving is done by hand, and the sheaves of wheat, the basket of fruit,

Illus. 413.—Doorway in Larkin-Richter House, Portsmouth, about 1800.

and the flower-filled draperies are delicate and charming. It was put in the house in 1800, but the paper dates to 1747, the time when the house was built, and it was imported for this room from France.

A very charming doorway is shown in Illustration 413, from the Larkin-Richter house in Portsmouth. It has urns and festoons of flowers and wonderfully fine carvings upon the cornice. Illustration 414 shows a doorway leading into the hall in the "Octagon" in Washington, D. C. The house derives its name from its shape, built to conform to a triangular lot. Col. John Tayloe built it in 1800, and for twenty-five years the entertainments given

Illus. 414.—Doorway in the "Octagon," Washington.

in the Octagon were famous. It is now occupied by the American Institute of Architects. The entrance to the house is in a circular tower of three stories in height, thus utilizing the shape of the triangle. This gives a large, circular vestibule from which a wide, arched doorway leads into the hall

Illus. 415.—Mantel in the "Octagon," Washington.

with the stairs, which are very simple, with plain small balusters, and a mahogany rail. The doorway is very fine, with fluted columns and carved capitals and on the inside of the arch a row of carving, making a beautiful entrance to the house.

The mantel in Illustration 415 is in the "Octagon" house, and is made of a cement composition, cast in a mould, and painted white. The cement is fine and the effect is much as if it were wood or stone. The designs are graceful and well modelled. This style of

Illus. 416.—Mantel in Schuyler House, Albany.

mantel with figures at the sides was used more in the South, and one would hardly find in a Northern home a mantel the motif of which was a frankly portrayed praise of wine, with the centre panel quite Bacchanalian in its joviality.

The mantel in Illustration 416 is in the Schuyler mansion in Albany, New York, which has been wisely and thoroughly restored to its original beauty, and stands a monument not only of the Albany life of the eighteenth century, but to the early efficiency of woman, for it was built in 1760 by the wife of Gen. Philip Schuyler, during the absence of her husband in England. This mantel is in the room called the Hamilton room, because it was here that the daughter of the house, Elizabeth Schuyler, was married to Alexander Hamilton. The wood of the mantel is, like that in the other rooms, pine, painted white, and the room is handsomely panelled, with a heavy cornice. The shelf is narrow with a panel above it which is surmounted by a cornice, with a broken pediment. The mantel is very dignified and does credit to the excellent taste of the colonial dame who chose it and superintended its instalment.

Illustration 417 shows a mantel in Philipse Manor in Yonkers, New York. The original house was built in the seventeenth century, but in 1745 it was greatly enlarged by Judge Philipse, the second lord of the Manor, and it was probably at about that time that the fine woodwork in the house was installed. Judge Philipse was the father of Mary Philipse, to whom in 1757 Washington paid court — unsuccessfully. She married Roger Morris in 1758, and in 1779 fled with him to England, attainted as Royalists, together with her brother, the third and last lord of the Manor, which then passed from the Philipse family. It was purchased in 1868 by the village of Yonkers, and remained in the possession of the city until

Illus. 417. — Mantel and Doorways in Manor Hall, Yonkers.

Doorways, Mantels, and Stairs 439

1908, when the title to the Manor was taken by the State of New York, and the American Scenic and Historic Preservation Society was appointed cus-

Illus. 418. — Mantel and Doorways in Manor Hall, Yonkers.

todian, thus insuring the preservation of this historic house. The mantel in Illustration 417 is in the East parlor, where Mary Philipse was married, and is, like all of the woodwork, painted white and very finely hand carved, with flowers in high relief. The iron fire back which was originally in the fireplace is still there, but the tiles are new. The pilasters have composite capitals, and are used as a part of the decoration of the side of the room with the mantel.

Illus. 419.— Mantel in Manor Hall, Yonkers.

The ceiling in this room, a glimpse of which may be seen in the illustration, is elaborately decorated with rococo scrolls, framing medallions, in two of which are portrait heads. The entire house bears evidence of the wealth of the lords of the Manor.

Doorways, Mantels, and Stairs 441

Illustration 418 shows the mantel in the chamber over the East parlor, also beautifully carved with flowers and fruit and scrolls, after the fashion of the period. The three feathers above were an indication of loyalty to the crown, as they were placed there years before the division of parties for the King and the Prince of Wales, when the use of the three feathers meant allegiance to the latter. Over the doors is a carved scroll with the broken pediment, and a small scroll in the centre.

Illustration 419 shows another mantel in Manor Hall of a less ornate type, very

Illus. 420.—Doorway and Stairs, Independence Hall.

dignified and fine with its simple pilasters and the smaller ones at the sides of the panel. The cornice over the doors is one that was used often in fine houses. These doorways and mantels are restored,

442   Furniture of the Olden Time

but the greater part was intact or simply out of repair. Illustration 420 shows the beautiful panelled arch to the doorway, and the stairs in Independence Hall in Philadelphia, with a glimpse of the frame of the window upon the landing. The balusters are plain and substantial, with a mahog-

Illus. 421.—Stairs at "Graeme Park," Horsham.

Doorways, Mantels, and Stairs 443

any rail, and the rise of the stairs is very gradual. The thickness of the wall allows wide panels in the inside of the arch, and the doorway and the pillars at the side are of imposing height.

Illustration 421 shows the stairway at "Graeme Park," the house built in 1722 by Sir William Keith,

Illus. 422.— Mantel and Doorways, Graeme Park.

Governor of Penn's Colony, at Horsham, Pennsylvania. The place is named from Dr. Graeme, who married the step-daughter of Gov. Keith, and occupied the house after 1727. Gov. Keith lived here in great style, with a large household, as his inventory implies, with "60 bedsteads, 144 chairs, 32 tables and 15 looking-glasses." The discrepancy between the number of bedsteads and looking-glasses is accounted for by the pric of glass, and the probability that many of the sixty occupants of the bedsteads were servants or slaves, whose toilet was not important, and who did not live in the mansion, but in the out-buildings around it. The house was built in accordance with the manner of life of the Governor, and contained large rooms, handsomely panelled and finished in oak, unpainted. The stairs in Illustration 421 are all of oak, stairs, balusters, and rail, and are of an entirely different style from the twisted balusters and newels of the northern seaport towns, but of a solidity and simplicity that is attractive.

Illustration 422 shows the side wall of a chamber at Graeme Park, also of oak. The fireplace is surrounded by tiles, and the chimney-piece is panelled above, but there is no shelf. The doorways at each side of the mantel are charming, with the arch above and the semicircular window. The old hinges and latches are still upon the doors.

The doorway in Illustration 423 is from the Chase house in Annapolis, Maryland, and is in a room with several doors and windows, all with their deeply carved frames, painted white, with solid mahogany doors, and hinges and latches of silver. The heavy wooden inside shutters have large rosettes carved upon them, and the effect of all this carving is extremely rich. The Chase house was built in 1769, by Samuel Chase, afterwards a Signer of the Declaration of Independence, and Associate Justice of the Supreme Court. It was sold soon after its completion, but in 1847 came back into the possession of Chase descendants, and finally, in 1888, it was left by will to found the Chase Home for Aged Women,

Illus. 423. — Doorway in Chase House, Annapolis.

446   Furniture of the Olden Time

together with furniture and china, much of which still remains there. A looking-glass from this house is shown in Illustration 374. The door latch of solid silver is of the shape of handles shown in Illustration 11, letter F.

Illustration 424 shows the noble entrance from the outer hall to the inner hall with the stairs, at

Illus. 424.—Entrance and Stairs, "Cliveden."

Illus. 425.—Mantel in Cliveden, Germantown.

"Cliveden," in Germantown, Pennsylvania. The house was built in 1761 by Chief Justice Benjamin Chew, and is now owned by Mrs. Samuel Chew.

Cliveden was famous for its entertainments, and during the Revolutionary War was the scene of the Battle of Germantown, when the house was seized by the British. The marks of bullets may still be seen in the wall at the right of the illustration. One of the daughters of Chief Justice Chew was the lovely Peggy Chew, who was one of the belles of the Mischianza fête, where Major André was her knight.

Cliveden had many famous guests — Washington, Lafayette, John Adams, and others, who came to Philadelphia while it was the seat of the administration. The door at the right of the stair in Illustration 240 opens into

Illus. 426. — Fretwork Balustrade, Garrett House, Williamsburg.

Doorways, Mantels, and Stairs 449

a parlor, the mantel in which is shown in Illustration 425. It is plain, but attractive for its simplicity.

The balustrade in Illustration 426 is in the house of the Misses Garrett in Williamsburg, Virginia, and is in a Chinese fretwork design. There is one with the same fretwork in the Paca house in Annapolis, and probably of the same date, about 1765. The winding staircase in Illustration 427 is in the house now occupied by the Valentine Museum, in Richmond, Virginia. It was built about 1812, and was given to the

Illus. 427.— Stairs, Valentine Museum, Richmond.

city for a museum, by the Valentine family. It is a very good example of the stairway known as a "winder." Illustration 428 shows a beautiful mantel

2 G

in the residence of Barton Myers, Esq., in Norfolk, Virginia. The mantel is in the Adam style, with festoons of flowers and scrolls beneath the shelf,

Illus. 428.— Mantel in Myers House, Norfolk.

in applied ornaments, and long lines of the bell-flower, looped in graceful lines upon the panel. The chandelier is brass, of about 1850–1860.

GLOSSARY OF TERMS USED IN CABINET WORK

A

Acanthus. The conventionalized leaf of the acanthus plant.
Anthemion. A Greek form of ornament made from the conventionalized flower of the honeysuckle.
Apron. The ornamental wooden piece extending between the legs of a table, below the body frame.
Applied ornament. One which is carved or sawed separately and fastened upon the surface.
Armoire. The French term for cupboard.

B

Bail. The part of a handle, in ring or hoop shape, which is taken hold of.
Bandy or **Cabriole leg.** One which is made in a double curve.
Banister back. A chair back made of vertical pieces of wood extending between an upper and lower rail.
Baroque. A term applied to a style of extravagant over-ornamentation.
Bead or **Beading.** A small convex moulding, sometimes divided and cut like beads.
Beaufat or **Bowfatt.** A corner cupboard, extending to the floor.
Bergère. A French chair with a very wide seat.
Bible box. A box, usually of oak, for holding the Bible.
Block front. A term applied to the front of a desk or chest of drawers, to indicate the blocked shape in which the drawer fronts are carved or sawed.

Bombé. Kettle-shaped.
Bonnet top. A top made with a broken arch or pediment.
Bracket. The piece of wood of bracket shape, used in the angle made by the top and the leg.
Bracket foot. A foot in bracket form.
Broken arch or **Pediment.** One in which the cornice is not complete, but lacks the central section.
Buffet. A sideboard, or piece of furniture used as a sideboard.
Buhl. A form of inlaying engraved brass upon a thin layer of tortoise shell, over a colored background. Named from its inventor, Buhl, or Boulle.
Bureau. In early time, and even now in England, a desk with a slanting lid. Now used chiefly to indicate a chest of drawers.
Bureau-table. A small chest of drawers made like a desk, but with a flat top.
Butterfly table. A small table with turned legs and stretchers and drop leaves, which are held up by swinging brackets with the outer edge curved like a butterfly wing.

C

Cabinet. The interior of a desk, fitted with drawers and compartments.
Cabriole leg. Bandy leg, curved or bent.
Capital. The upper part of a column or pillar.
Carcase. The main body of a piece of furniture.
Cellaret. A low, metal-lined piece of furniture, sometimes with the interior divided into sections, used as a wine cooler.
Chaise longue. The French term for a day bed or couch.
Chamfer. A corner cut off, so as to form a flat surface with two angles.
Claw-and-ball foot. The termination of a leg with a ball held in a claw, usually that of a bird.
Comb back. A Windsor chair back, with an extension top, shaped like a comb.
Commode. A chest of drawers.

Glossary of Terms used in Cabinet Work

Console table. One to be placed below a looking-glass, sometimes with a glass between the back legs.

Court or **Press cupboard.** A very early cupboard with doors and drawers below and a smaller cupboard above, the top being supported by heavy turned columns at the corners.

D

Day bed or **Chaise longue.** A long narrow seat used as a couch or settee, usually with four legs upon each side, and a chair back at the head.

Dentils. An architectural ornament made of a series of small detached cubes.

Desk. A piece of furniture with conveniences for writing.

Desk box. A box similar to a Bible box, made to hold books or papers.

Diaper. A small pattern or design, repeated indefinitely on a surface.

Dish top. A table top with a plain raised rim.

Dovetail. Fastening together with mortise and tenon.

Dowel. A wooden pin used to fasten sections together.

Dresser. A set of shelves for dishes.

Dutch foot. A foot which spreads from the leg in a circular termination.

E

Egg and dart. A form of ornament made of egg-shaped pieces with dart-shaped pieces between.

Empire style. A style which became popular during the First Empire, largely formed upon Egyptian styles, found by Napoleon during his Egyptian campaign. Later the term was applied to the heavy furniture with coarse carving, of the first quarter of the nineteenth century.

Escritoire. A secretary.

Escutcheon. The metal plate of a key-hole.

F

Fan back. The back of a Windsor chair with the spindles flaring like an open fan.

Fender. A guard of pierced metal, or wire, to place before an open fire.
Field bedstead. One with half high posts which uphold a frame covered with netting or cloth.
Finial. The ornament which is used at the top of a pointed effect as a finish.
Flemish foot or **leg.** An early scroll form with one scroll turning in and the other turning out; found upon Jacobean furniture.
Fluting. A series of concave grooves.
French foot. In Chippendale's time, a scroll foot terminating a cabriole leg; in Hepplewhite's time, a delicate form of a bracket foot.
Fret-work. A form of ornament in furniture, sawed or carved in an open design.

G

Gadroon or **Godroon.** A form of ornament consisting of a series of convex flutings, chiefly used in a twisted form as a finish to the edge.
Gallery. The raised and pierced rim upon a table top, usually in Chinese fret-work.
Gate-legged, hundred-legged, or **forty-legged table.** An early table with drop leaves and stretchers between the legs, of which there are six stationary upon the middle section, and one or two which swing out to hold up the drop leaves.
Girandole. A mirror with fixtures for candles.
Guéridon. A stand to hold a candelabra, — a candle-stand.
Guilloche. An ornamental pattern formed by interlacing curves.

H

High-boy. A tall-boy or chest of drawers upon high legs.
Hood. The bonnet top of a high-boy.
Husk. The form of ornament made from the bell-flower, much used by Hepplewhite.

J

Jacobean. A term applied to furniture of the last quarter of the seventeenth century, although properly it should apply to the period of James I.

Japanning or **Lacquering.** In the eighteenth century a process copied from the Chinese and Japanese lacquer; in Hepplewhite's time a method of painting and gilding with a thin varnish.

K

Kas or **Kos.** A Dutch high case with drawers and doors, made to hold linen, and extending to the floor, from which it was sometimes held up by large balls.

Kettle front or **bombé.** A form of chest of drawers or secretary, in which the lower drawers, toward the base, swell out in a curve.

Knee. The term applied to the upper curve, next the body, of a bandy leg.

Knee-hole desk. A desk with a table top, and an open space below with drawers at each side.

L

Lacquer. A Chinese and Japanese process of coating with many layers of varnish.

Ladder back. A chair back of the Chippendale period, with horizontal carved or sawed pieces across the back.

Low-boy. A dressing-table, made to go with a high-boy.

M

Marquetry. Inlay in different woods.

Mortise. The form cut in a piece of wood to receive the tenon, to form a joint.

Mounts. The metal handles, escutcheons, or ornaments fastened upon a piece of furniture.

O

Ogee. A cyma, or double curve, as of a moulding.
Ormolu. Mountings of gilded bronze or brass, used as ornaments.

P

Pie-crust table. A table with a raised edge made in a series of curves.
Pier-glass. A large looking-glass.
Pigeon-hole. A small open compartment in the cabinet of a desk or secretary.
Patina. The surface of wood or metal acquired by age or long use.
Pediment. The part above the body of a book-case or chest of drawers, with an outline low at the sides and high in the middle, similar to the Greek pediment.
Pembroke table. A small table with drop leaves, to use as a breakfast table.

R

Rail. The horizontal pieces across a frame or panel.
Reeding. Parallel convex groovings.
Ribband or **Ribbon-back.** A chair back of the Chippendale period, with the back formed of carved ribbon forms.
Rococo. A name derived from two words, rock and shell — applied to a style of ornamentation chiefly composed of scrolls and shells, used in irregular forms, often carried to extremes.
Roundabout or **Corner chair.** An armchair, the back of which extends around two sides, leaving two sides and a corner in front.

S

Scroll-top. A top made of two curves broken at the center, a bonnet top.
Secretary. A desk with a top enclosed by doors, with shelves and compartments behind them.

Serpentine or **Yoke front.** A term applied to drawer fronts sawed or carved in a double curve.

Settee. A long seat with wooden arms and back, the latter sometimes upholstered.

Settle. A seat, usually for two, made with high wooden arms and back, to stand in front of a fire. Often the back turned over upon pivots to form a table top.

Slat-back. A chair back very commonly found, with plain horizontal pieces of wood across the back in varying numbers.

Spade foot. A foot used by Hepplewhite and Sheraton, the tapering leg increasing suddenly about two inches from the end, and tapering again forming a foot the sides of which are somewhat spade-shaped.

Spandrels. The triangular pieces formed by the outlines of the circular face of a clock and the square corners.

Spanish foot. An angular, grooved foot with a scroll base turning inward.

Spindle. A slender, round, turned piece of wood.

Splat. The upright wide piece of wood in the middle of a chair-back.

Squab. A hard cushion.

Stiles. The vertical pieces of a panel, into which the upper and lower rails are set, with mortise and tenon.

Strainers or **Stretchers.** The pieces of wood extending between the legs of chairs or tables to strengthen them, and in early times to rest the feet upon, to keep them from the cold floor.

Swell front. A front curved in a slightly circular form.

T

Tambour. A term applied to a door or cover made from small strips of wood glued to a piece of cloth which is fastened so that it is flexible.

Tenon. The form of a cut which fits into a mortise so as to make a firm joint.

Torchère. A candle stand.

V

Veneer. A very thin piece of wood glued upon another heavier piece.

Vernis Martin. A French varnish with a golden hue, named for its inventor.

W

Wainscot chair. An early chair, usually of oak, with the seat and back formed of solid panels.

INDEX OF THE OWNERS OF FURNITURE

A

Albany Historical Society, Girandole, 395; forty-legged table, 247.
Alexander Ladd House, Portsmouth. Chair, 161; double chair, 224.
Allen House. Stairs, 427.
American Antiquarian Society, Worcester. Desk 127; double chair, 225; high chair, 156; looking-glass, 376; slate-top table, 245; tall clock, 354.
American Philosophical Society, Philadelphia. Chair, 177.

B

Barrell, Mrs. Charles C., York Corners. Looking-glass, 380, 382.
Baxter, James Phinney, Portland. Sideboard, 97; dressing-glass, 50.
Bigelow, Francis H., Cambridge. Andirons, 319; candelabra, 345; cellaret, 111; chairs, 183, 185, 197, 206, 207; clock, 359; desk, 129, 151; lamps, 344; looking-glass, 41, 403, 406; secretary, 150; sconce, 340; settee, 228; sideboard, 104, 105; sofa, 230; table, 251, 253, 269; timepiece, 368; wash-stand, 60.
Bigelow, Mrs. H. H., Worcester. Looking-glass, 10.
Bigelow, Irving, Worcester, Clock, 362; table, 266.
Blaney, Dwight, Boston. Andirons, 318; bureau, 52; chair, 163, 198; desk, 133; high chest, 26; looking-glass, 400; music-stand, 303; settle, 215; sideboard, 108; table, 243, 244, 245, 246, 253, 262, 276; what-not, 267.
Boston Art Museum. Clock, 354; looking-glass, 402.
Bostonian Society. Clocks, 356.
Burnside, Miss H. P. F., Worcester. Looking-glass, 64; table, 275.

C

Carroll, Mrs. Elbert H., Worcester. Bureau, 48.
Chase Mansion, Annapolis. Doorway, 445.
Chickering & Co. Piano, 302, 310.
Clark, Charles D., Philadelphia. Clock, 357.
"Cliveden," Germantown. Entrance and stairs, 446; mantel, 447.
Coates, Miss Mary, Philadelphia. Chair, 161, 176, 187, 189, 204; table, 253.
Colonial Dames of Pennsylvania. Bedstead, 79; sideboard, 110; sofa, 220.
Concord Antiquarian Society. Bedstead, 69; chair, 190; couch, 217; looking-glass, 242; settee, 234; table, 262, 264.
Connecticut Historical Society, Hartford. Chest, 14.
Cook-Oliver House, Salem. Mantel and doorway, 413.
Corbett, George H., Worcester. Bedstead, 82.

460 Index of the Owners of Furniture

Crowninshield, Frederic B., Marblehead. Settee, 233.
Cutter, Mrs. J. C., Worcester. Chair, 209.

D

Dalton House, Newburyport. Doorway, 414; mantel, 416, 417; stairs, 418.
Darlington, Dr. James H., Brooklyn. Piano, 294, 327.
Deerfield Museum. "Beaufatt," 90; chair, 182; chest, 11, 15; dulcimer, 304; settle, 214; spinet, 282.
Dyer, Clinton M., Worcester. Table, 258; table and chair, 267.

E

Earle, Mrs. Alice Morse, Brooklyn. Chair, 187; desk, 138.
Essex Institute, Salem. Chair, 158; cupboard, 88; settee, 216.

F

Faulkner, Dr. G., Roxbury. Clock, 363.
Flagler, Harry Harkness, Millbrook. Andirons, 320; candle-stand, 343; chair, 164, 186, 188, 195; clock, 359; double-chair, 222; dressing-table, 39; fender, 320; high chest, 37; lantern, 346; looking-glass, 39; 386, 404; side table, 93; settee, 221; table, 254, 255, 256, 258, 261; writing table, 136.

G

Gage, Mrs. Thomas H., Worcester. Bureau, 53, 56; case of drawers, 55; desk, 152; looking-glass, 398; sofa, 239.
Gage, Miss Mabel C., Worcester. Desk, 120.
Garrett, The Misses, Williamsburg. Mixing table, 116; stairs, 448.
Gay, Calvin, Worcester. Clock, 372.
Gilbert, J. J., Baltimore. Bedstead 71; bookcase, 143; chair, 199; table, 256; music-stand, 306.
Gilman, Daniel, Exeter. Chest of drawers, 36.
Girard College. Settee, 229.
Graeme Park, Horsford. Mantel, 443; stairs, 442.
Grisier, Mrs. Ada, Auburn. Piano, 295.

H

Harrison, Mrs. Charles Custis, St. David's. Mixing-table, 115.
Henry, Mrs. J. H., Winchendon. Desk, 153.
Herreshoff, J. B. F., New York. Double-chest, 33.
Historical Society of Pennsylvania. Chair, 173, 201; desk, 112.
Hogg, Mrs. W. J., Worcester. Settee, 227.
Holmes, George W., Charleston. Bookcase, 144; looking-glass, 409; side-table, 94.
Hosmer, The Misses, Concord. Couch, 218; sofa, 235; table, 268.
Hosmer, Walter, Wethersfield. Chair, 180; couch, 218; cupboard, 88; desk, 125, 126; dressing-table, 35.
Huntington, Dr. William R., New York. Desk with cabinet top, 130.
Hyde, Mrs. Clarence R., Brooklyn. Comb-back rocker, 175; chair, 202; knife-box, 100; settee, 232; table, 275.

I

Independence Hall. Doorway and stairs, 441.
Ipswich Historical Society. Bedstead, 67; chair, 170, 171.

Index of the Owners of Furniture 461

J

Johnson-Hudson, Mrs. Stratford. Bedstead, 66; bureau, 47; candleshades, 332; kas, 91; looking-glass, 332; screen, 338; table, 259.

K

Kennedy, W. S. G., Worcester. Chair, 190, 203; clock, 364; desk, 149; looking-glass, 392; piano, 293; sideboard, 113; sofa, 230.

Kimball House, Salem. Mantel, 431.

Knabe, William & Co., Baltimore. Harpsichord, 285.

Kohn, H. H., Albany. Looking-glass, 315.

L

Ladd House, Portsmouth. Chair, 161; settee, 224.

Lang, B. J., Boston. Piano, 308.

Larkin-Richter House, Portsmouth. Doorway, 433.

Lawrence, Walter Bowne, Flushing. Chair, 208.

Lawton, Mrs. Vaughan Reed, Worcester. Harp, 313.

Lee Mansion, Marblehead. Bedstead, 70; fireplace, 316; mantel, 422; stairs, 425.

Lemon, E. R., Sudbury. Chest of drawers, 19; fire-frame, 328; looking-glass, 349, 374.

Lincoln, Waldo, Worcester. Chair, 209, 210; sideboard, 109.

Lindall-Barnard-Andrews House, Salem. Mantel, 432.

M

MacInnes, J. C., Worcester. Side-table, 106.

Manor Hall, Yonkers. Mantel, 438, 439, 440.

Marsh, Mrs. Caroline Foote, Claremont-on-the-James. Chest, 13.

Meggatt, William, Wethersfield. Lantern clock, 349.

Metropolitan Museum of Art. Basin-stand, 59; chair, 191; dressing-table, 24; high-boy, 27; looking-glass, 393, 411; table, 262, 277.

Moffett, Charles A., Worcester. Clock, 369.

Moore, D. Thomas, Westbury. Clock, 371; chair, 196.

Morse, Charles H., Charlestown. Bureau, 58; clock, 366; dressing-table, 54.

Morse, Mrs. E. A., Worcester. Bedstead, 77; chair, 194, 208; clock, 361, 364; table, 279; washstand, 62.

Morse, Miss Frances C., Worcester. Andirons, 324; bedstead, 78, 81; bureau, 45, 51; candlesticks, 333; chairs, 166–168, 169, 172, 174, 178, 184, 193, 200, 212; clock, 350, 357, 360, 362, 364; coasters, 102, 252; desk, 146; high chest, 30; lamps, 329; looking-glass, 84, 280, 378, 392, 396, 407, 410; low-boy, 30, 40, 378; mirror-knobs, 394; night-table, 62; piano, 290; piano-stool, 298, 300; secretary desk, 147; settee, 321; sideboard, 102; sofa, 236; table, 250, 252, 260, 265; washstand, 61, 63.

Mount Vernon. Lamp, 335; mantel, 324.

Myers, Barton, Norfolk. Mantel, 450; settee, 232; table, 274.

N

Newburyport Historical Association. Cradle, 65; desk with cabinet top, 137; table, 244.

Newman, Mrs. M., New York. Sofa, 241.
Nichols, The Misses, Salem. Chair, 205; looking-glass, 399.

O

"Oak Hill." Peabody. Stairs, 428.
"Octagon," Washington. Doorway, 434; mantel, 435.
Ogle House, Annapolis. Looking-glass, 390.
Orth, John, Boston. Clavichord, 288.
Otis, Harrison Gray, House, Boston. Mantel, 425; stairs, 424.

P

Parker-Inches-Emery House, Boston. Doorway, 420.
Pendleton Collection, Providence. Hall lantern, 348; knife urn, 99.
Pennsylvania Historical Society. Chair, 173, 183, 184; desk, 124.
Penny-Hallett House, Boston. Mantel. 419.
Philadelphia Library Association. Looking-glass, 384.
Pilgrim Society, Plymouth. Chairs, 157; cradle, 65.
Poore, Ben: Perley, Byfield. Bedstead, 72, 75; candle-stand, 330, 342; cellaret, 111; chair, 159, 160, 162, 172, 181, 186, 204; chest on frame, 18; clock, 352; looking-glass, 117, 154; screen, 342; sofa, 240.
Potter, Mrs. M. G., Worcester. Looking-glass, 213.
Pratt, Miss Emma A., Worcester. Miniature tall clock, 360.
Prentice, Mrs. Charles H., Worcester. Dutch chair, 179.
Preston, Mrs. William, Richmond. Looking-glass, 397.

Priest, Mrs. Louis M., Salem. Piano, 296.
Pringle House, Charleston. Chandelier, 336.
Prouty, Dwight M., Boston. Andirons, 322; chair, 166, 192, 202; chest, 17; chest of drawers, 20; clock, 368; bureau, 42; hall lantern, 347; looking-glass, 375, 384, 388, 408; music-stand, 307; screen, 341; settee, 219; side-table, 107; stool, 167; table, 248, 263, 270.

R

Rankin, Mrs. F. W., Albany. Desk, 119, 120; table, 249.
Rines, Albert S., Portland. Chair, 192; secretary, 135; settee, 226.
Robart, F. A., Boston. Dressing-table 23; high-chest, 22.
Robinson House, Saunderstown. Stairs, 426.
Rogers, Mrs. N. F., Worcester. Cheval glass, 405.

S

Sargent-Murray-Gilman House Gloucester. Mantel, 429; stairs, 430.
Schoeffer, Dr. Charles, Philadelphia. Sofa, 212.
Schuyler House, Albany. Mantel, 436.
Shapiro, L. J., Norfolk. Sideboard, 114, table, 272.
Sibley, Charles, Worcester. Bureau, 46.
Smith, John, Worcester. Table, 273.
Stevenson, Cornelius, Philadelphia. Screen, 341.

T

Tappan, Mrs. Sanford, Newburyport. Piano, 292.

Index of the Owners of Furniture

Tilton, Miss M. E., Newburyport. Table, 251.

Turner, Frank C., Norwich. Clock, 369.

U

Unitarian Church, Leicester. Chair, 200.

V

Valentine Museum, Richmond. Stairs, 449.

Verplanck, Samuel, Fishkill. Desk with cabinet top, frontispiece.

W

Warner House, Portsmouth. Bedstead, 76; bill of lading, 139; bookcase, 142; bureau, 43; chandelier, 334; double chest, 32; dressing-table, 34; high chest, 28; sofa, 237; stove, 327.

Waters, Charles R., Salem. Bedstead, 74; bureau, 44; candelabra, 325; chair, 155, 160, 194, 196, 203; chest, 16; chest upon frame, 18; cupboard, 87; desk box, 118; desk with cabinet top, 128; hob grate, 325; looking-glass, 383; lantern clock, 350.

Wing, Mrs. John D., Millbrook. Music stand, 303.

Woodward, Mrs. Rufus, Worcester. High chest, 29.

Woodward, Mrs. Samuel B., Worcester. Bedstead, 80; bureau, 57; table, 268.

Worcester Art Museum. Table, 274.

Wyman, Bayard, looking-glass, 389.

GENERAL INDEX

A

Adam, Robert and J., 4, 5, 99, 184.
Adam leg, 235, 241.
Adams, John, quoted, 284.
Allen house, 427.
Andirons, 317.
Argand lamp, 334.
Astor piano, 292.

B

Baldwin, Christopher Columbus, quoted, 314.
Banister-back chair, 168.
"Banjo" clock, 366.
Bason stand, 58.
Beaufet or beaufatt, 89, 90.
Bedstead, claw-and-ball foot, 69; cording of, 73; coverlid for, 78; early, 65; field, 67; French, 82; Hepplewhite, 73; low post, 80; ornaments for concealing bed screws, 77; press, 66; sleigh, 83; steps for, 73, 79.
Bell-flower, 197.
Belter, John, 290.
Betty lamp, 328.
Bevelling, 375.
Bible box, 118.
"Biglow Papers," quoted, 31.
"Bilboa" looking-glass, 401.
Bill of lading, 189.
Bird-cage clock, 349.
Bliss, Rev. Daniel, 190.
Block, front, 42, 128, 129.
Blythe, Samuel, 286.

Bolles collection, 25, 26, 155, **242.**
Bonaparte chair, 209.
Books on furniture, 4.
Bowley, Devereux, 355.
Bracket clock, 352.
Brass beading, 237.
Brewster chair, 157.
Broadwood harpsichord, 287.
Brown, Gawen, 355.
Brown, John, Joseph, Nicholas, Moses, 34, 195.
Bulkeley, Rev. Peter, 217.
Bureau, 41, 113, 146.
Burney, Dr., quoted, 281.
Burnt work on chest, 12.
Butterfly table, 245.

C

Candelabra, 373, 375.
Candle beam, 337.
Candle extinguisher, 334.
Candle shades, 332.
Candle-stand, mahogany, 343; **iron,** 331.
Candlestick, 327, 333.
Carroll, Charles, 235.
Carver chair, 157.
Cellaret, 111.
Chair, bandy-leg, 177; banister, 168, cane, 159; Carver and Brewster, 157; comb-back, 175; Dutch, 178; easy, 182; fan-back, 175; Flemish, 160; leather, 158; Queen Anne, 167; rocking, 173; roundabout, 170; slat-back, 171; turned, 156;

General Index

Turkey work, 160; wainscot, 157; Windsor, 175; writing, 177.
Chair table, 243.
Chaise longue, 217.
Chambers, Sir William, 4.
Chandelier, 334, 336.
Chandler, John, 225, 355.
Charters, John, 300.
Chase, Samuel, 444.
Chase house, 444.
Chest, 10.
Chest of drawers, 19.
Chest on frame, 18.
Cheval glass, 405.
Chew, Benjamin, 447.
Chickering & Co., 301, 310.
China steps, 25.
Chinese taste, 193, 223, 379.
Chippendale, Thomas, 4, 184.
Clavichord, 287.
Claw-and-ball foot, 178.
Clementi, 291.
Cleopatra's Barge, 233.
Cliveden, 446.
Clocks, 348.
Coasters, 103, 251.
Comb-back, 175.
Commode, 41, 66; table, 41.
Cook-Oliver house, 412.
Cording a bed, 73.
Corner chair, 170.
Cornucopia sofa, 238.
Couch, 217.
Cradle, 65.
Creepers, 321.
Cupboard, almery, 84; corner, 90; court, 86; livery, 86; press, 84.
Cupboard cloths or cushions, 89.

D

Dalton, Tristram, 415.
Darby and Joan seat, 220.
Darly, Matthias, 4.

Day bed, 217.
Dearborn, General Henry, **167.**
Derby house, 411.
Desk, 107, 108.
Desk-box, 108.
Dish-top table, 252.
Dodd & Claus, 289.
Double chair, 222, 225.
Double chest, 32.
Drawing-table, 243.
Dressing-glass, 50.
Dulcimer, 304.
Dutch marquetrie, 46.
Dutch tea-table, 251.

E

Easy-chair, 182, 183.
Edwards and Darley, 379.
Emerson, Rev. William, 190.
Empire bureau, 56, 57, 58; sideboard, 114; dining-table, 272.
Erben, Peter, 297.
Extension-top chair, 191.

F

Fan-back, 175.
Fancy chair, 210.
Faneuil, Peter, 347.
Fender, 320.
Fireback, 323.
Fire-frame, 326.
Fireplace, 316, 319.
Flemish chairs, 160.
Flucker, Lucy, 49.
Foot, claw-and-ball, 178; Dutch, 171; Flemish, 163; French, 48, 222; spade, 210; Spanish, 165.
Forms, 139.
Forty-legged table, 248.
Franklin, Benjamin, 306, 326.
Franklin stove, 326.
French foot, Hepplewhite, 48; scroll, 186, 222.

General Index

Frets, 288.
Friesland clock, 341.
Fringe, netted, 68.

G

Gas, 344.
Gate-leg, 248.
Gibbon, Dr., 3.
Gilman, Rev. Samuel, 431.
Girandole, 395.
Girard, Stephen, 229.
Graeme Park, 442.
Guilloche, 200.

H

Hadley chest, 16.
Haircloth covering, 204, 241.
Hall lantern, 346, 347.
Hamilton, Alexander, 437.
Hancock, John, 126, 225, 267, 211, 346, 353.
Hancock, Thomas, 353.
Handles, 21, 49.
Harmonica, 305.
Harp, 313.
Harp-shaped piano, 311.
Harpsichord, 286.
Harris, John, 286.
Hassam, Stephen, 365.
Haward, Charles, 281.
Hawkey, Henry, 312.
Hawthorne, Nathaniel, quoted, 38.
Heaton, J. Aldam, quoted, 9.
Hepplewhite, 4, 6, 196.
Hessians, 318.
High-boy, 24, 31.
Hipkins, A. J., 283.
Hitchcock, John, 284; Thomas, 281, 283.
Hob-grate, 323.
Holmes, O. W., quoted, 1, 132, 155.
Howard, Edward, 364.

Hundred-legged table, 2, 248.
Huntington, Dr. William R., 133.

I

Ince and Mayhew, 4, 184, 379.
Independence Hall, 441.
Irish Chippendale, 93.

J

Jacobean furniture, 159.
Japanning, 24, 123, 204.
Japan work, 24, 123, 376.
Jefferson, Thomas, 177, 334.
Johnson, Dr. Samuel, 91; Dr. William Samuel, 258, 338.
Johnson, Thomas, 4, 5, 379.
Joint or joined furniture, 10.
Jones, William, 4.

K

Kas or kasse, 91.
Keene, Stephen, 281, 282.
Keith, Sir William, 443.
Kettle-shape, 44, 135.
Kettle-stand, 257.
Kimball house, 431.
Knife-boxes, 99, 100.
Knobs for looking-glasses, 394.
Knox, General, 50, 98.

L

Lacquered furniture, 24, 123.
Lafayette, 238.
Lamp, betty, 328; mantel, 345; silver, 335.
Langdale, Josiah, 162.
Lantern, 346.
Lantern clock, 348.
Larkin-Richter house, 433.
Lee, Col. Jeremiah, 423.
Lee mansion, 317, 423.
Light-stand, 257.

Lindall-Barnard-Andrews house, 432.
Lock, Matthias, 4, 5, 379.
Logan, James, 110.
Looking-glasses, 374.
Low-boy, 24, 31.
Lowell, James Russell, quoted, 21.

M

Macphaedris, Archibald, 140.
Mahogany, 3, 4.
Manor hall, 437.
Mantel lamps, 345.
Manwaring, Robert, 4, 184.
Marie Antoinette, 97, 227.
Marquetrie, 46.
McIntire, 207, 411.
Mather, Richard, 156.
Mayhew, Ince and, 4, 184.
Melville, David, 344.
Miniature bureau, 53; sofa, 239.
Mirror knobs, 394.
Mischianza fête, 385, 448.
Mixing table, 115, 116.
Morgan, Lady, 308, 314.
Morris, Robert, 116.
Mouldings, 19, 47.
Mount Vernon, chair, 205; fireplace, 324; lamp, 335.
Murray, Rev. John, 431.
Musical clock, 361, 363.
Musical glasses, 305.
Music-stand, 303, 306, 307.
Myers, Barton, house, 450.

N

Newport chest, 33; bureau, 45; writing table, 136.
Night table, 62.

O

Oak, 3, 19.
Oak Hill, 428.
Octagon house, 434.

Oliver, Gen. 412.
Osborne, Sir Danvers, 122.
Otis, Harrison Gray, house, 424.

P

Parker-Inches-Emery house, 420.
"Parson Turell's Legacy," quoted, 155.
Pembroke table, 262.
Pendleton collection, 100, 347.
Penn, William, 125.
Penny-Hallet house, 419.
Pepperell, Sir William, 160.
Pepys, Samuel, quoted, 281.
Philipse, Mary, 437.
Philipse Manor house, 437.
Phyfe, Duncan, 275.
Piano, 289.
Piano-stool, 298, 300.
Pie-crust table, 252.
Pillar-and-claw table, 272.
Pipe-case, 36.
Pollen, Hungerford, quoted, 375.
Popkin, Dr. John Smelling, 129.
Portuguese twist, 168.
Preston, John, 245.
Prince of Wales feathers, 197.
Pringle house, 337.
Province House, 332.
Putnam cupboard, 86.

Q

Quadrille, 258.
Queen Anne chair, 167.
Quill work, 339.
Quincy, Eliza Susan Morton, quoted, 335.

R

Ripley, Dr. Ezra, 190, 234.
Rittenhouse, David, 358.
Robinson, G. T., quoted, 3.
Robinson house, 426.

General Index

Rockers, 173, 177.
Roundabout chair, 170.
Rumford, Count, 320.

S

Sally, ship, 96, 226.
Sargent-Murray-Gilman house, 429.
Satinwood, 6.
Schuyler, Gen. Philip, 437.
Schuyler house, 437.
Sconce, 377.
Screen, 338, 341.
Scrutoir, 118.
Secret drawers, 132, 136.
Settee, 216, 221.
Settle, 214.
Sewall, Judge Samuel, 280, 321, 377.
Shaw, Miss Rebecca, 137, 189.
Shearer, Thomas, 5, 96, 264.
Sheraton, Thomas, 4, 184, 205.
Sheraton quoted, 3, 7, 106, 146, 150, 295.
Sherburne, John, 28.
Sideboard, 91; Shearer, 96; Hepplewhite, 101; Sheraton, 105; measurements of, 106; woods used in, 99.
Side table, Chippendale, 93, 94.
Slat-back chair, 171.
Slate-top table, 245.
Slaw-bank, 66.
Smoker's tongs, 331.
Spade foot, 210.
Spandrels, 353.
Spanish foot, 165.
Spindle-leg, 249.
Spinet, 281.
Splat, 179, 184.
Squabs, 238.
Stand, candle, 343; Dutch, 251; kettle, 257; light, 257.
Stein, André, 398.
Stenton, 110, 221.
Steps for beds, 73, 79.

Storr, Marmaduke, 355.
Strong, Governor Caleb, 190.
Swan, Colonel, 96.

T

Table, butterfly, 246; card, 257, 264; chair, 243; dish-top, 252; drawing, 243; Dutch tea, 251; framed, 248; forty, gate or hundred-legged, 243; joined, 243; Pembroke, 262; piecrust, 252; pillar-and-claw, 272; slate-top, 245; spindle-legged, 249; work, 268.
Table borde, 242.
Table piano, 301.
Tall clocks, 354.
Tambour, 150.
Tayloe, Col. John, 434.
Tea-tray, mahogany, 264; Sheffield, 249.
Terry, Eli, 370.
Thomas, Seth, 370.
Turkey work, 159, 216.

U

Unitarian church, Leicester, 200.
Upright piano, 309.

V

Valentine Museum, 449.
Vanderbilt, Mrs., quoted, 72.
Van Rensselaer, Killian, 120.
Van Rensselaer, Philip, 120.
Virginal, 280.

W

Wainscot chair, 157.
Walnut, 3.
Ware, Isaac, quoted, 423.
Warner, Colonel Jonathan, 140.
Warville, Brissot de, quoted, 289.
Washington, George, 103, 151, 201, 205, 323, 378.

Washstand, 57.
Watson's Annals, quoted, 306.
Wendell, Elizabeth Hunt, 283.
Wentworth, Governor John, 223.
Whatnot, 267.
Whipple house, 171, 319.
Wig stand, 58.

Willard, Aaron, Benjamin, Simon. 362.
Windsor, chair, 174.
Wood, Small & Co., 300.
Work-table, 270.
Writing-chair, 177.
Writing-table, 136.